IMAGES
of America

TROY'S LITTLE ITALY

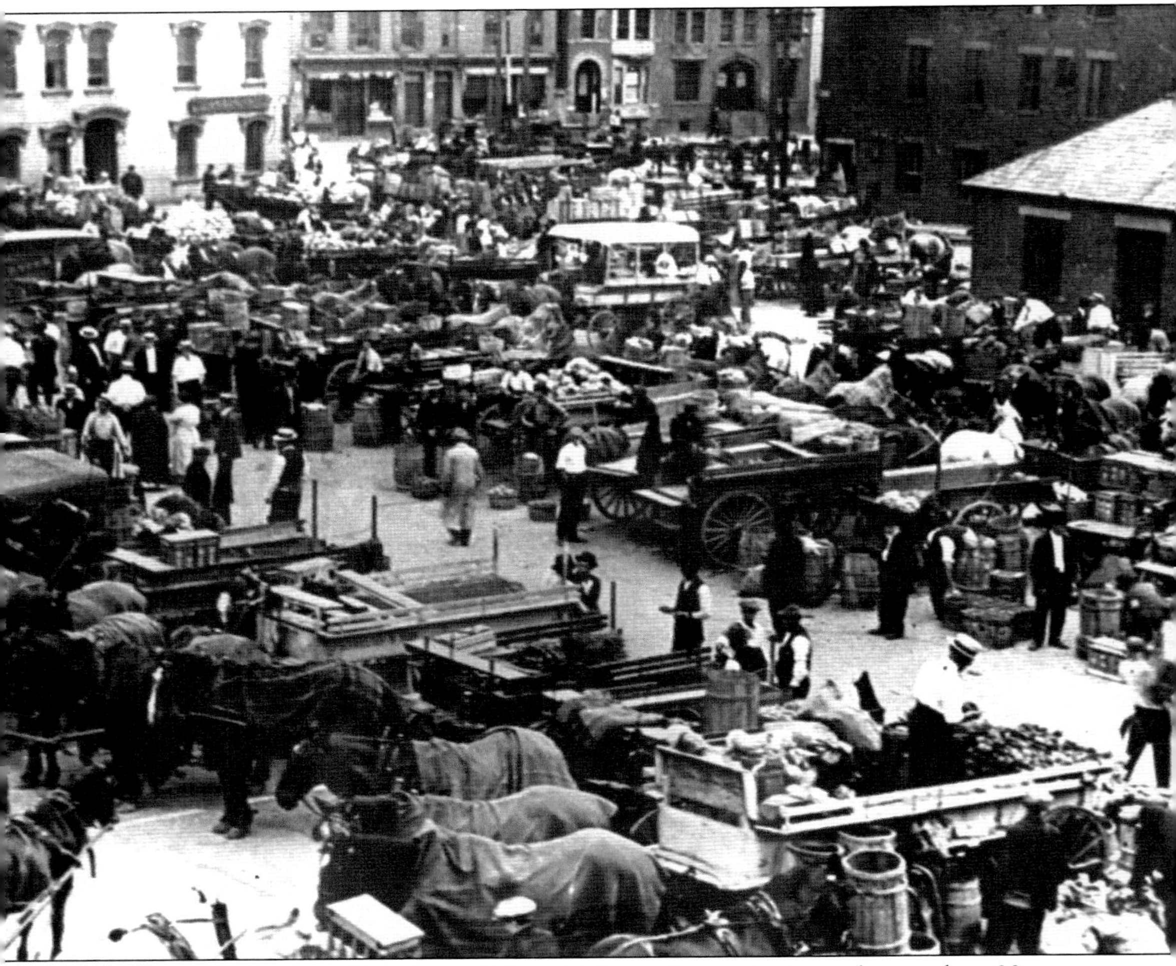

The Troy Public Retail Market at Hill and Liberty Streets is pictured more than 90 years ago with dozens of horse-drawn carts filled with fruits and vegetables grown by local farmers. By the time the market was organized, the residents of the surrounding blocks were primarily Italian immigrants, people from the warm climate of the Mediterranean region, who were accustomed to fresh produce as an important part of their diet and would be frequent customers at the market. (Courtesy of the Rensselaer County Historical Society.)

On the cover: The Troy Public Retail Market at Hill and Liberty Streets, a few blocks south of the city's central business district, opened on July 5, 1918, at the instigation of women of Troy who expressed great interest in obtaining fresh produce from local farmers. The one-acre site, which initially contained 150 stalls, had been the location of a stoneware factory from 1816 to 1837 and of the Troy Gas Light Company from 1848 to 1899. (Courtesy of the Bevevino family.)

IMAGES
of America

TROY'S LITTLE ITALY

Michael A. Esposito

ARCADIA
PUBLISHING

ISBN 978-0-7385-6513-2

Published by Arcadia Publishing
Charleston, South Carolina

Printed in the United States of America

Library of Congress Control Number: 2008942676

For all general information contact Arcadia Publishing at:
Telephone 843-853-2070
Fax 843-853-0044
E-mail sales@arcadiapublishing.com
For customer service and orders:
Toll-Free 1-888-313-2665

Visit us on the Internet at www.arcadiapublishing.com

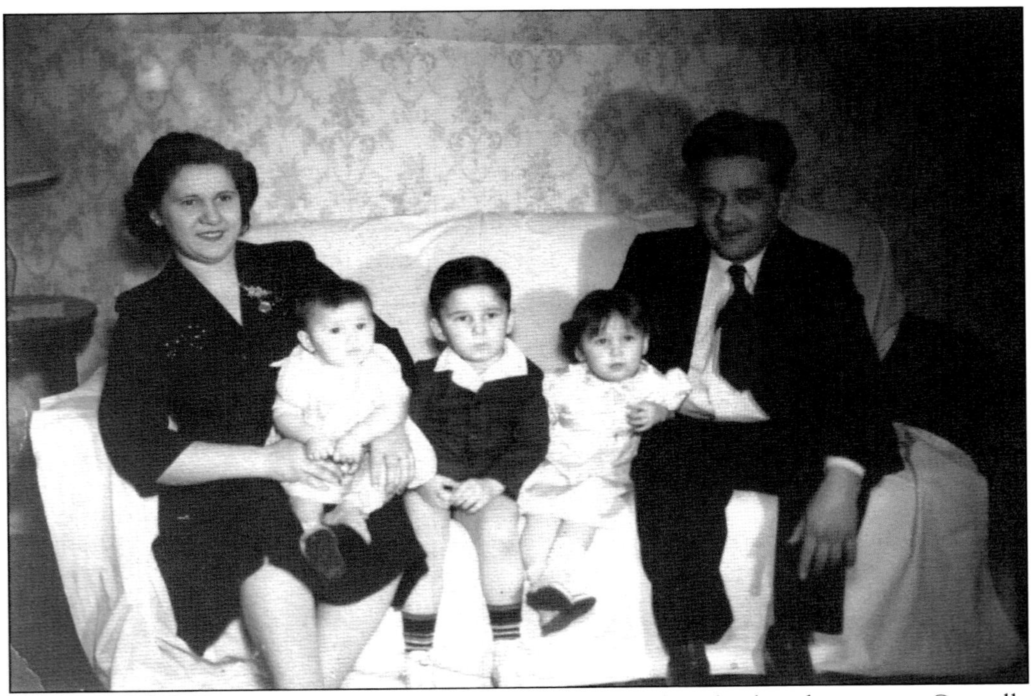

This book is lovingly dedicated to my parents, Antoinette and Michael, and my sisters, Carmella and Nancy. Antoinette and Michael Esposito are shown with their three children, from left to right, Carmella, Michael Jr., and Nancy, in 1943 in their apartment at 30 Havermans Avenue, the home of Antoinette's parents. In 1946, Michael purchased a home for his family in the same neighborhood at 7 St. Mary's Avenue. (Author's collection.)

Contents

Acknowledgments 6

Introduction 7

1. The Formative Years 9

2. Their Faith Sustained Them 19

3. But Sister Said 35

4. Always Ready to Serve 49

5. Open for Business 61

6. The Neighborhood 79

7. The People of Little Italy 87

8. A Lot to Celebrate 123

ACKNOWLEDGMENTS

How often have we heard the expression "A picture is worth a thousand words?" Hundreds of neighbors were gracious in allowing me to use photographs and images that help tell the story of the wonderful, warm, colorful community I was privileged to be born into and where I have spent so many years of my life. I am most thankful to the many family members and friends whose shared life experiences helped add substance to the book.

The Rensselaer County Historical Society and the Troy Public Library provided me with resources used in research for this book. Their collections and the staff that diligently acquires, preserves, and provides access to our history offer an invaluable public service. The archives at St. Anthony's Church, St. Mary's Church, LaSalle Institute, the Italian Community Center, and the local veterans' post, Ciccarelli, Rea, Agars, Bevevino Garrison 1954, provided many photographs important for our collection. My gateway to information about local Italian immigrants was provided by Pat Connors and her volunteers, who are faithfully transcribing available New York State and federal census data on Troy.

I am particularly grateful to Arlene Bouras, Marion Field, Dan Lennon, and Frank Visco for assisting me in acquiring, organizing, and compiling photographs and information. I am in awe of Dan's computer skills—they served us well as he carefully scanned and organized more than 1,400 photographs and images into folders and files, cropping hundreds used in the book—and of Arlene's expertise in copyediting the narrative sections of the book. Marion and I grew up in Troy's Little Italy and it was initially her encouragement that prompted the book. Frank's many years of experience in advertising was a valuable asset to our endeavor. I have very much appreciated their friendship and enthusiasm for the project.

During the early months of the planning process, I had the counsel of longtime family friend Frank Laiacona, author of *Tory Hill and Other Stories*, a personal remembrance of our historic neighborhood. I mourn his untimely passing.

INTRODUCTION

In his colorful and detailed description *Troy's One Hundred Years, 1789–1889,* published in 1891, historian Arthur James Weise makes reference to the area called the upper, middle, and lower farms owned by heirs of the prominent 17th-century Dutch family the Van der Heydens. The lower farm, "the southern allotment," inherited by Matthias Van der Heyden, is the area now referred to as South Central Troy. Matthias lived in the home of his grandfather, also named Matthias, in a brick building originally built in 1752 on the east side of River Road at what is now the corner of Division and River Streets. A 1789 map of Vanderheyden, the earlier name of Troy, consisted of 289 lots along the riverbank in the approximate area that is now the central business district. The population of the settlement was estimated at 150.

Weise tells that "Jan Barentsen Wemp, a provident Dutchman, whose services to the patron of Rensselaerswyck were recorded in the Great Book of the colony as early as 1644, bought from the Indians, in 1659, the Great Meadow Ground, between the Poesten Kill and Meadow Creek, now a part of the site of Troy." According to the early records of Rensselaerswyck, a sawmill built on the Poesten Kill by Wemp is cited in a patent confirmed in 1667 by Richard Nicolls, the English governor of the province of New York. At his death in 1663, Wemp left his property to his wife, Maria, and his two sons and three daughters. Maria remarried and in the years that followed, the huge farm was sold several times. In 1707, the property was purchased by Dirk Van der Heyden. It remained in the Van der Heyden family through the remainder of the 18th century, was surveyed (the south farm was divided into lots and mapped as early as 1793), and gradually sold. One of the first large sections purchased was the area around Washington Park developed in the 1830s and 1840s by a group of prominent Troy businessmen.

By all accounts, the growth of Troy was remarkable. "From the older states the tide of emigration continued, and Troy became more attractive. The influx of eastern emigrants continued," states Weise, referring to the Yankees from New England who resettled in Troy. By the time the city was incorporated on April 12, 1816, its population was more than 4,000. The first of its six wards was from Ferry Street to the Poestenkill, the city's southern boundary. The opening of the Erie Canal in the area on October 8, 1823, was to create further prosperity for the city, which expanded both south and north along the Hudson. Historically, industry in the South Central neighborhood grew primarily along the river—bell foundries, iron and stove works, lumberyards, railroad freight yards, and garment shops. Some large businesses were scattered on the periphery of the neighborhood, below the western slopes of Mount Ida and near the Poestenkill.

Mount Ida, the dominant geographic feature of the city, would play a prominent part in the history of Troy. Clay from its slopes was used for pottery and for bricks. But there were also frequent and sometimes disastrous landslides. Between 1816 and 1837, a stoneware factory was in operation in the lower part of Troy at the intersection of Hill and Washington Streets just below Mount Ida. The first recorded landslide, on January 1, 1837, destroyed the pottery works and killed seven people.

Between 1845 and 1848, Irish immigrants were arriving in America by the tens of thousands due to the tragic famine in their homeland. In response to the obvious needs of the newly arrived immigrants, Rev. Peter Havermans, a Dutch priest, established a hospital, several schools, asylums for orphans, and two Catholic churches, all within a few blocks of Washington Street. This was accomplished over a period of two decades beginning in the mid-1840s. By 1854, part of the route of the Troy Union Railroad cut diagonally through the South Central neighborhood from Sixth Avenue to First Street. In 1848, a decade after the pottery works was destroyed, the site became the location of the Troy Gas Light Company, which remained in operation until 1899. In 1872, several blocks south, in what was then a sparsely populated area near the Poestenkill, at Fifth Avenue and Jefferson Street, the company erected a huge circular gasholder house, one of a few of its kind still standing. For more than 100 years, the flour mill and gristmill of Andrew Ruff, a prominent member of Troy's German community who immigrated to America in 1841, was located near Hill Street at the Poestenkill. A block away, William Connors, the manufacturer of American Seal paint, established a factory in 1878 at Hill and Ida Streets.

By 1880, Troy was the 29th-largest city in the country, with a population of 56,747, of whom 39,809 were native-born residents and 16,938 were foreign born. During the next several dozen years, Troy's population would swell with the arrival of even more immigrants and with the annexation of the village of Lansingburgh in 1900. By 1902, the city had acquired the Warren and Vail family estates on Mount Ida for parkland and turned it into a beautifully landscaped public space, Prospect Park. The early Italian immigrants, either by chance or by choice, chose wisely in settling where they did in Troy.

One

The Formative Years

Among the 48,253 names in the 1875 New York State census of Troy, 27 individuals from 11 families listed their country of origin as Italy. All resided in the First and Second Wards. Nine men were listed as head of household: three were musicians, three were barbers, and one each was a cook, a glazier, and a saloon keeper. According to the 1880 United States census, 49 individuals reported that they or one or both of their parents had been born in Italy. Fourteen men were listed as head of household: six worked as hucksters (primarily fruit peddlers), four were barbers, three were peanut vendors, and one worked for a real-estate salesman. They lived in just 5 of Troy's 13 wards.

By 1900, half of the 465 Italian immigrants in the city resided in several dozen buildings on Church and William Streets in the First and Eighth Wards. Each federal census for 1910, 1920, and 1930 reported 1,500 to 1,900 people in Troy who identified themselves as "Italian born." They were primarily unskilled laborers; few had professions, some had trades—tailors, barbers, masons. They were comfortable living among their large extended families and among *paesans*. They came primarily from the regions of Campania, Calabria, Sicily, and Apulia.

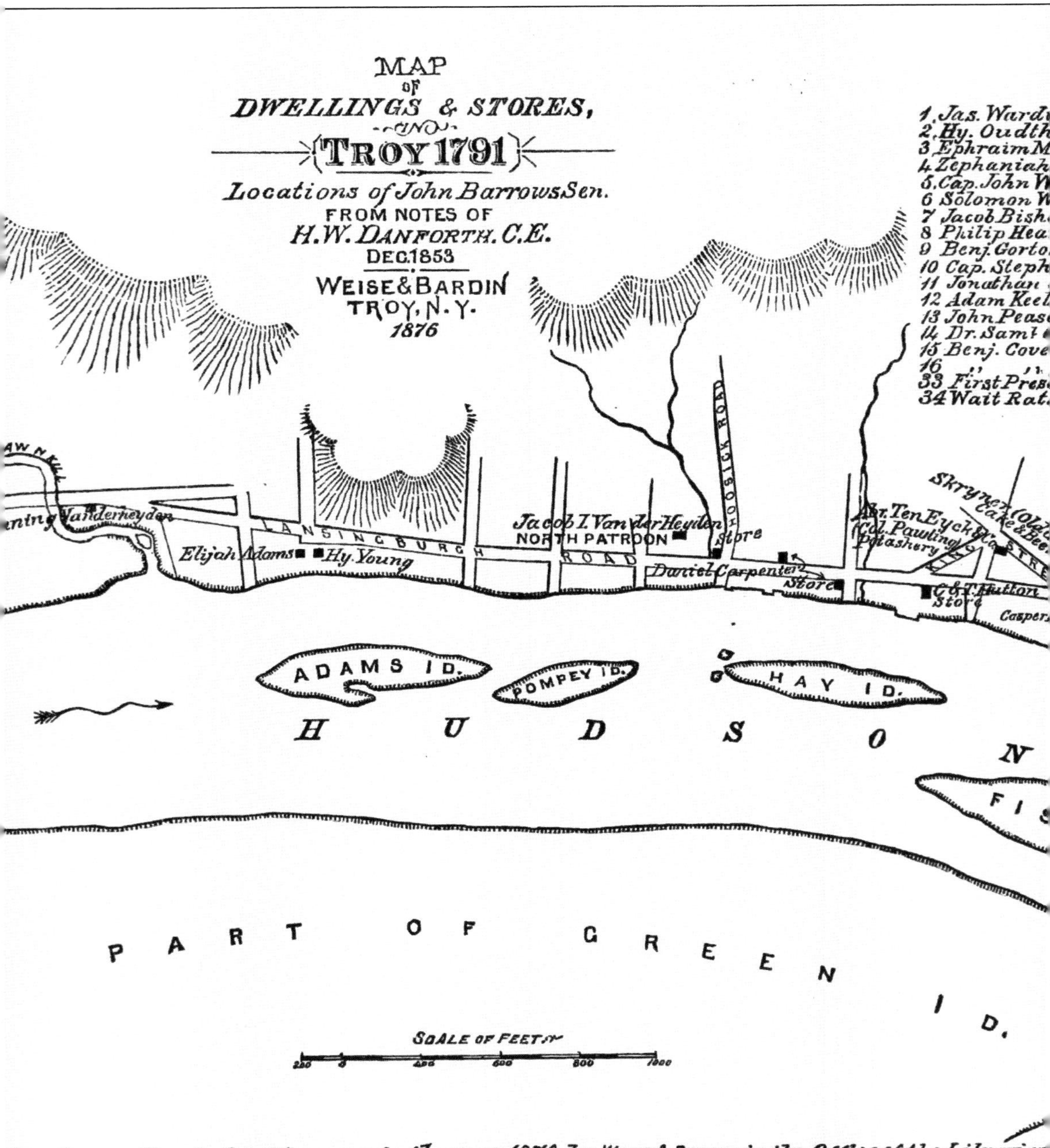

This is an 1876 composite of the map of Troy in 1791, when much of the land was still owned by the Van der Heyden family. The area was the aboriginal domain of the Mohegan Indians, who referred to it as the Great Meadow. It would eventually be surveyed and mapped by John E. Van Alen. A few miles north was the junction of the Hudson and Mohawk Rivers, and seven miles

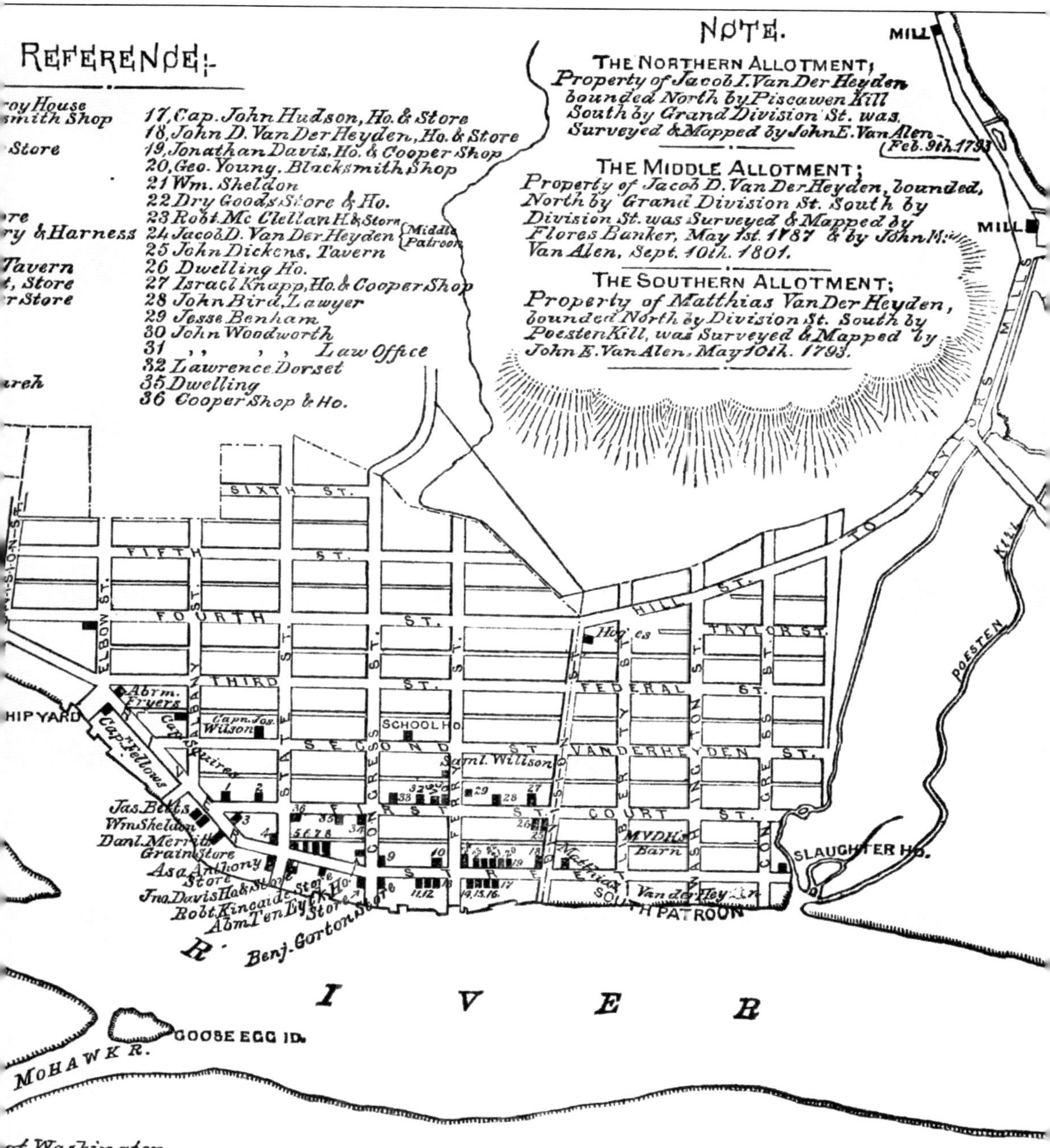

south was Fort Orange (later called Albany). The area designated as the southern allotment is now referred to as Troy's South Central neighborhood. Little Italy is located below the slope of Mount Ida from Ferry Street to Fourth Street to the Poesten Kill. (*History of the City of Troy* by Arthur James Weise.)

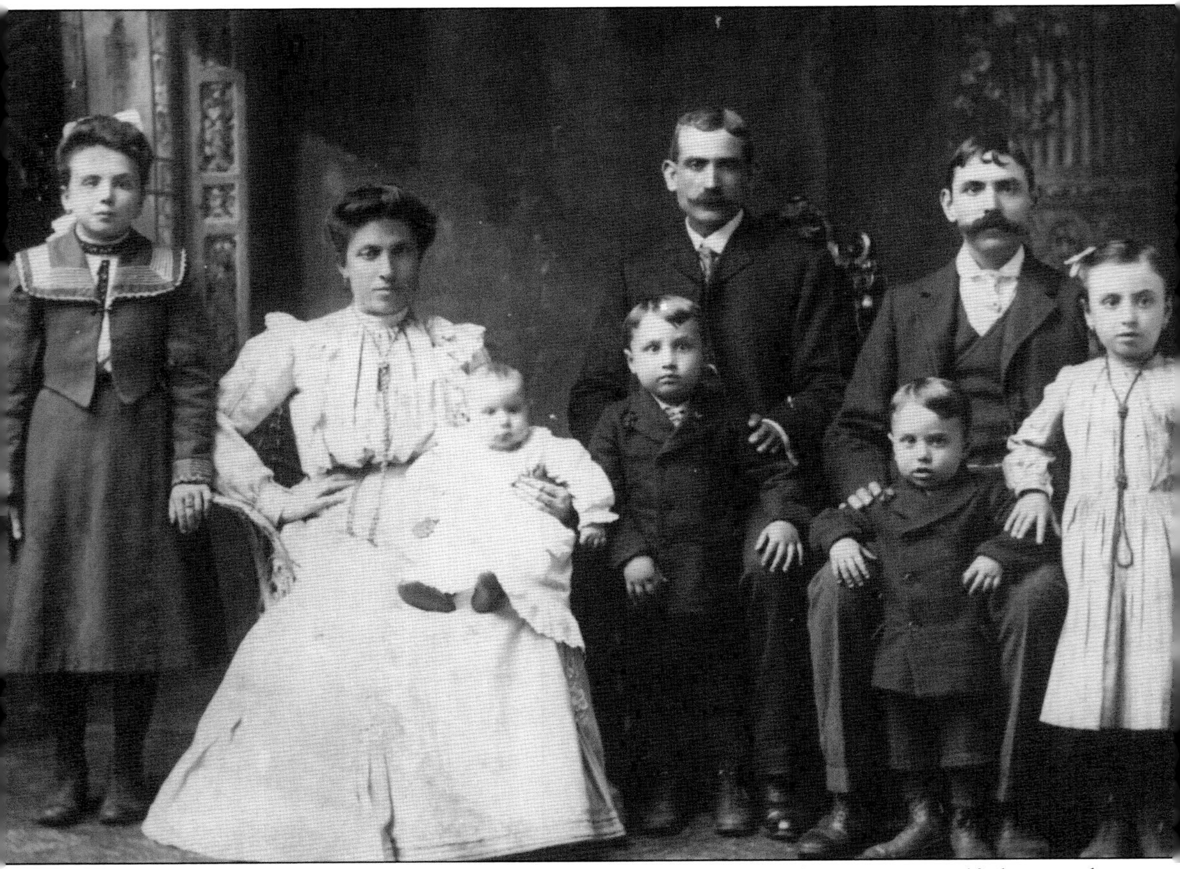

Parents Philomena and Antonio Visco bracket the unidentified patron, or godfather, as they pose with the first five of their eight children, from left to right, Elizabeth, baby Mary, Vincenzo "Jimmy," Gaetano "Guy," and Rose. In 1892, the Visco family was one of 23 Italian immigrant families who joined Rev. Giovanni Santoro to establish a parish community dedicated to St. Anthony of Padua. The second generation would become known as the Visk family and would continue to support the Italian church, St. Anthony's, as parishioners, trustees, ushers, and show-producing fund-raisers. (Courtesy of the Visk family.)

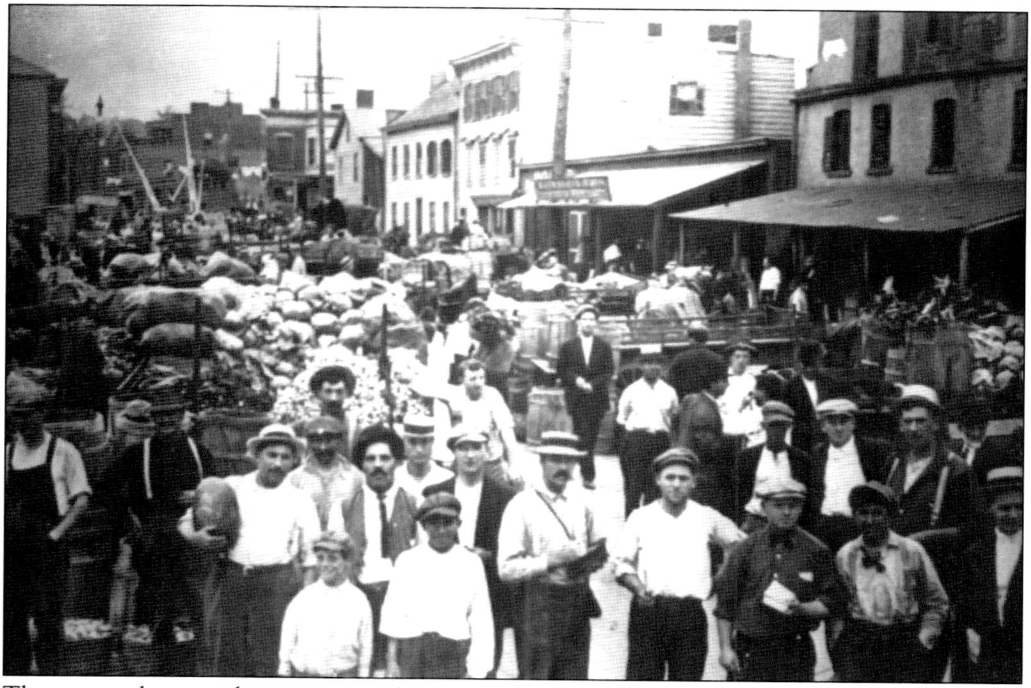

These two photographs are views of the Troy Public Retail Market. Between 1905 and 1920, several successful produce establishments opened on the west side of Hill Street from Liberty to Washington Streets. The women of the city expressed a great interest in a retail farmers' market for the huge vacant lot adjacent to the wholesale establishments. On July 5, 1918, 500 women eagerly awaited the opening of the Troy Public Retail Market, which contained 150 stalls. The retail farmers' market gradually lost business when the Menands Regional Market opened in 1932, and by the 1950s, its use as a farmers' market had ceased. (Above, courtesy of the Marchese family; below, courtesy of Mayor Harry Tutunjian.)

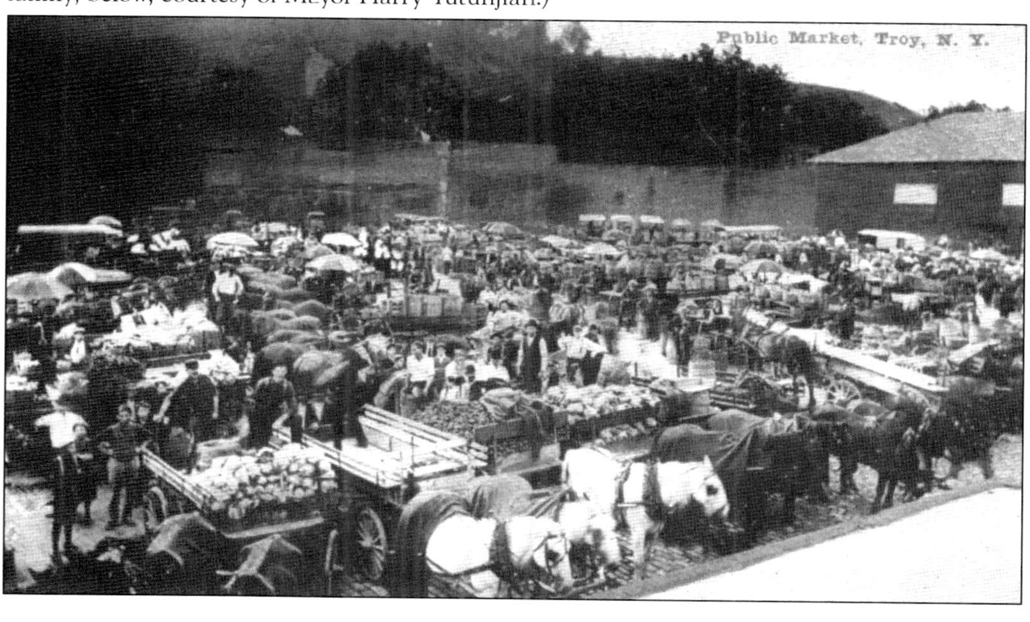

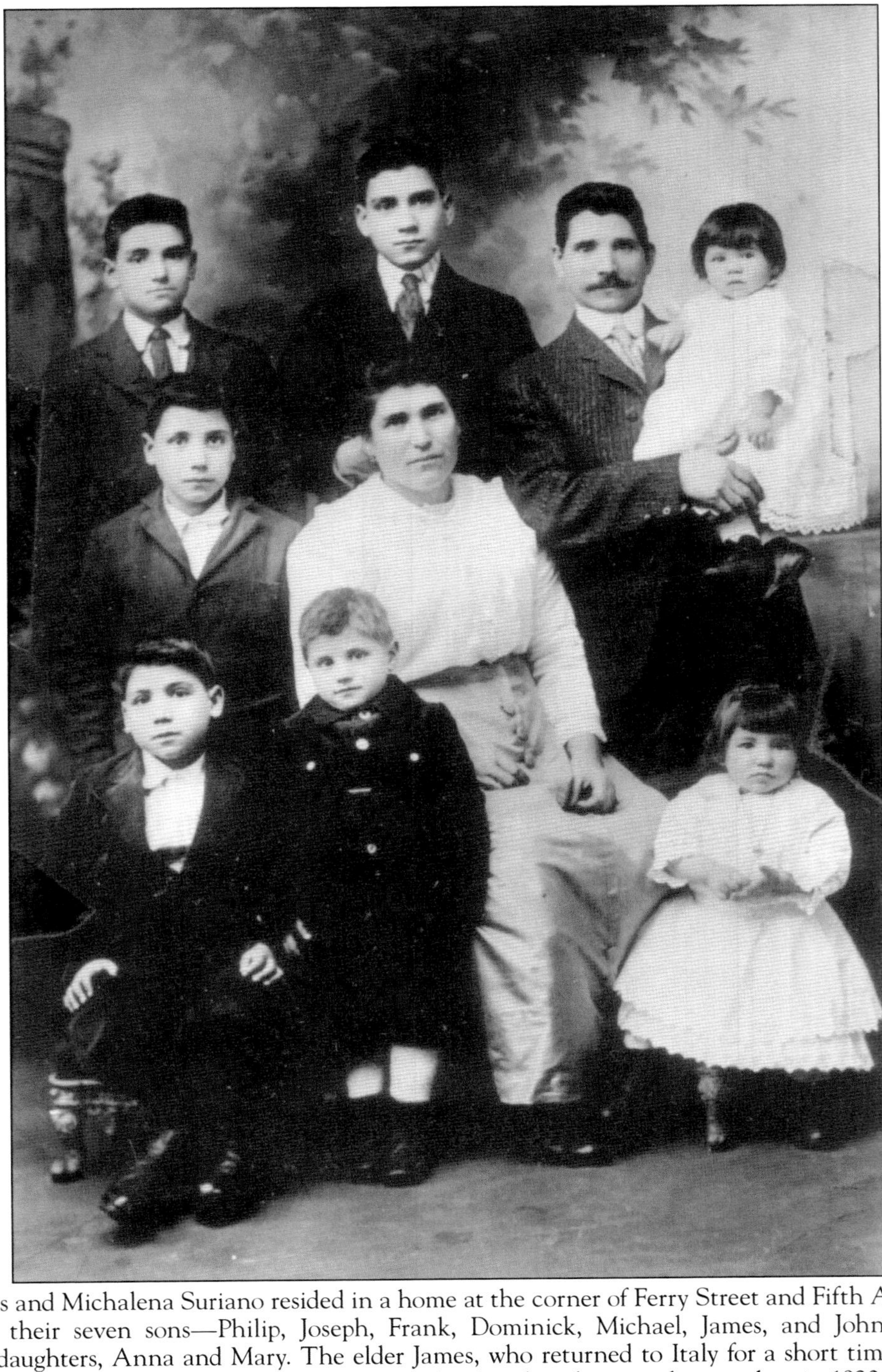

James and Michalena Suriano resided in a home at the corner of Ferry Street and Fifth Avenue with their seven sons—Philip, Joseph, Frank, Dominick, Michael, James, and John—and two daughters, Anna and Mary. The elder James, who returned to Italy for a short time after immigrating to Troy, died at an early age shortly after this photograph was taken in 1920. Their home was an equal distance from the Ferry Street homestead of Samuel "Uncle Sam" Wilson, Troy's nationally known folk hero, and residences on William Street off Ferry Street that housed hundreds of Troy's earliest Italian immigrants. (Courtesy of James Suriano.)

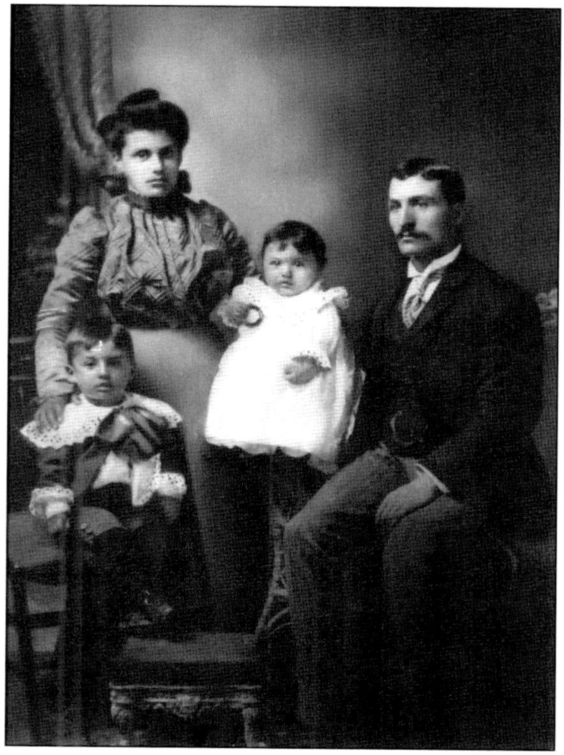

Frank LaPosta emigrated from Frosolone, a mountain town in the Italian region of Molise, before Ellis Island was the eastern United States entry point. From a family of scissors makers, he settled for menial jobs until he and his wife, Rose DeMarino LaPosta, opened their confectionery and raised a large family. Four generations later, there is still a LaPosta's store in the family. (Courtesy of the LaPosta family.)

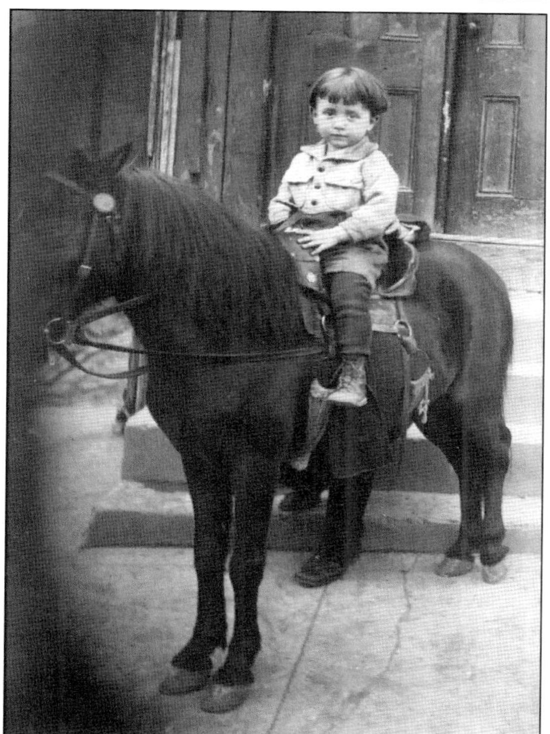

Joseph Mosca poses on a pony in Troy's public market on Hill Street in the early 1920s. Usually, an old-timer who owned a pony and a camera would visit the neighborhood and, for a coin or two, would provide children with a pony ride and a memorable photograph for the family album. Joseph and his brothers, Salvatore and James, were the sons of Carmela and Antonio Mosca from Aqua Viva, Sicily. (Courtesy of Robert Mosca.)

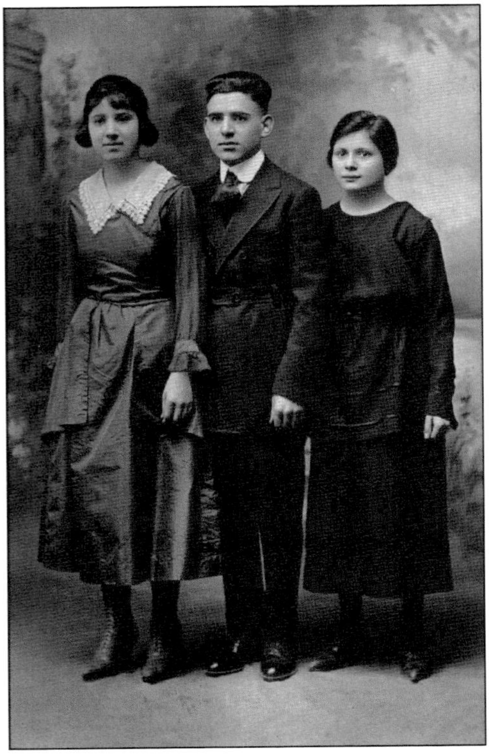

Studio photographs by professional photographers provided longtime keepsakes for families. From left to right, Rebecca Terribile poses with her brother, Michele, and his sister-in-law, Assunta. All were born in Candela, Italy. Rebecca married Luigi Favata; Assunta married Nicolo Cavallo. Both women and their husbands worked for many years in Troy's garment industry. Michele married Clelia "Clara" Comegna and after many years as a laborer, worked in the Allegheny Ludlum steel mill. (Courtesy of Michael Dinova.)

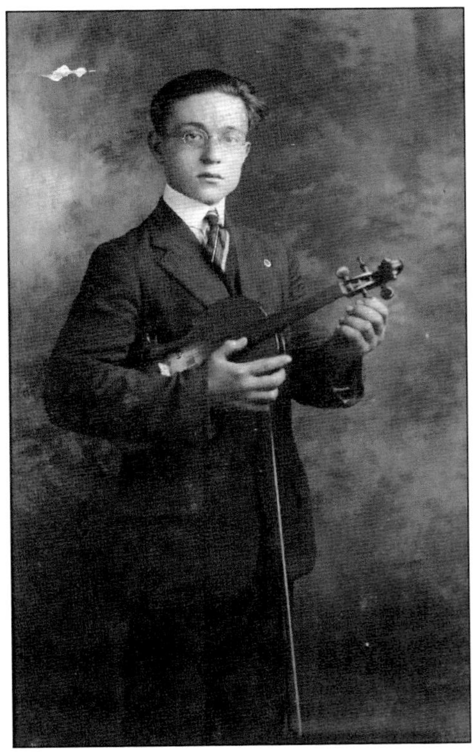

Louis Favata Sr. (right) was an accomplished musician, specializing in guitar, banjo, and mandolin. He played guitar on the local Forrest Willis show on radio station WOKO for several years. He often accompanied his four sons, who played piano, saxophone, and violin. His son Ted, a graduate of the Troy Conservatory of Music, played professionally with a trio. Louis was a presser in Troy's garment industry. (Courtesy of Michael Dinova.)

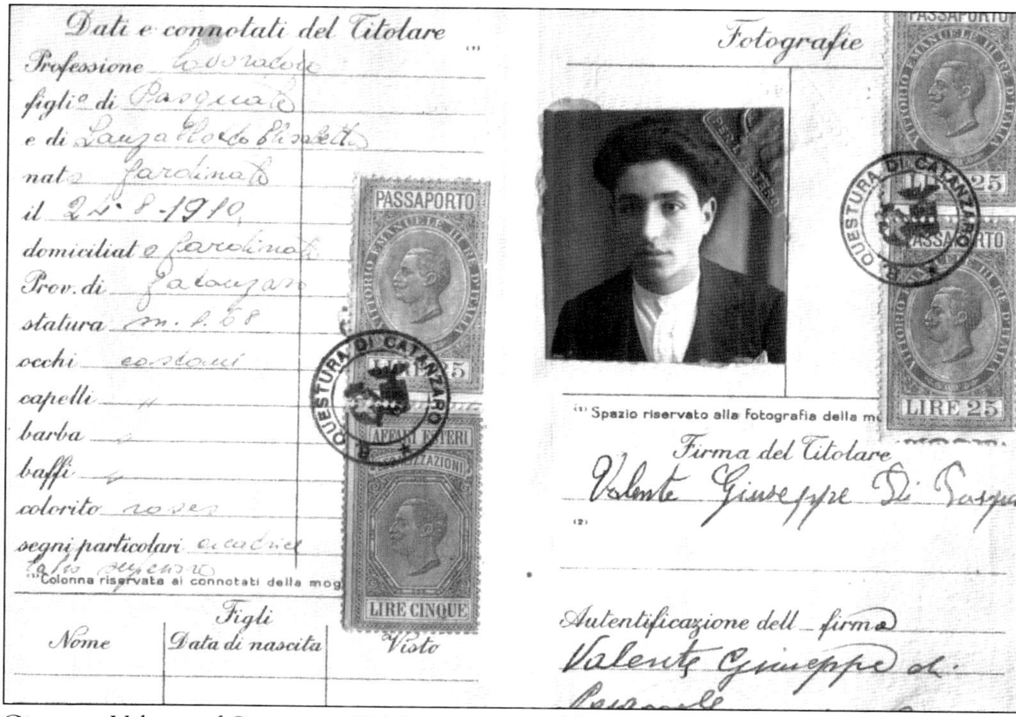

Giuseppe Valente of Catanzaro, Calabria, was issued his passport at the age of 19 in June 1927. Upon his arrival in America, he resided in Westchester County but eventually moved to Troy and became a longtime resident of Havermans Avenue and a skilled shoe repairman at the Fulton Shoe Repair Shop in downtown Troy. He married Victoria Rachielle and was father of Patrick, Joseph, and Elizabeth. (Courtesy of Patrick Valente.)

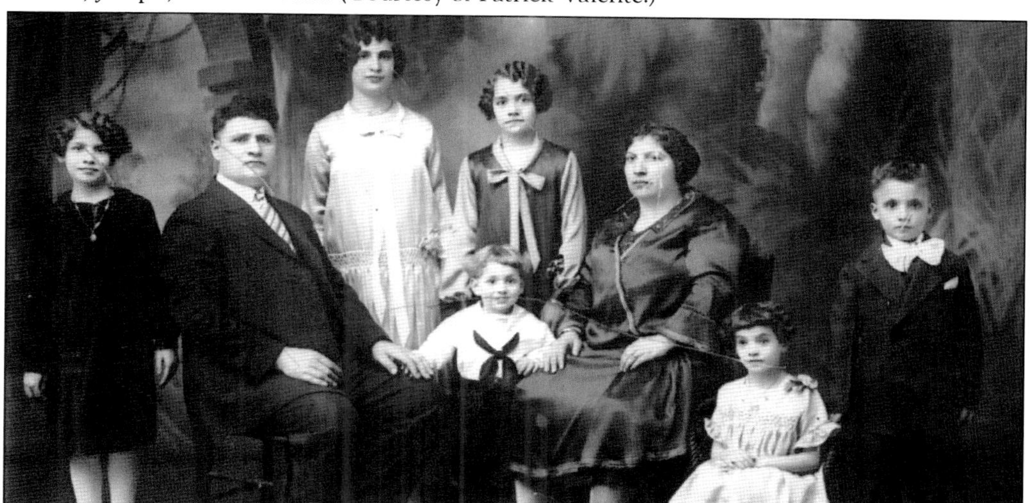

Dominic and Stella Lombardo are photographed with their children. From left to right are Jennie, Madeline, Julie, Anthony, Mary (seated), and Dominic Jr. A fifth daughter, Anne, was born several years later. Their sons Dominic and Anthony were owners of the Airport Inn (later called Mario's Theatre Restaurant), Paul's Restaurant, Manory's Luncheonette, and other successful Troy businesses. (Courtesy of Anne Lombardo Rymanowski.)

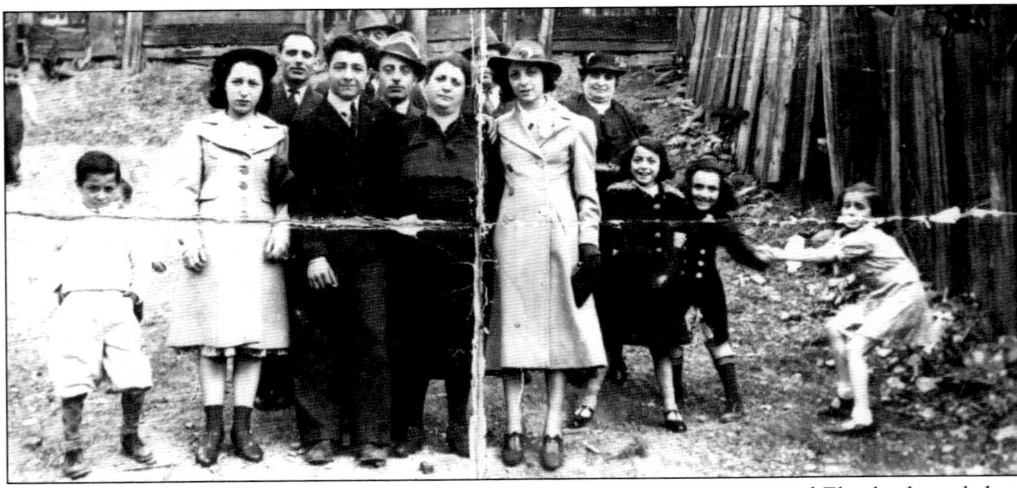

The Bevevinos have been a family of neighborhood stalwarts. Dominic and Elizabeth and their children are photographed in the late 1930s near their home at 3 St. Mary's Avenue. From 1940 to 2004, their family residence was at 65 Hill Street. As the children—sons Bruno, Dominic Jr., James, Joseph, Nicholas, and Frank and daughters Marion, Rose, Catherine, and Mary—married, they in turn raised their children within the confines of the Little Italy neighborhood. (Courtesy of the Bevevino family.)

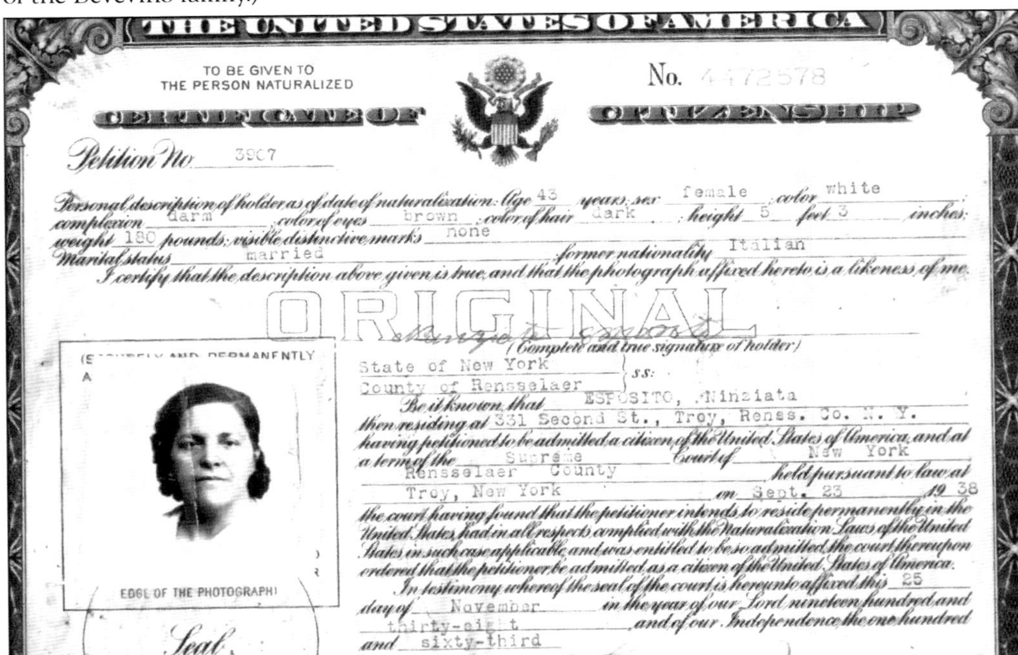

THE UNITED STATES OF AMERICA

TO BE GIVEN TO THE PERSON NATURALIZED

No. 4472578

CERTIFICATE OF CITIZENSHIP

Petition No. 3907

Personal description of holder as of date of naturalization: Age 43 years; sex female color white complexion dark color of eyes brown color of hair dark height 5 feet 3 inches; weight 180 pounds; visible distinctive marks none

Marital status married former nationality Italian

I certify that the description above given is true, and that the photograph affixed hereto is a likeness of me.

ORIGINAL

(Complete and true signature of holder)

State of New York } ss:
County of Rensselaer }

Be it known, that ESPOSITO, Ninziata then residing at 331 Second St., Troy, Renss. Co. N. Y. having petitioned to be admitted a citizen of the United States of America, and at a term of the Supreme Court of New York Rensselaer County held pursuant to law at Troy, New York on Sept. 23 1938 the court having found that the petitioner intends to reside permanently in the United States, had in all respects complied with the Naturalization Laws of the United States in such case applicable, and was entitled to be so admitted the court thereupon ordered that the petitioner be admitted as a citizen of the United States of America.

In testimony whereof the seal of the court is hereunto affixed this 25 day of November in the year of our Lord nineteen hundred and thirty-eight and of our Independence the one hundred and sixty-third

EDGE OF THE PHOTOGRAPH

Seal.

Nunziata Santora Esposito was born in the region of Campania, Italy, in 1895 and immigrated to America in 1924 to marry Giuseppe Esposito, a widower with eight children. She received her Certificate of Citizenship in 1938. The large family—the children of Nunziata and Giuseppe and Giuseppe's children by his first wife—resided in Little Italy. In the 1940s, Giuseppe purchased vacant land adjacent to the Troy Airport and built a small farmhouse. (Courtesy of Nancy Esposito Farley.)

Two

Their Faith Sustained Them

In 1843, 50 years before there were many Italian immigrants in Troy, a Dutch priest, Rev. Peter Havermans, organized the city's second Catholic church, St. Mary's. He immediately concerned himself with the spiritual, social, and economic needs of thousands of immigrants in South Troy: first the Irish, then the French Canadians and the Germans. During his 55 years as pastor of St. Mary's, prominent local historians who were his contemporaries recorded that the Catholic community in Troy was created through the efforts and achievements of this remarkable priest. His priorities were a school, an asylum for orphans, and a place for the sick, all of which he organized in a relatively short time at institutions on the blocks adjacent to Washington Street. Reverend Havermans encouraged members of several religious orders to come to Troy to educate the children and care for the orphans, the elderly, and the sick. French-Canadian, German, and later Italian immigrants worshiped in their native languages at St. Mary's Church until each group organized a parish—St. Jean's in 1850, St. Lawrence's in 1870, St. Anthony's in 1892. Family stories handed down from generation to generation repeat the uncomfortable facts about the intolerance of one group toward another; but there is little doubt about Rev. Havermans's care of and devotion to all under his ministry during his many years in the priesthood.

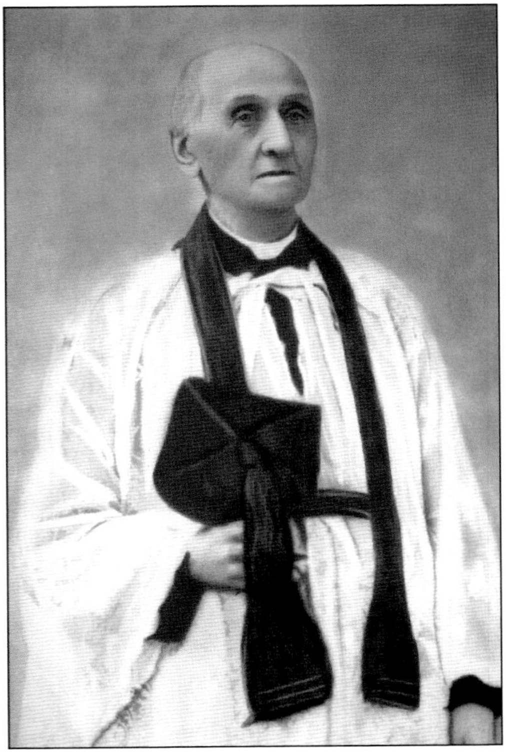

Rev. Peter Havermans was born in 1806 in Baarle Nassau, North Brabent, Holland, near the Belgian border. He entered the priesthood in 1824, immigrated to America in 1830, and was assigned as pastor of St. Peter's Catholic Church in Troy in 1842. He was founder and first pastor of St. Mary's Church and served there for 55 years (1843–1897). The inscription on his monument in St. Mary's Cemetery reads, "Father of Troy's Catholic Institutions." (Courtesy of the St. Mary's Church Archives.)

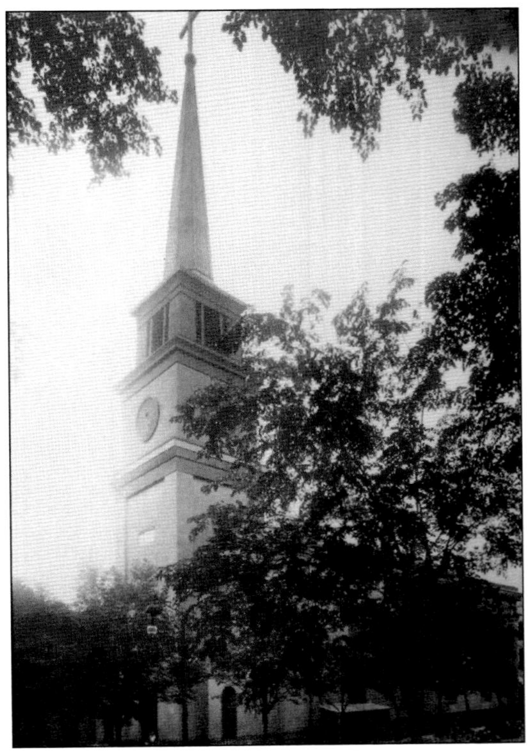

St. Mary's Church was founded in 1843 by Rev. Peter Havermans to serve the spiritual needs of an influx of Irish Catholic immigrants in the southern neighborhoods of Troy. The former church, a wooden structure located on the southeast corner of Washington and Third Streets, was demolished in 1898. The parish flourished and by 1900 consisted of 1,350 families. The present church, built on the same site, was dedicated on May 8, 1904. (Courtesy of the St. Mary's Church Archives.)

Rev. Giovanni Santoro, first pastor of St. Anthony of Padua Church, was a priest of the Albany Catholic Diocese appointed by Bishop Francis McNierny to organize 23 Italian immigrant families as the nucleus of a new parish. The small storefront where they met at 106 Ferry Street was listed from 1893 to 1904 in the city directory as simply the Italian chapel. There is no known photograph of the small chapel. (Courtesy of John Capano Jr.)

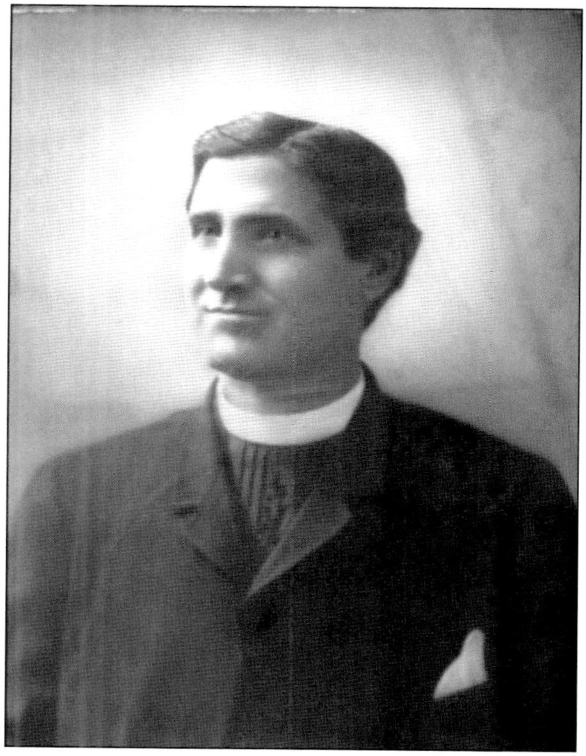

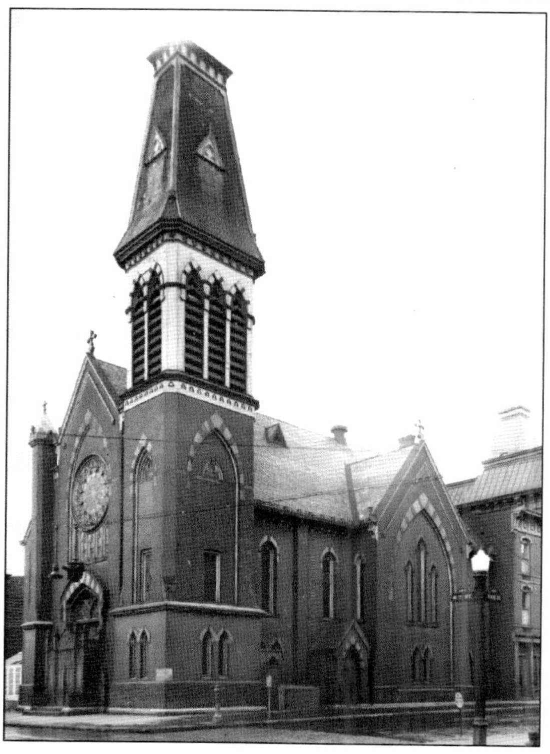

In 1905, the growing congregation of St. Anthony's purchased a church built in 1876 by the Unitarian Society at the corner of Fourth and State Streets. It was to be the second of three church buildings accommodating the parish. Following an elaborate renovation of the interior, the church in the photograph was solemnly dedicated in 1907. It was not until 1925 that the parish was offered to the care of the Franciscans of the Commissary of the Immaculate Conception of New York. (Courtesy of the St. Anthony's Church Archives.)

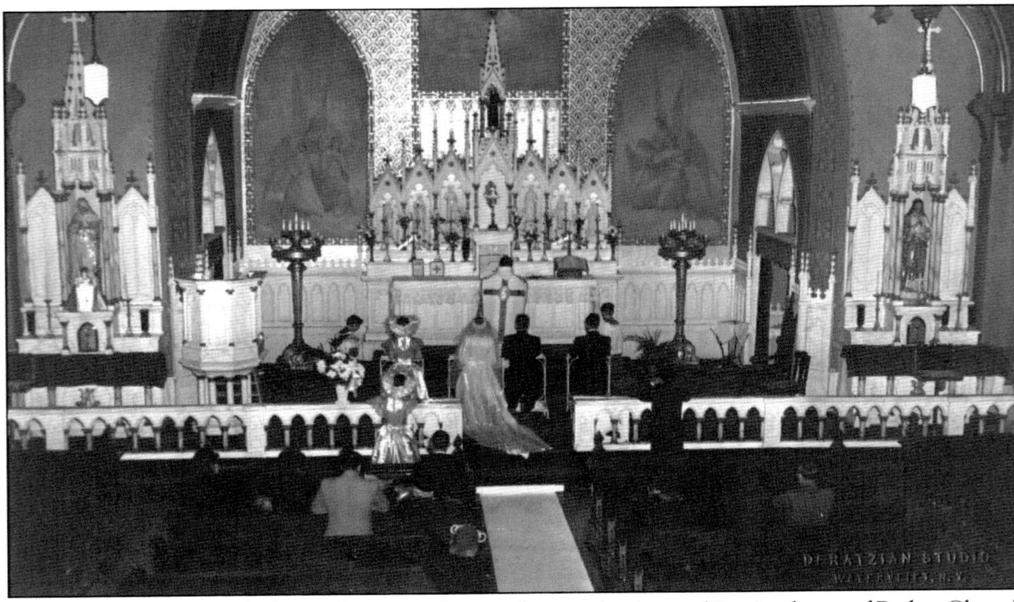

An interior photograph shows the main altar and two side altars of St. Anthony of Padua Church at its location on the corner of Fourth and State Streets. Among the active church organizations always ready to assist each pastor were the Holy Name Society, the Altar-Rosary Society, the Third Order of St. Francis (St. Louis and St. Elizabeth fraternities), the Mother's Club, and the Parent Teacher Association. (Courtesy of A. V. Costa.)

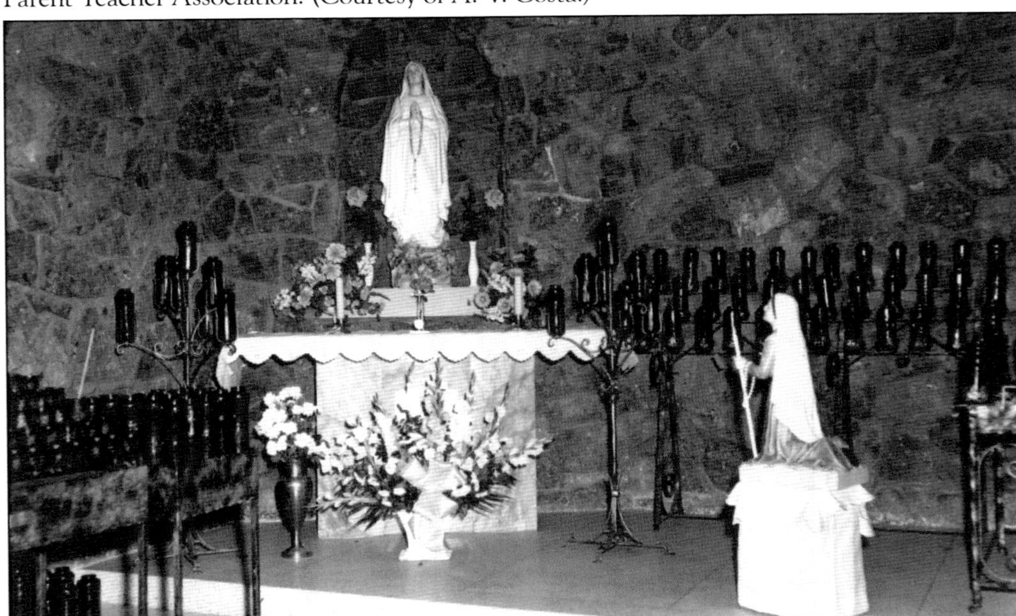

Our Lady of Lourdes Shrine, a replica of the site in southern France where Bernadette Soubirous received her message from "the beautiful lady," was first constructed for the lower-level chapel in St. Anthony's Church on Fourth Street. When the new church was built on State Street, the shrine was reconstructed and continues to serve as a special place to venerate and worship. (Courtesy of the St. Anthony's Church Archives.)

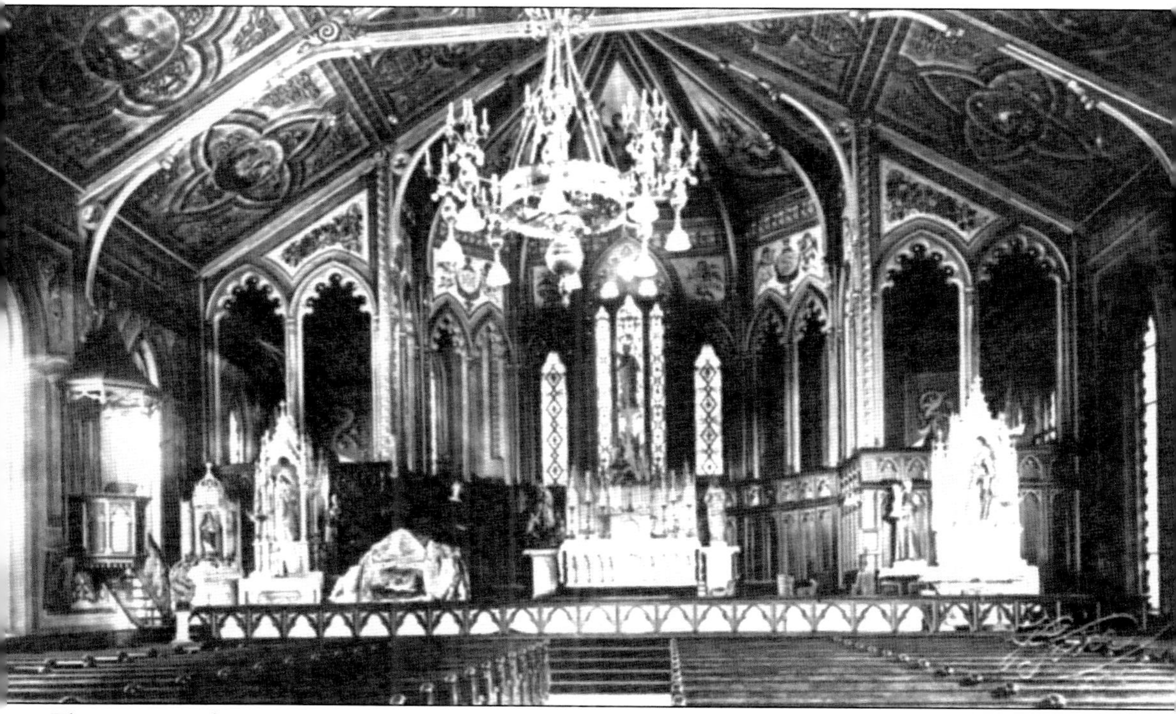

The interior of St. Jean Baptiste Church, located on the east side of Second Street between Adams and Jefferson Streets, was dedicated in 1869. The French congregation, organized in 1850, first worshipped in the basement of St. Mary's Church. Several years later, it purchased a former Universalist church between First and Second Streets. When the old structure burned to the ground, parishioners worshipped at St. Joseph's Church until the new one was built. In 1880, when St. Jean's opened its school, the Sisters of Ste. Anne of Lachine, Canada, and for a time, the Sisters of Jesus and Mary, a French order, taught there. St. Jean's maintained separate buildings for boys and girls. When a new school was built in 1914, the Sisters of St. Joseph of Carondelet began teaching there and remained until the school closed in 1934. The church closed in 1970. (Courtesy of the Joe Connors postcard collection.)

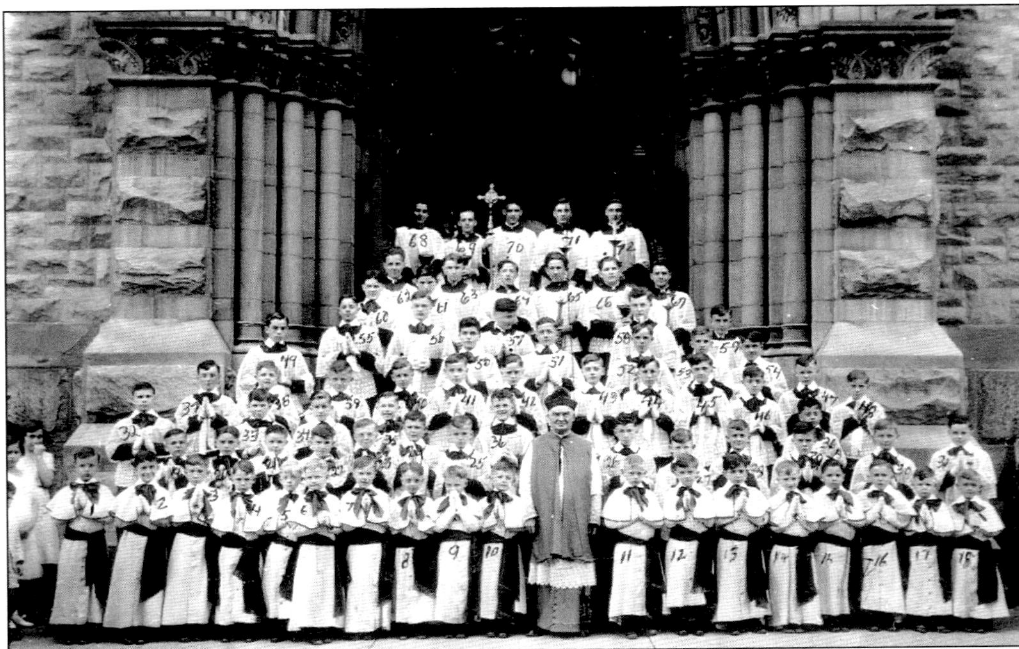

The steps of St. Mary's Church at Third and Washington Streets provide the gathering site in 1931 for the 72 members of the combined altar boys and choirboys of the parish. Prior to Vatican II, it was essential for the young people who served mass or sang in the choir to know and understand Latin. Standing among the young people is Msgr. William P. Fitzgerald, pastor from 1919 to 1938. (Courtesy of Rev. Edward Ryan.)

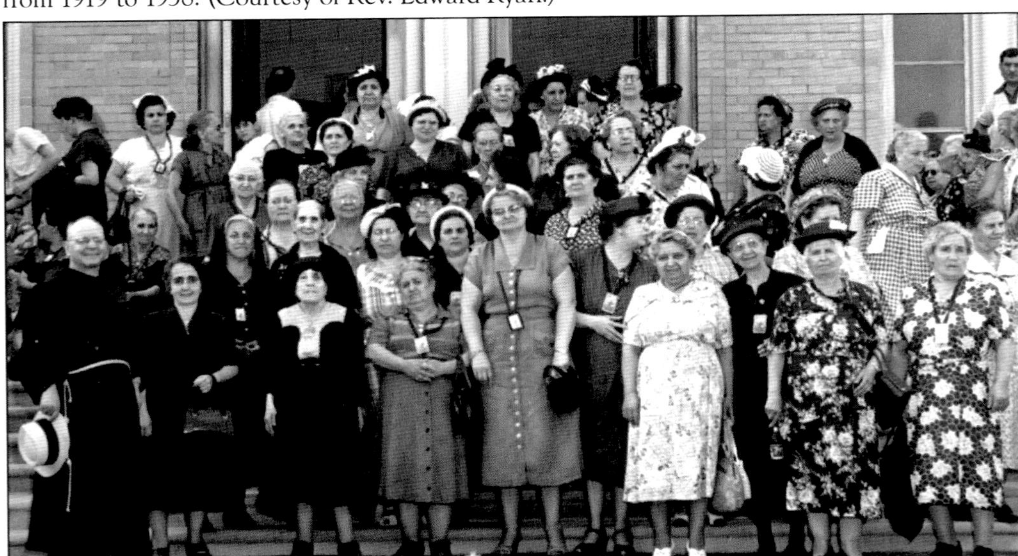

The Third Order of St. Francis, established in 1925, is an association of the faithful, the laity, who seek to pattern their lives after Christ in the spirit of St. Francis of Assisi, the founder of the group. Members are photographed following a 1946 spiritual retreat. Retreats were frequently held at the Franciscan Monastery of the Immaculate Conception in South Troy. All were devout people and active in the community. (Author's collection.)

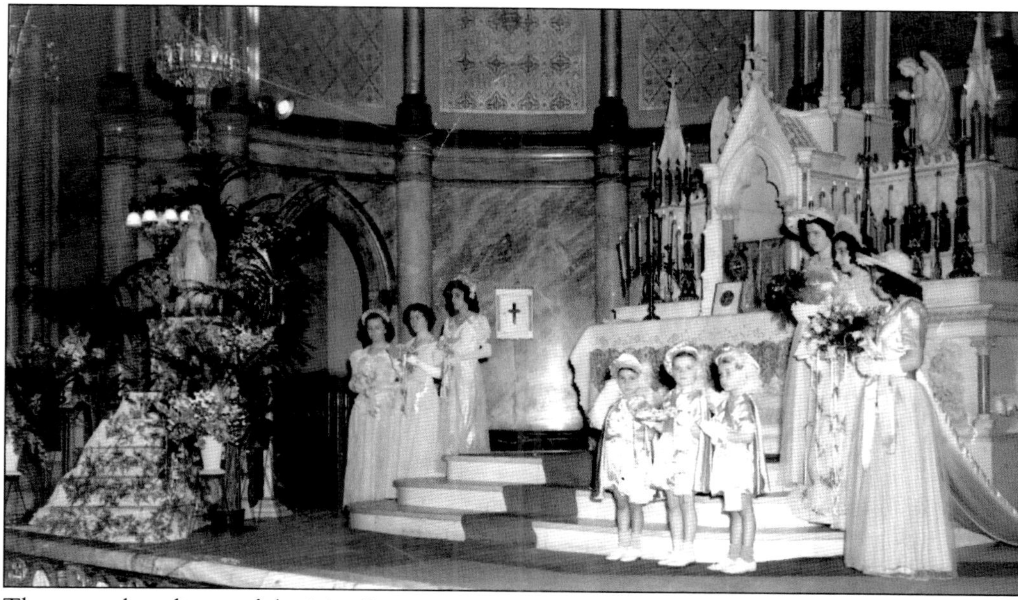

The annual tradition of the May Day crowning of a statue of the Virgin Mary attracted several thousand area residents to the neighborhood. The procession of parish children would begin at the church, walk around and through Washington Park, then return to the church for the crowning ceremony. There would be standing room only in the church, which seated more than 500. People would line the streets around Washington Park as well. (Author's collection.)

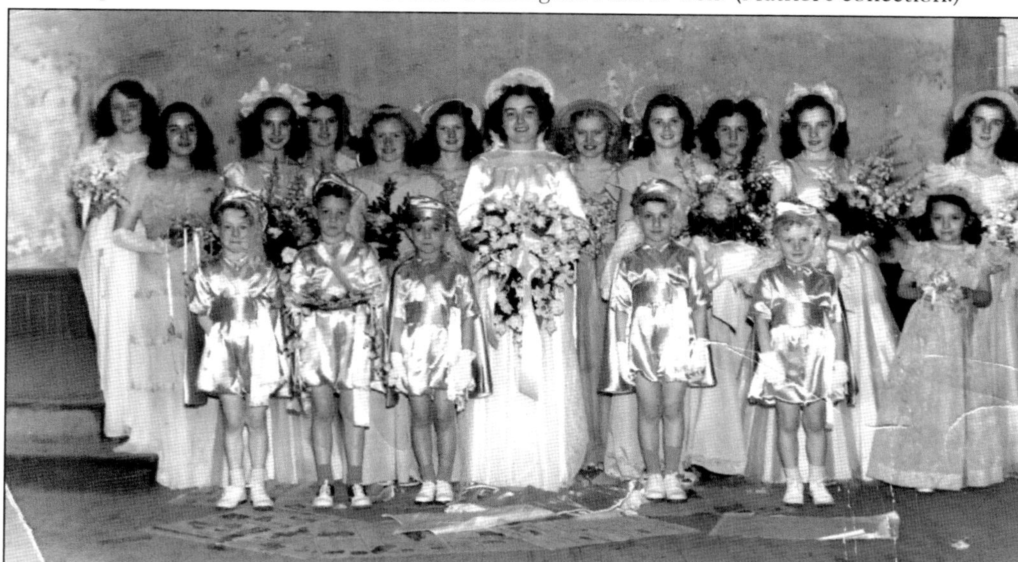

The crowning of a statue of the Virgin Mary was a sizable production for the good sisters, the Daughters of Charity, who taught at St. Mary's School (originally St. Mary's Academy). While the entire student body would participate in the ceremony, a court was assembled consisting of a young woman who would crown the statue with a wreath of fresh flowers. She would have several assistants. Young boys would be assigned as pages for the court. (Courtesy of Marion Church Field.)

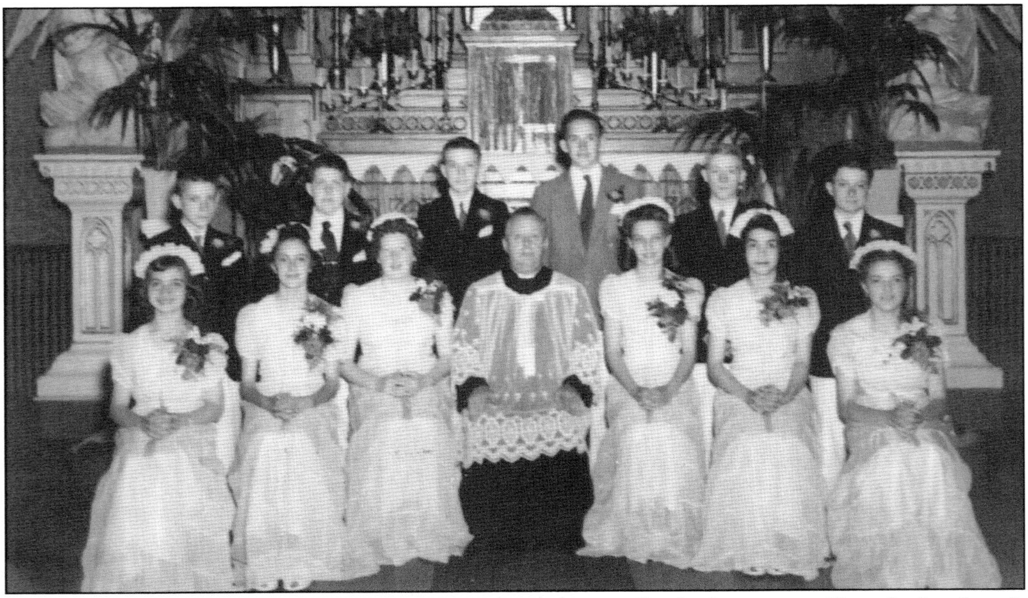

The 1947 graduating class of St. Lawrence School (originally St. Lawrence Church Academy), which includes Anne Lombardo, gathers for a class photograph in front of the altar of the German Catholic church with Rev. Francis J. Buechler, who served for many years as pastor. The Albany Catholic Diocese closed the church in 1987. The building was sold and is now home to the United Ordained Church of Christ, an active congregation. (Courtesy of Anne Lombardo Rymanowski.)

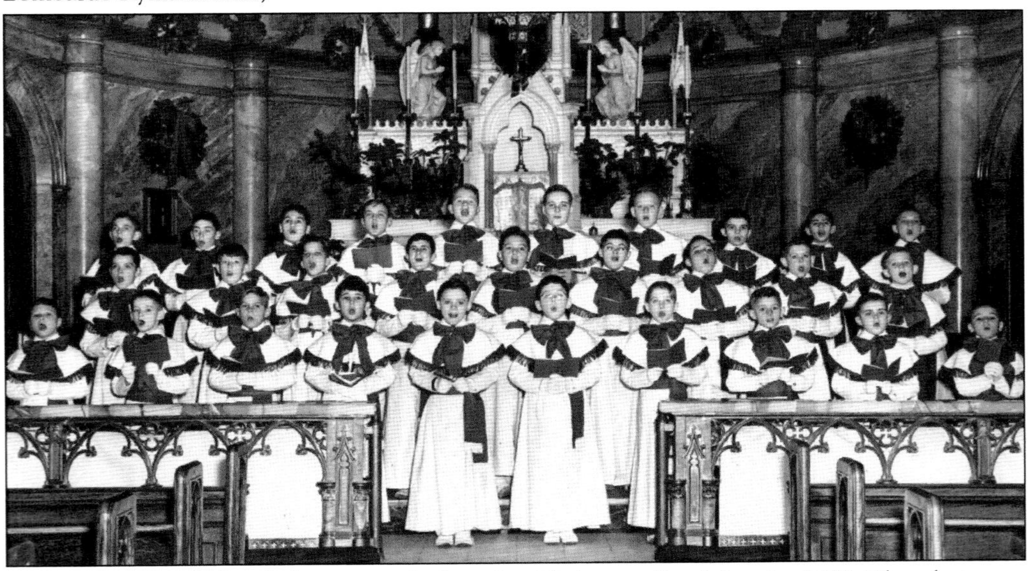

St. Mary's Church boys' choir sings before the Christmas Eve Mass in 1949. The choir was led by director and organist Agnes Sheeran. Early-Saturday-morning practice was held in a small alcove on an upper level of the church. Sheeran is remembered fondly as a gracious and devoted parishioner. She would often treat choir members to ice cream from the local Stewart's Ice Cream Shop after they helped her put away songbooks and tidy up the practice room. (Author's collection.)

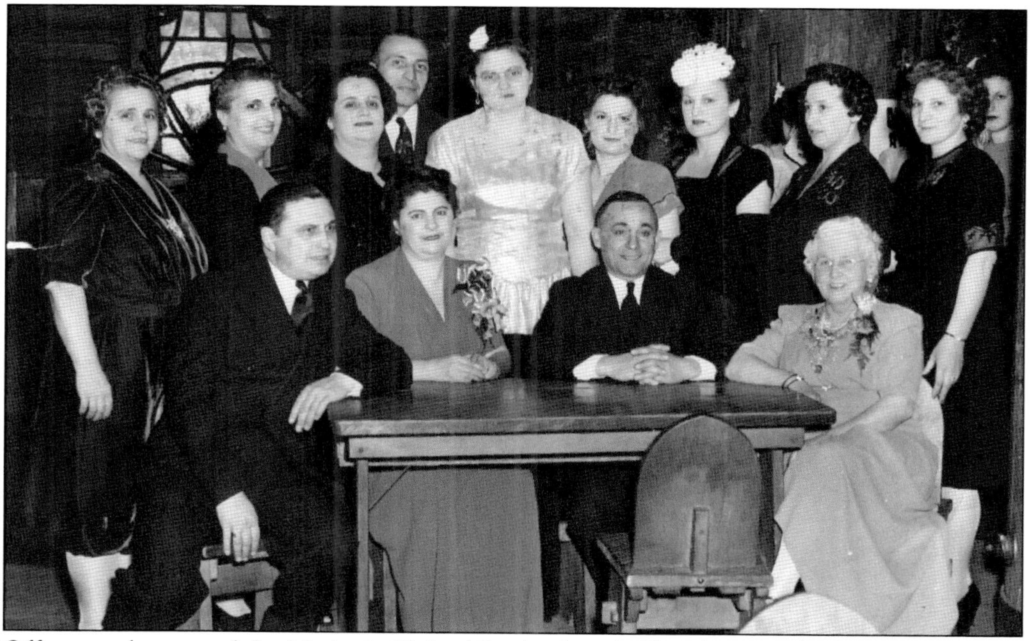

Officers and guests of the Mother's Club of St. Anthony's Church enjoy the hospitality of one of downtown Troy's premier establishments, the Hendrick Hudson Hotel, at a church-sponsored fashion show. Among those in the attractive Half-Moon Lounge are (first row) James (Jimmy) Visk, Josephine Rea, Dominic Pafundi, and Kay Gardner; (second row) Angie Mele, Jennie and Ted Cantanucci, Anna Fazioli, Julia Rizzo, Mrs. Frank Mai, and Minnie Dinova. (Courtesy of Mickey Visk.)

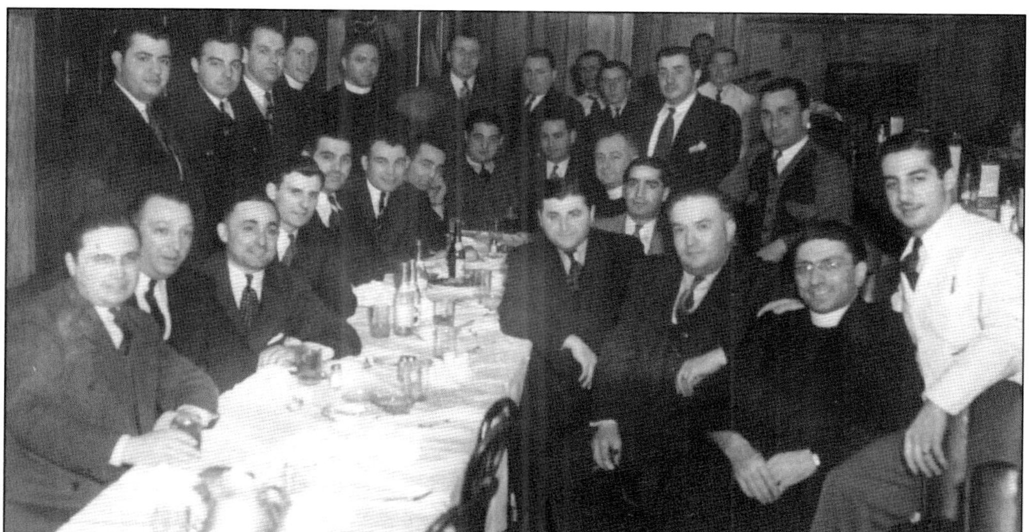

Rev. Thomas DeLuca, O.F.M., joins with St. Anthony's bowling team at its annual banquet. The Franciscan served as pastor of St. Anthony of Padua Church from 1937 to 1940 and from 1955 to 1967. While each pastor contributed to the spiritual and physical well-being of the small parish, Father Tom brought a remarkable vitality to the parish and is especially remembered for his ministry. (Courtesy of the St. Anthony's Church Archives.)

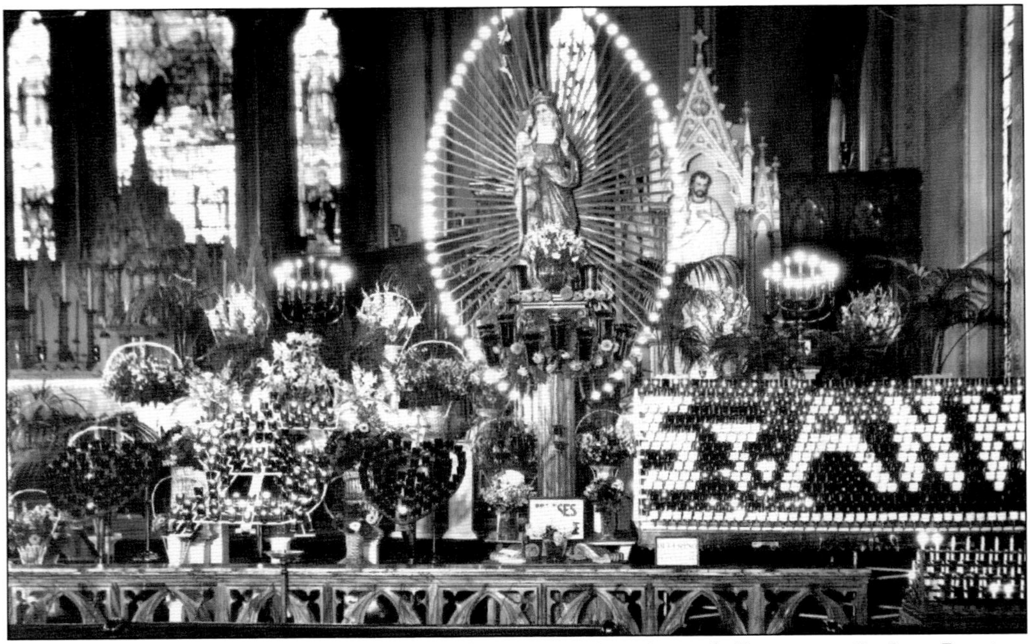

The altar is decorated in 1950 for the annual novena to Ste. Anne de Beaupré at St. Jean Baptiste Church. Devotion to Ste. Anne began with the foundation of the parish in 1865. When the church closed in 1970, its records were transferred to St. Mary's parish and the annual novena, which had begun in 1889, was continued each July at St. Mary's Church during the week of the feast day of Ste. Anne. (Courtesy of Rosemary Oathout.)

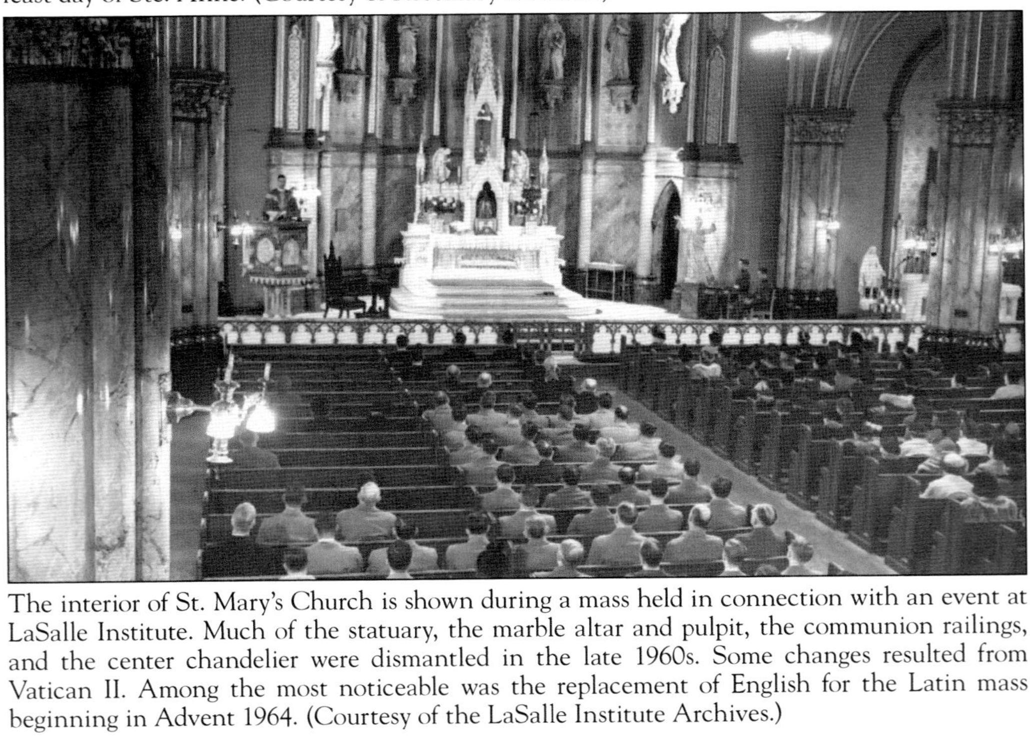

The interior of St. Mary's Church is shown during a mass held in connection with an event at LaSalle Institute. Much of the statuary, the marble altar and pulpit, the communion railings, and the center chandelier were dismantled in the late 1960s. Some changes resulted from Vatican II. Among the most noticeable was the replacement of English for the Latin mass beginning in Advent 1964. (Courtesy of the LaSalle Institute Archives.)

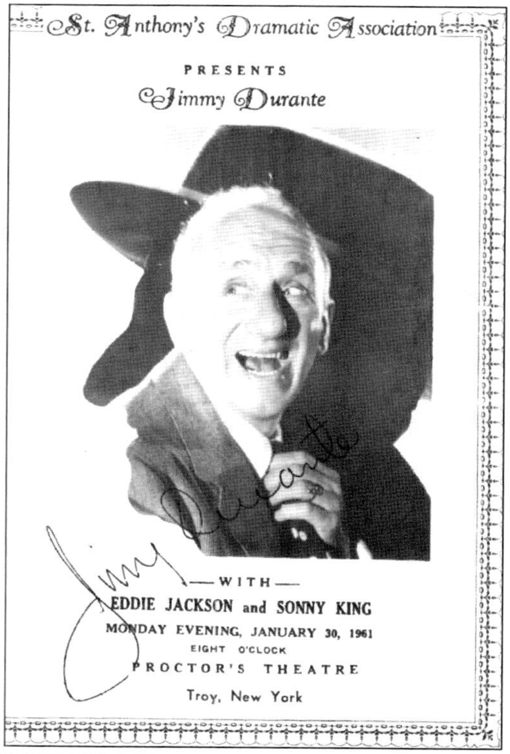

Jimmy Durante, one of the most famous and lovable entertainers in America and longtime friend of St. Anthony's pastor Rev. Thomas DeLuca, headlined two fund-raisers for the parish—at Proctor's Theater in 1961 and at the Rensselaer Polytechnic Institute Field House in 1963. Durante was introduced to his second wife, Margie Little, whom he married in 1960, by Reverend DeLuca. (Courtesy of Mickey Visk.)

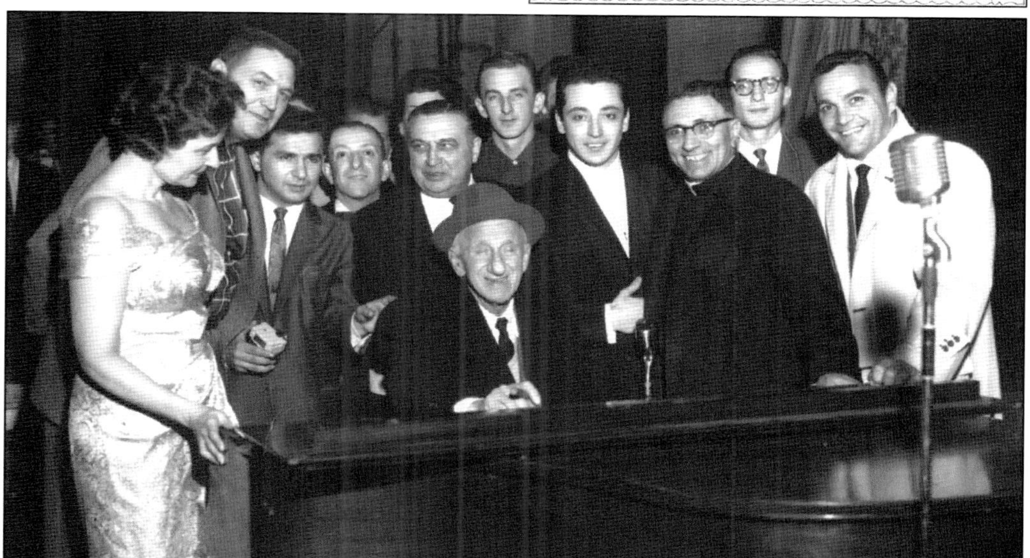

Jimmy Durante is at the piano. Included in this photograph are Lillian Teta, Anthony Furciniti, James (Jimmy) Visk, Rev. Thomas DeLuca, and accompanist Jules Bufano on January 30, 1961, at the Proctor's Theater benefit fund-raiser for St. Anthony's Church. Local talent provided the entertainment for the first half of the program. The second half was all Durante and his troupe. Both the 1961 and 1963 fund-raisers were sellouts. (Courtesy of the St. Anthony's Church Archives.)

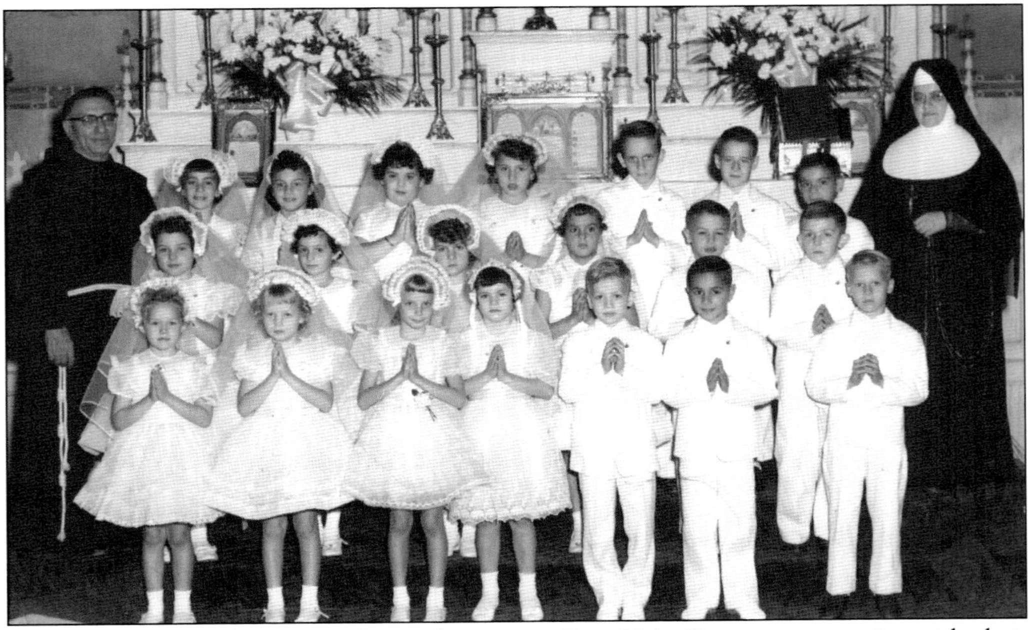

Children of St. Anthony's parish are shown at a First Holy Communion service with their pastor, Rev. Thomas DeLuca, and their teacher, Sr. Antonia. Those who can be identified are (first row) Sue Osborne, Linda Agars, Tom Mazzariello, and Mario Julian, who would become the pastor of St. Anthony's Church; (second row) Lisa Bevevino and Lucy Miele; (third row) Fran Lanzillo, Geraldine DeBonis, Mary Rose Magnetto, Louise Miele, Anthony Morey, and Joe Rizzo. (Courtesy of Rose Julian.)

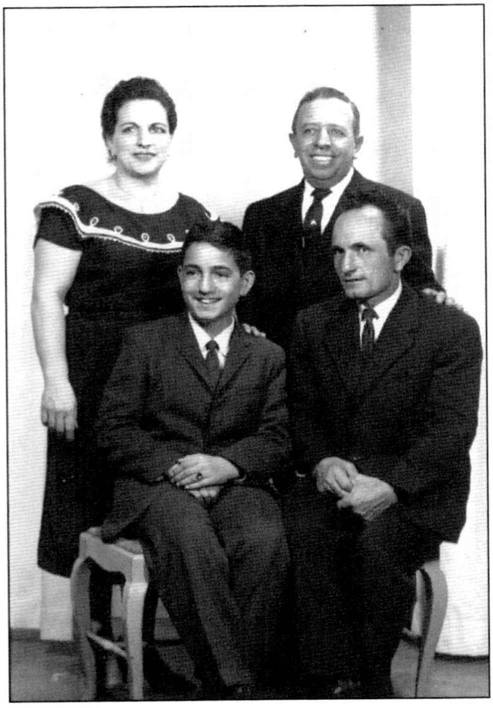

Theresa Mantello and her husband, James, are photographed with Dominick and Bruno Russomanno at the confirmation of young Dominick. James sponsored Dominick, who immigrated with his father to the United States in mid-1950 from the region of Calabria. The Russomannos were soon followed by the remainder of their family. The sponsorship established the tradition of *compare*, one of kinship between the Mantello and Russomanno families. (Courtesy of Isabella Mantello Miles.)

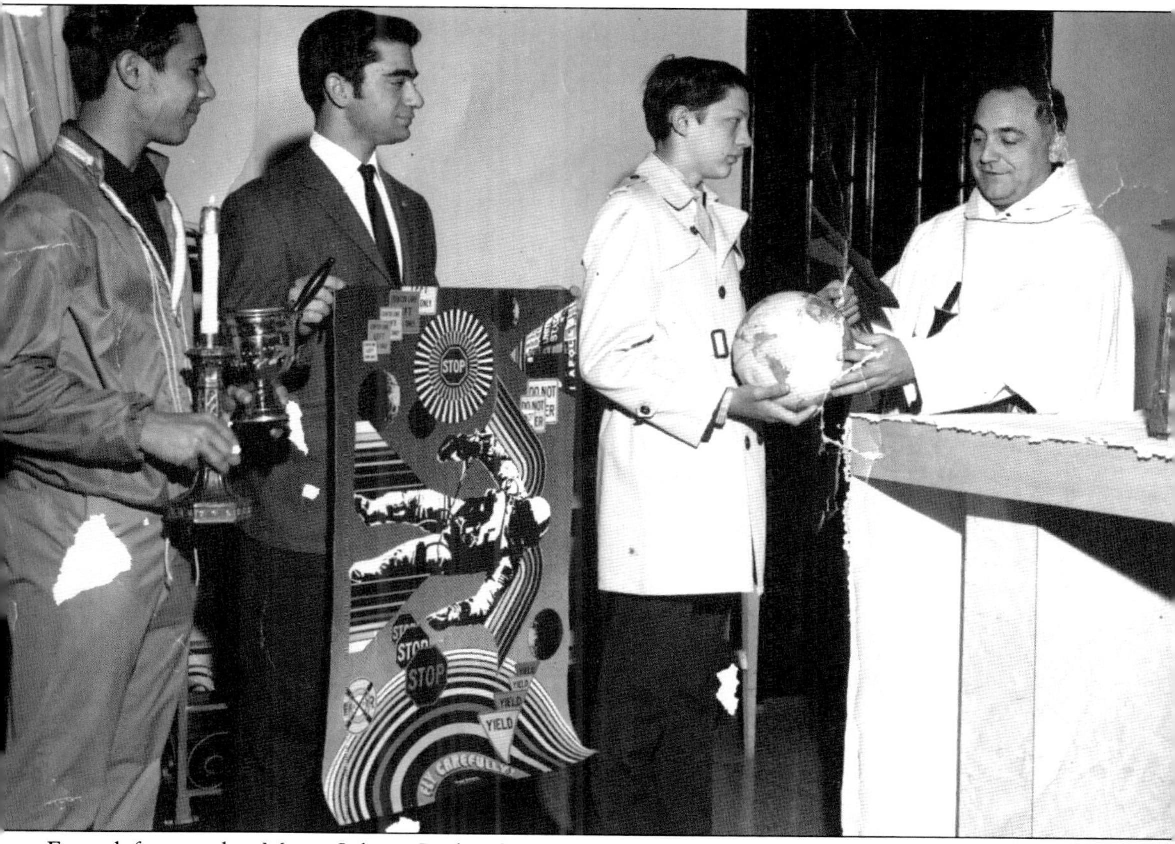

From left to right, Mario Julian, Richard Carlino, and John Edwards assist in serving with Rev. Bebe Ferraro at an Earth Day Mass at St. Francis Friary, Andover, Massachusetts. Rev. Mario Julian, who grew up on Fifth Avenue, is pastor of Troy's St. Anthony of Padua Church, and Rev. Richard Carlino is pastor of St. John the Evangelist and St. Anthony's in Schenectady. Other men from the neighborhood who entered the Franciscan order included Rev. Angelo Bucciero, O.F.M., also a former resident of Fifth Avenue, who served for many years at St. Anthony's Church in Toronto, and Revs. Francis DeLorenzo, Arnold Martenisi, and Francis Prezio. (Courtesy of Rose Julian.)

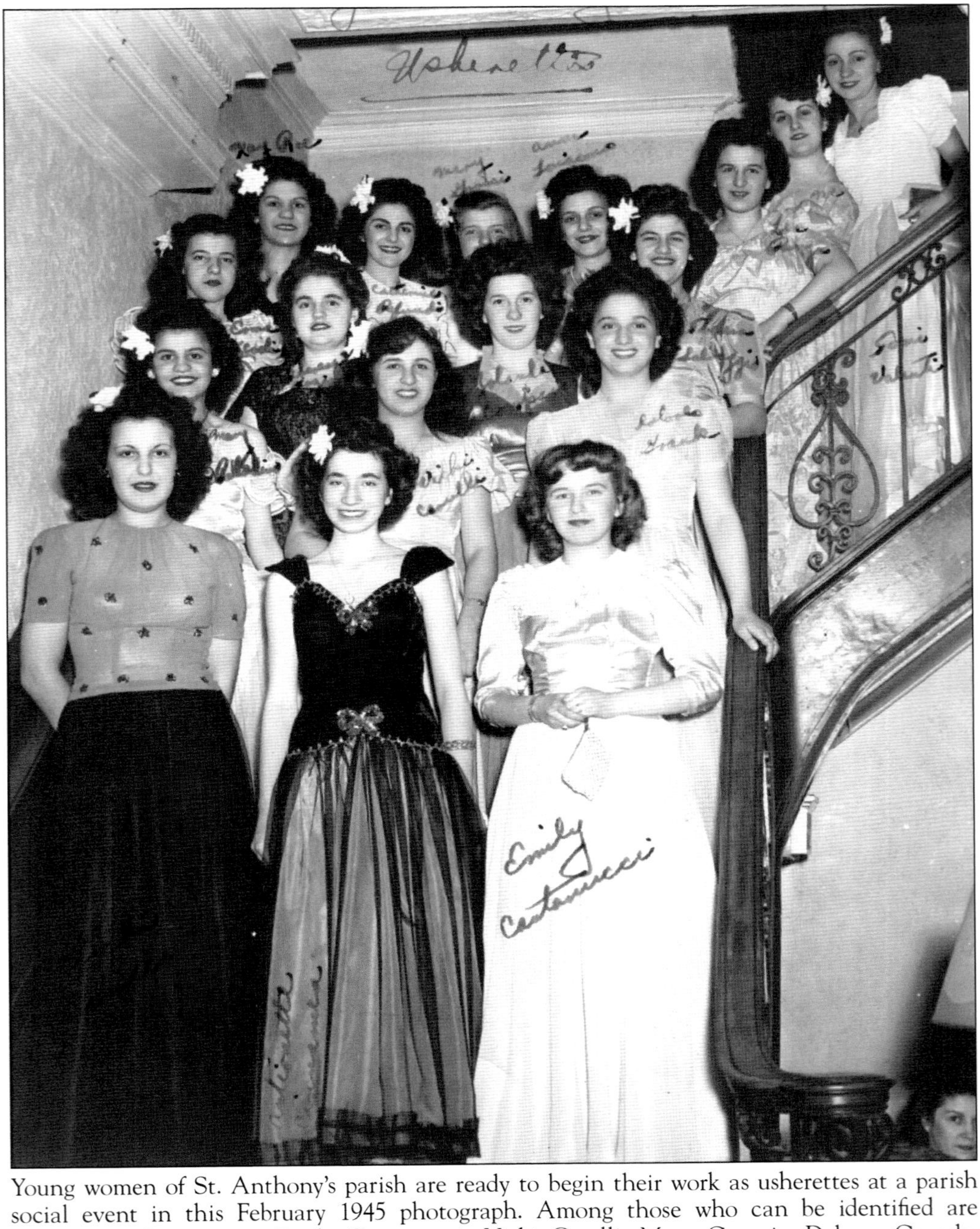

Young women of St. Anthony's parish are ready to begin their work as usherettes at a parish social event in this February 1945 photograph. Among those who can be identified are Antoinette Ciannamea, Emily Cantenucci, Vicki Carelli, Mary Gervais, Delores Grande, Ann Laiacona, Kay Rea, Theresa Salvaggio, and Toni Valenti. (Courtesy of the St. Anthony's Church Archives.)

Sr. Mary Joanne (left) and Sr. Carmelite Germinerio are photographed visiting the Franciscan Monastery in Washington, D.C. Sr. Carmelite, raised on Hill Street, served as principal of St. Mary's School, which she had attended as a child, and served 25 years in pastoral care at St. Mary's Hospital, where, according to an article in the Albany Diocesan paper the *Evangelist*, "she opened her Mediterranean heart to the sick." (Courtesy of Marietta DePaoli.)

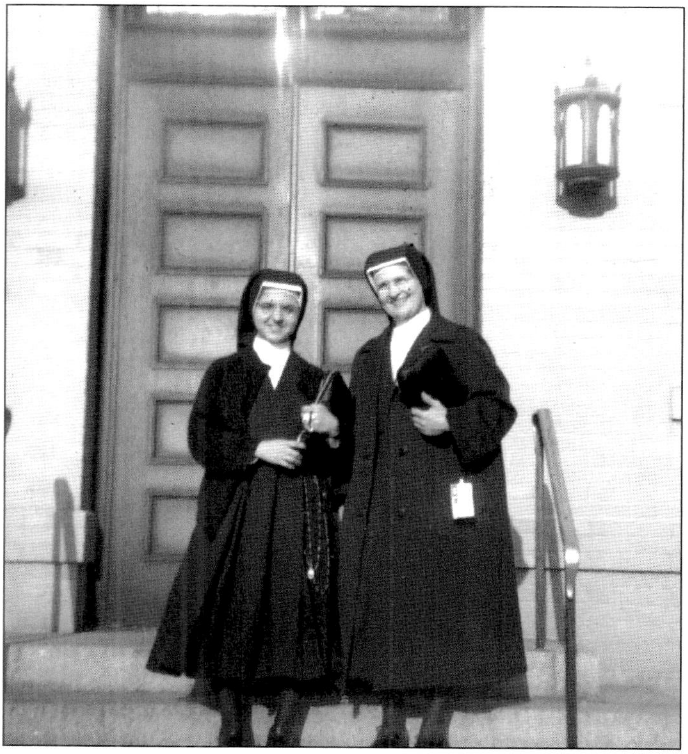

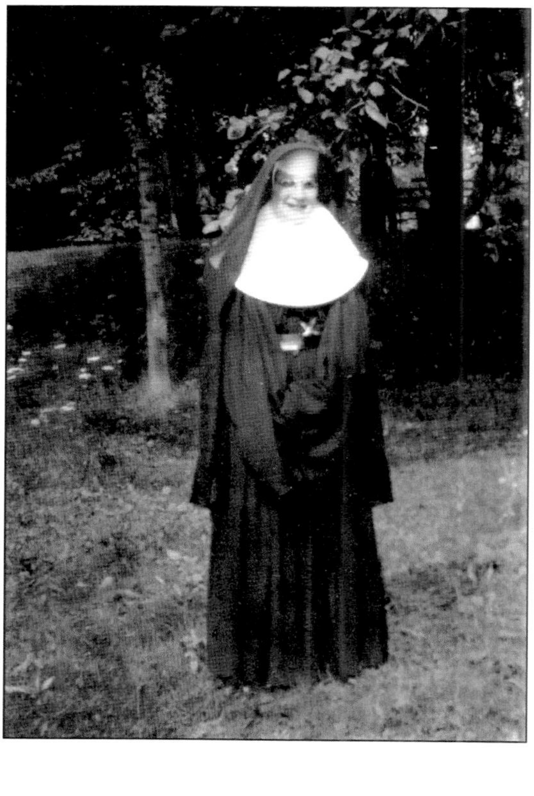

Sr. Mary Jane Manzerra, daughter of Louise Marie and Joseph Manzerra of Fourth Street, entered the Religious of the Sisters of Mercy in 1945 and was assigned to teaching positions in the Albany Catholic Diocese, where she taught kindergarten to eighth grade for more than 34 years. In 1980, Sr. Mary Jane left teaching but continued a ministry visiting and counseling the sick in hospitals and homes. (Courtesy of the Manzerra family.)

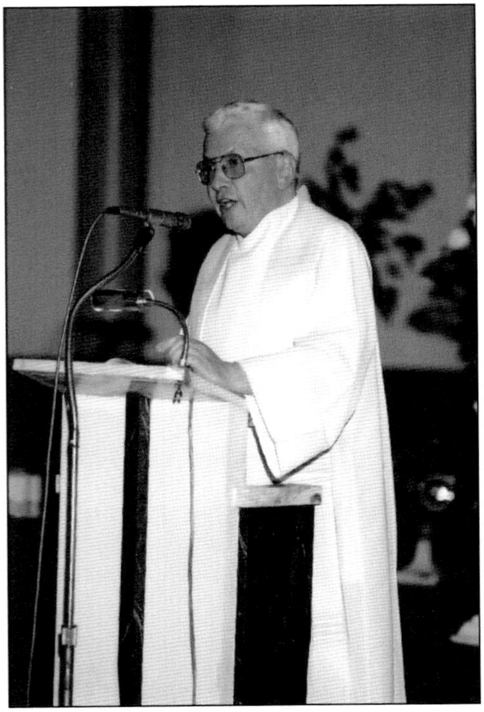

Rev. Harry Donaghy was born in Dungannon, County Tyrone, Ireland, and served as pastor of St. Mary's Church for 22 years (1981–2003), until his untimely death. He was pastor, counselor, neighbor, and friend to all who knew him, serving with the Catholic Youth Organization in Troy before his longtime pastorate at St. Mary's. Father Harry would refer to the church as the sign of God's presence in the community. (Photograph by Christopher Cioffi.)

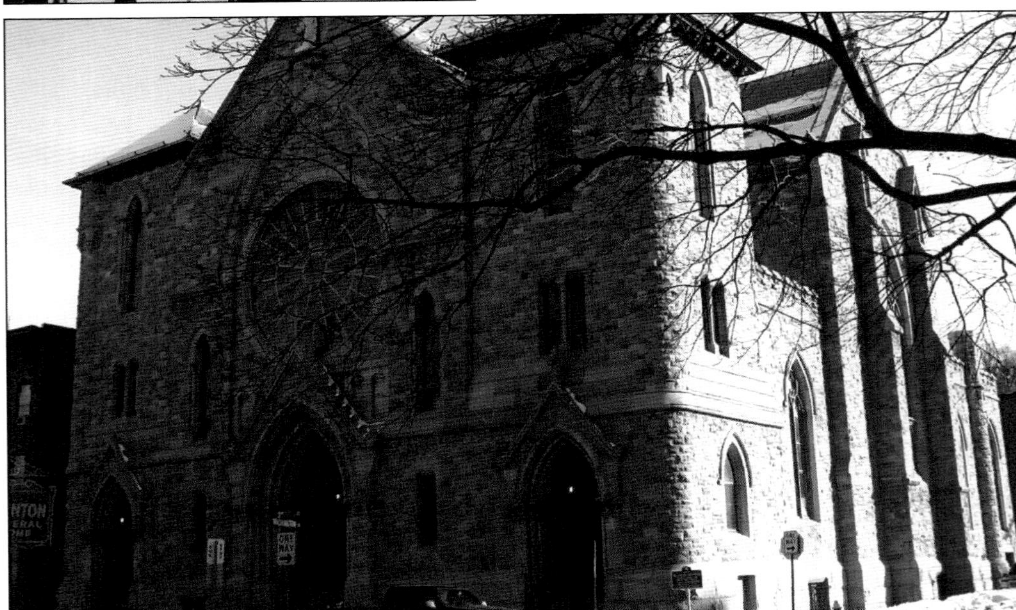

From its founding in 1843 to the present, St. Mary's Church has been a positive element in the neighborhood. In addition to its priority to fill the spiritual needs of the community, since the 1970s it has maintained a soup kitchen and a food pantry and provided other services for the needy families of the area. The cornerstone of the present church was dedicated on May 27, 1900. The solemn dedication of the new church was held on May 8, 1904. (Photograph by Dan Lennon.)

Three

But Sister Said

There were once seven elementary schools—four parochial institutions and three public schools—within the neighborhood adjacent to Troy's Italian section. St. Mary's first parish school, built in 1859, was located on St. Mary's Avenue. By 1866, the school moved to 185 Third Street and then in 1917 to a building at 212 Third Street. The school closed in the mid-1970s. St. Joseph's Academy began educating young men in 1850, and by 1880, it became LaSalle Institute, remaining on Fourth Street until 1965. St. Jean's opened its school in 1880 and built a new one in 1914, which closed in 1934. By 1890, St. Lawrence's had established a small parish school. The abandoned Public School No. 8 at 1471 Fifth Avenue became home to St. Anthony's elementary school in 1916. The children at St. Mary's were taught by the Daughters of Charity; the Sisters of St. Joseph of Carondelet taught at St. Lawrence's, St. Jean's, and St. Anthony's parish schools; and the Christian Brothers taught at LaSalle. The three public elementary schools—School No. 8 on Fifth Avenue, School No. 9 at Liberty and River Streets, and School No. 11 at Third and Adams streets—eventually merged when a new building was constructed at the former site of School No. 11 and became Public School No. 10. Each parochial school offered religious instruction for Catholic students who attended the public school system.

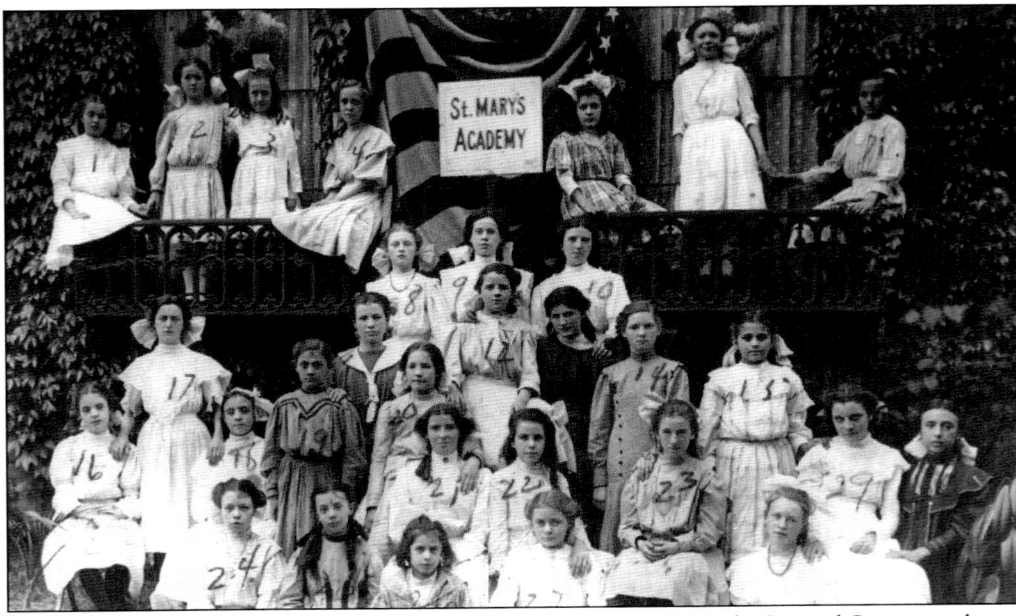

The 1911 graduating class of St. Mary's Academy gathers in front of a Second Street residence. The parish school consisted of grades 1 through 12, including high school until 1925, two years after Troy's Catholic High School on Eighth Street was established. At the time of the photograph, the school was located at 185 Third Street. Four of the 30 graduates in the class were children of Italian immigrants: Louise Mangione, Stella Pasinella, A. Colarusso, and Rose Visk. (Courtesy of Grace Hoffman.)

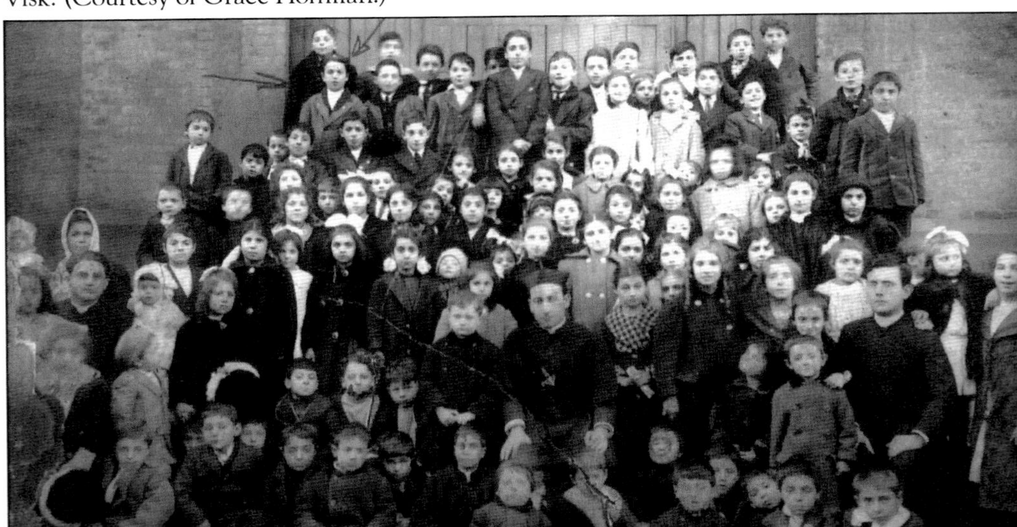

Realizing that education and Americanization were important for the children, in 1913, Rev. Metello Galante, the second pastor of St. Anthony's Church, acquired the abandoned Public School No. 8 at 1471 Fifth Avenue, just south of Ferry Street, and opened an elementary school in 1916. The children were taught by the Sisters of St. Joseph of Carondelet. Children of the parish surround Reverend Galante in this 1916 photograph taken on the steps of the first parish school. (Courtesy of Anthony G. Visk.)

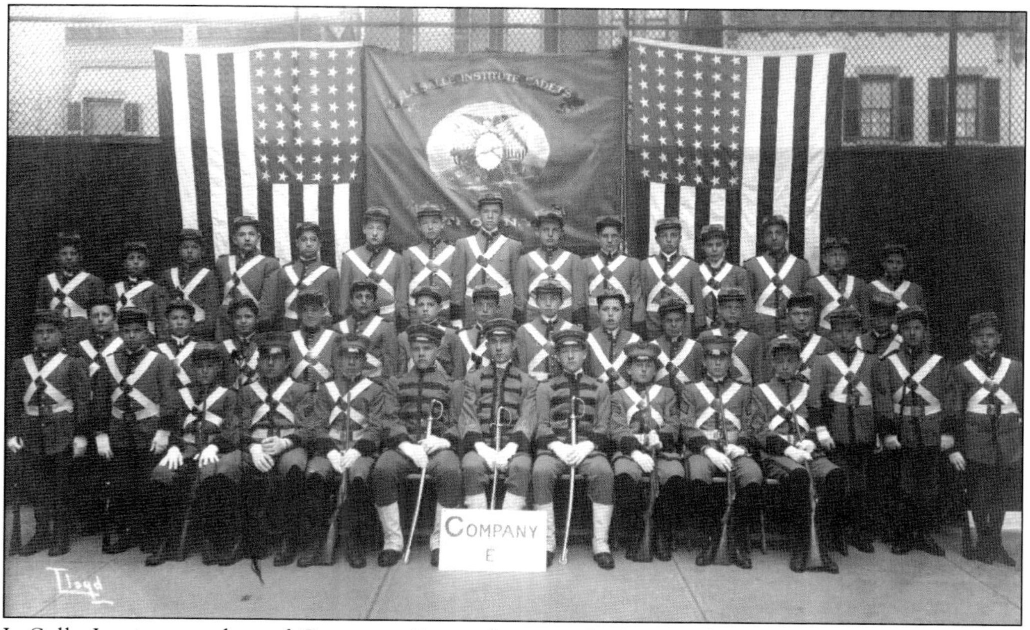

LaSalle Institute cadets of Company E are photographed around 1915 in the school's yard at the Fourth Street site. The cadets would assemble at the market space on Hill Street for an afternoon of drill, band practice, or marching. During warm-weather months, it was common to see dozens of neighborhood children with their grandparents viewing the cadets' maneuvers. The school was located two blocks from the public market. (Courtesy of the LaSalle Institute.)

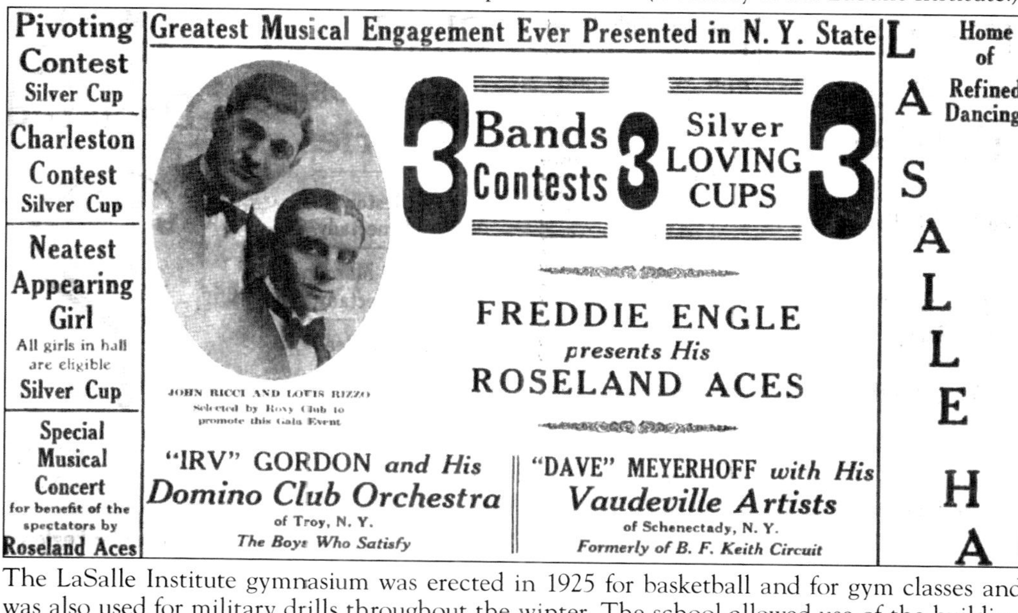

The LaSalle Institute gymnasium was erected in 1925 for basketball and for gym classes and was also used for military drills throughout the winter. The school allowed use of the building as a neighborhood meeting place and for social events. This advertisement is fairly descriptive of an extravaganza promoted by Fourth Street businessmen John Ricci and Louis Rizzo. When LaSalle Institute moved to its suburban complex in 1966, the building was acquired by the Catholic Youth Organization for its programs. (Courtesy of Annette Rizzo Sanders.)

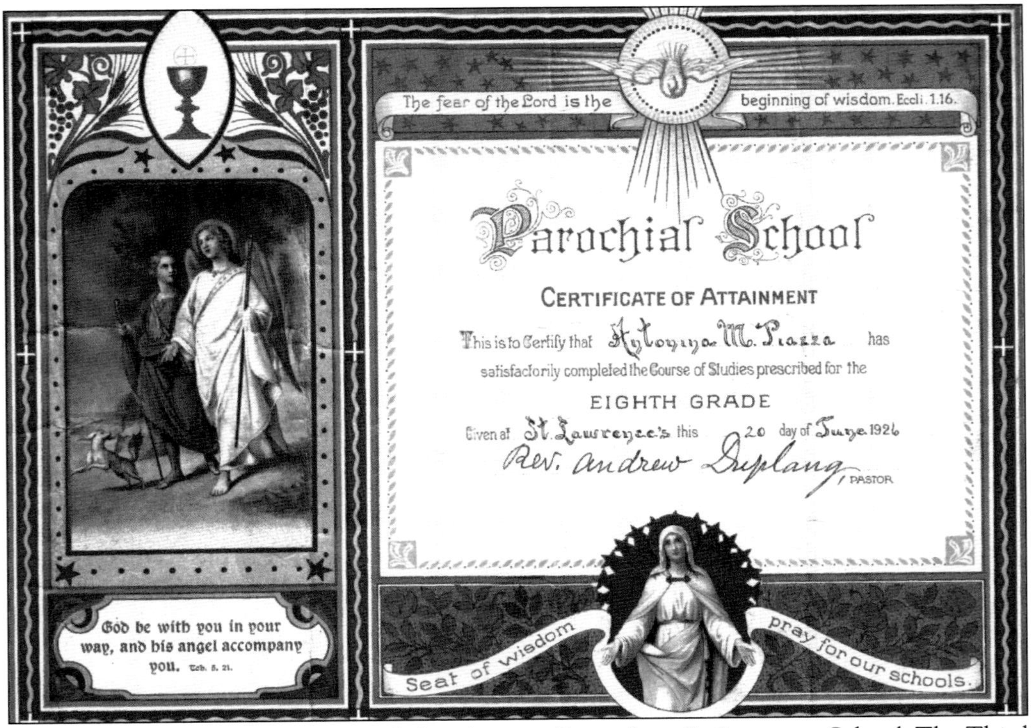

A Certificate of Attainment is awarded to Antonia Piazza from St. Lawrence School. The Third Street school, which opened in the early 1890s, was one of four parochial elementary schools available to children in the neighborhood. St. Jean Baptiste, which opened on Second Street in 1880, had separate buildings for boys and girls. St. Anthony's School opened in 1916 in a building on Fifth Avenue below Ferry Street. For a period of time, St. Mary's was located in two buildings on Third Street. (Courtesy of the Piazza family.)

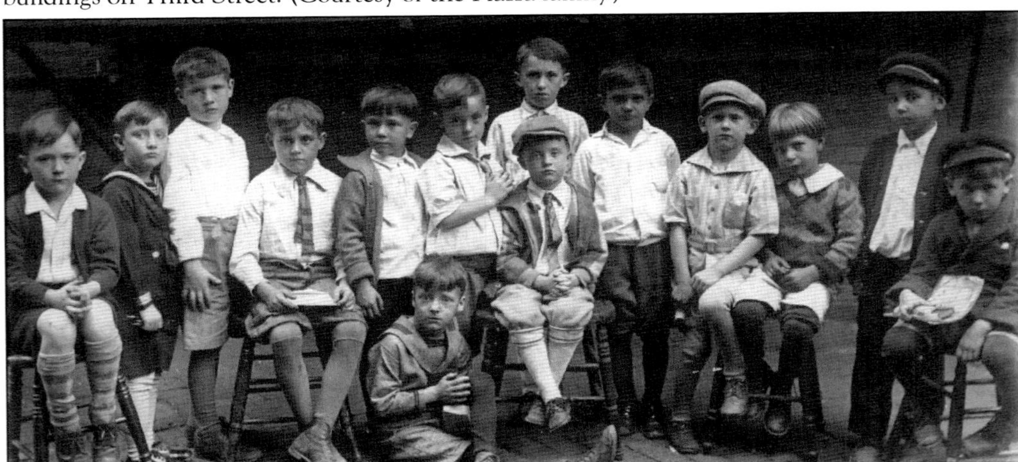

New pupils of St. Lawrence School begin their fall session in this 1927 photograph. Included in the group is Salvatore Piazza (standing, extreme right). Several Italian American families, including members of the Piazza, Lombardo, and Marro families—primarily those who lived within a block or two of St. Lawrence, the German Catholic parish on Third Street—attended the parish church and elementary school. (Courtesy of the Piazza family.)

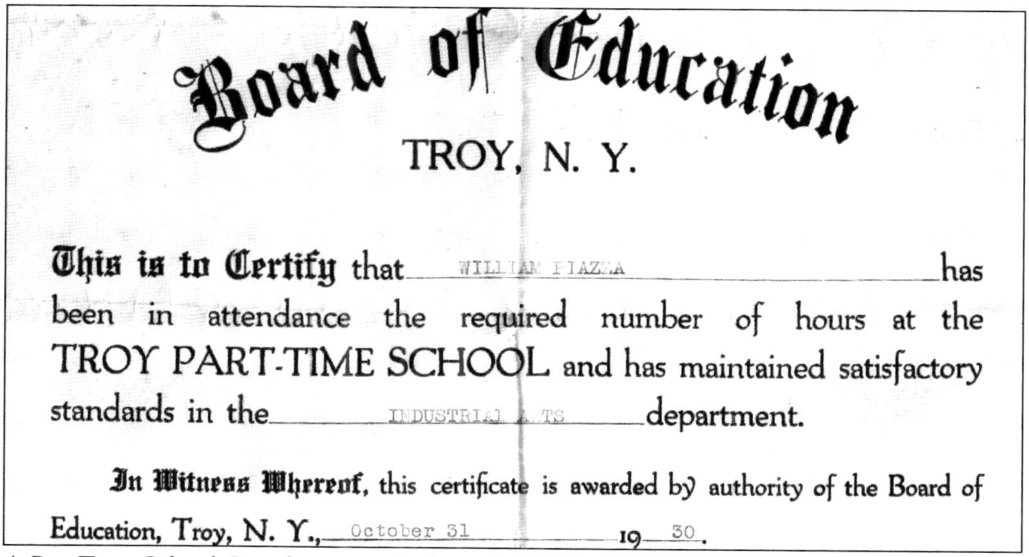

Board of Education

TROY, N. Y.

This is to Certify that WILLIAM PIAZZA has been in attendance the required number of hours at the TROY PART-TIME SCHOOL and has maintained satisfactory standards in the INDUSTRIAL ARTS department.

In Witness Whereof, this certificate is awarded by authority of the Board of Education, Troy, N. Y., October 31 19 30.

A Part-Time School Certification in Industrial Arts was awarded to William Piazza. This was a familiar educational route for many young immigrants who were required by family pressure or family responsibilities to both work and attend school. Affectionately known as PTU (part-time university), the Troy Continuing Education program was located in the former Public School No. 9 at the corner of River and Liberty Streets. (Courtesy of the Piazza family.)

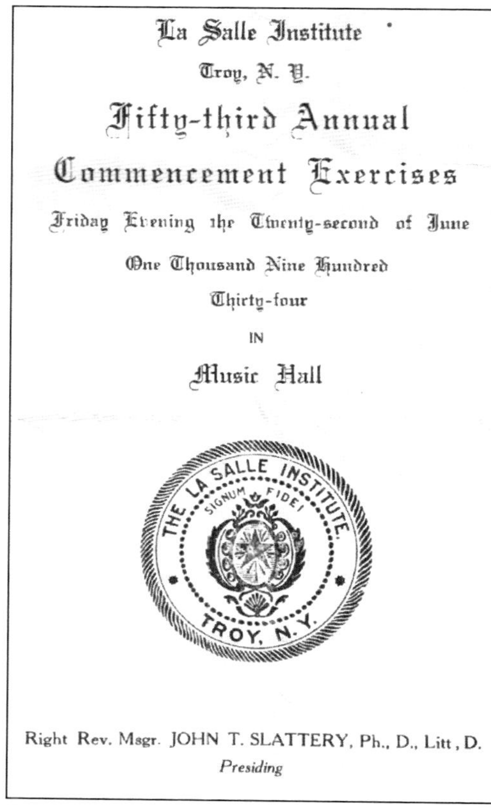

La Salle Institute

Troy, N. Y.

Fifty-third Annual

Commencement Exercises

Friday Evening the Twenty-second of June

One Thousand Nine Hundred

Thirty-four

IN

Music Hall

Right Rev. Msgr. JOHN T. SLATTERY, Ph., D., Litt, D.

Presiding

The program for the 53rd annual commencement exercises for LaSalle Institute described the ceremony held at the Troy Savings Bank Music Hall. Included in the graduating class of 1934 were Little Italy residents Eugene Bizzarro, Thomas Covatta, Frank Esposito, and Michael Farina. A longtime school tradition included assisting St. Mary's parish with toy drives, donations of food and money, and volunteering at the food pantry, the soup kitchen, and other parish-related activities. (Courtesy of Lucille DeMaria Salerno.)

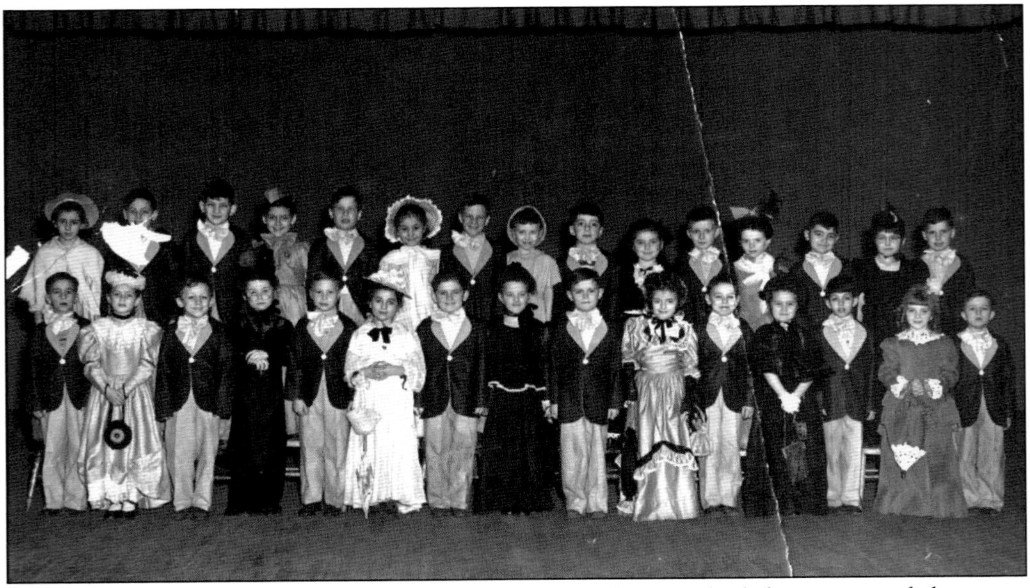

The 1945 kindergarten class of St. Mary's School is photographed during one of the many variety shows performed by classes over the years in the school's auditorium. The cast members who can be identified are Richard Warenchak, Frank Fitzgerald, Ronald Kerwin, Barbara Ryan, Rocco Testo, Lorraine Colvin, Nicholas Martone, Michael Yamin, Daniel Burns, Tina Pasinella, Barbara Fields, Peter Ricci, Marie Agostine, Nancy O'Brien, and Michael Rizzo. (Courtesy of Mary Ann Centofanti.)

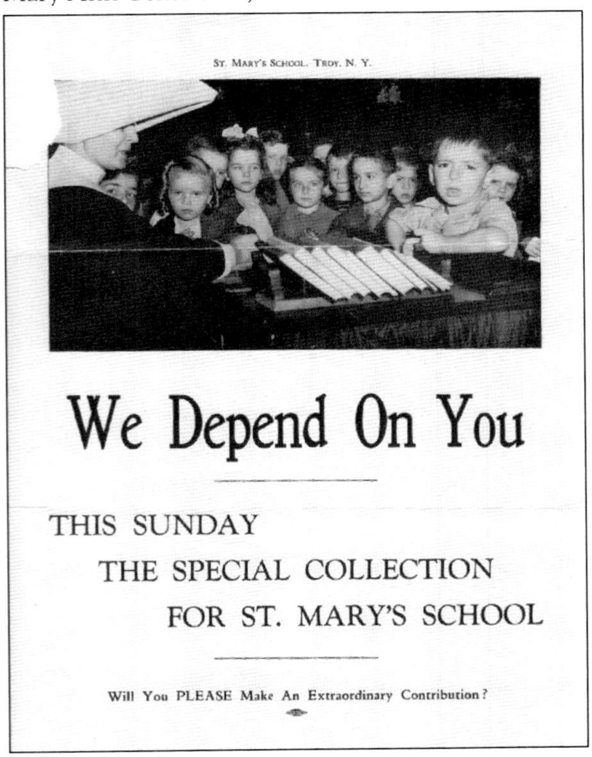

A special financial appeal is made to the parishioners of St. Mary's Church soliciting aid for its school and its church. Among the class members with kindergarten teacher Sr. Georgia are, from left to right, Marion Church, Nancy O'Brien, Danny Burns, Mary Ann Pommer, Marie Agostine, and Peter Ricci. (Courtesy of Marion Church Field.)

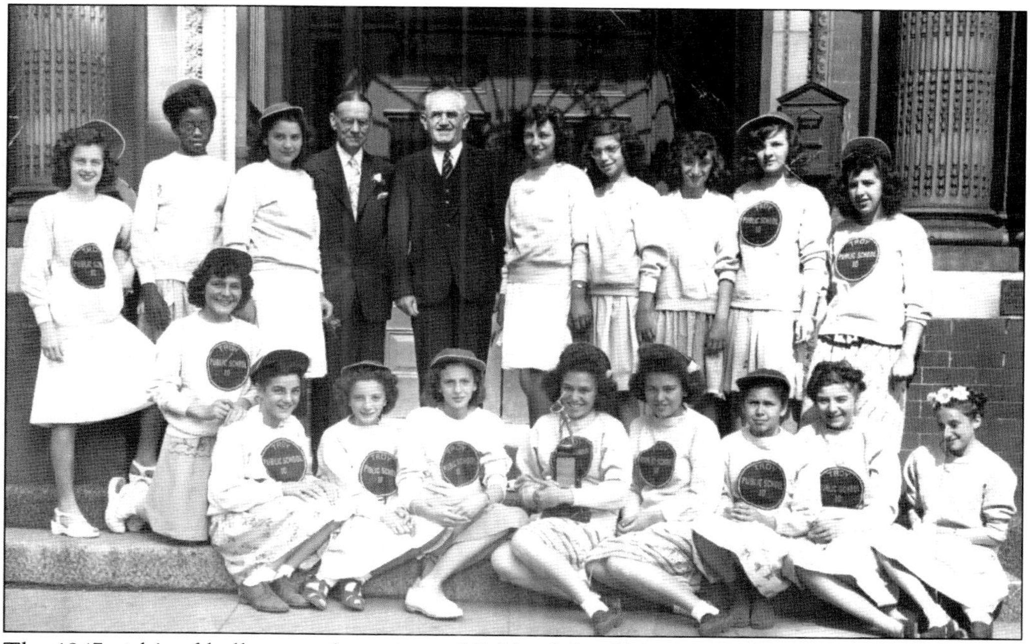

The 1947 girls' softball team, champions of Public School No. 10, celebrates with a photograph in front of the school at Third and Adams Streets. From left to right are (first row) Dolores Pasinella, Lorraine Delgiacco, Mary Casale, Louise Donato, twins Josephine and Ann Renna, Frances Gillespie, Roberta Cohen, unidentified, and Mary Ann Mamone; (second row) two unidentified, Patricia Finelli, principal Michael Kling, Troy mayor Francis Ahern, Antoinette Delgiacco, Carmella Germano, Nicolina Montello, Joan Duffney, and Emma Esposito. (Courtesy of Louise Donato Finelli.)

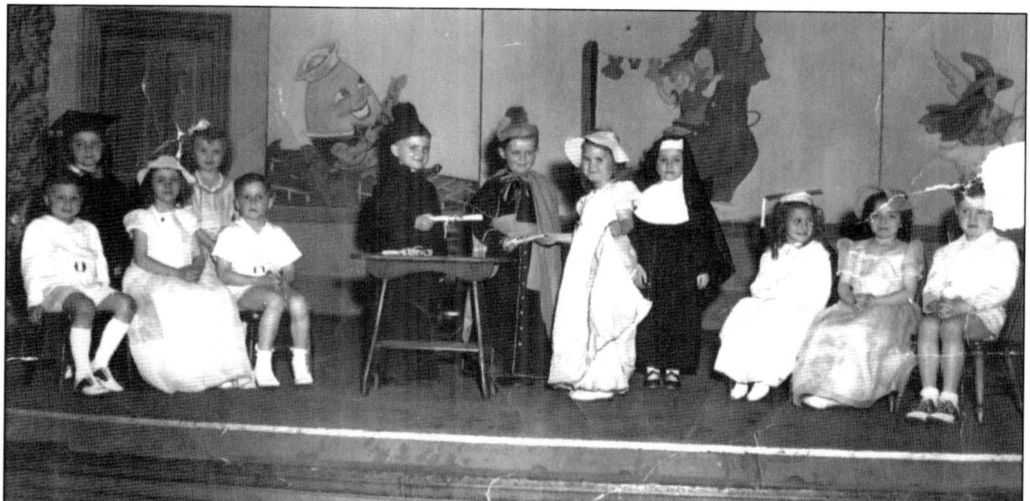

The 1945 kindergarten graduating class of St. Mary's School performs in a variety show for family and friends onstage in the school auditorium. From left to right are (seated) Richard Warenchak, unidentified, Daniel Burns, Barbara Ryan, Marion Church, and Leo Boland; (standing) Marie Agustine, Maryann Pommer, Frank Fitzgerald (as a priest), Ronald Kerwin (as a bishop), Patricia Snyder, and Georgianna McKenna (as a nun). (Courtesy of Marion Church Field.)

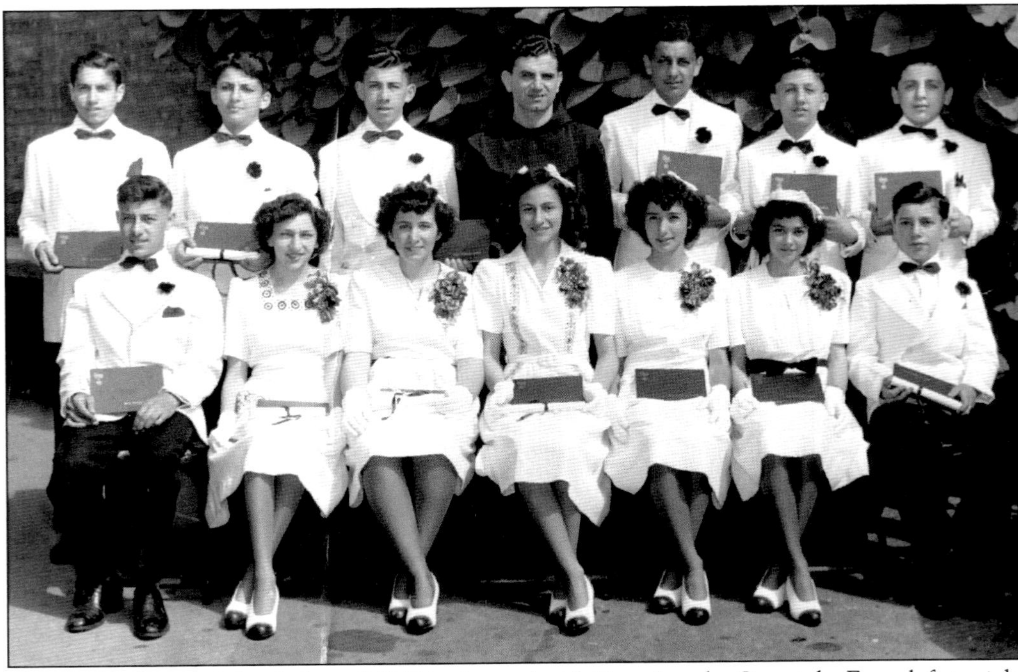

The St. Anthony's School class of 1945 is pictured with Rev. Anselm Sanniola. From left to right are (first row) Ralph Debboli, Anna Rose Farina, Thomasine Meddis, Mary Salvaggio, Marion Crispo, Jane Bonelli, and Leonard DeMeo; (second row) Joe Cirrincione, Mickey Milanese, Frank Mancini Jr., Reverend Sanniola, Bob Reo, O'Neil Valenti, and Jerry Valenti. The building at 1471 Fifth Avenue served as the parish school from 1916 to 1957. A new school was constructed at 107 Fourth Street, adjacent to the parish church. (Courtesy of Leonard DeMeo.)

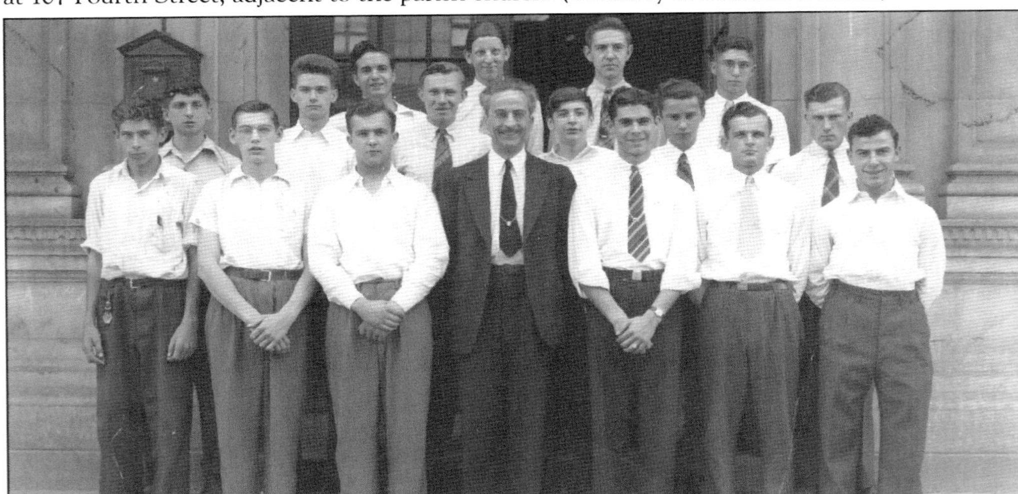

Students from the Electricity II shop gather for a class photograph in front of Troy High School, located at the time at Seventh Avenue and State Street, now the site of the Ned Pattison Government Center. Included in the photograph, the first student on the left in the third row is Joseph Campese of 27 Havermans Avenue, who eventually worked for the Ford Motor Company. (Courtesy of Geri Campese DeSeve.)

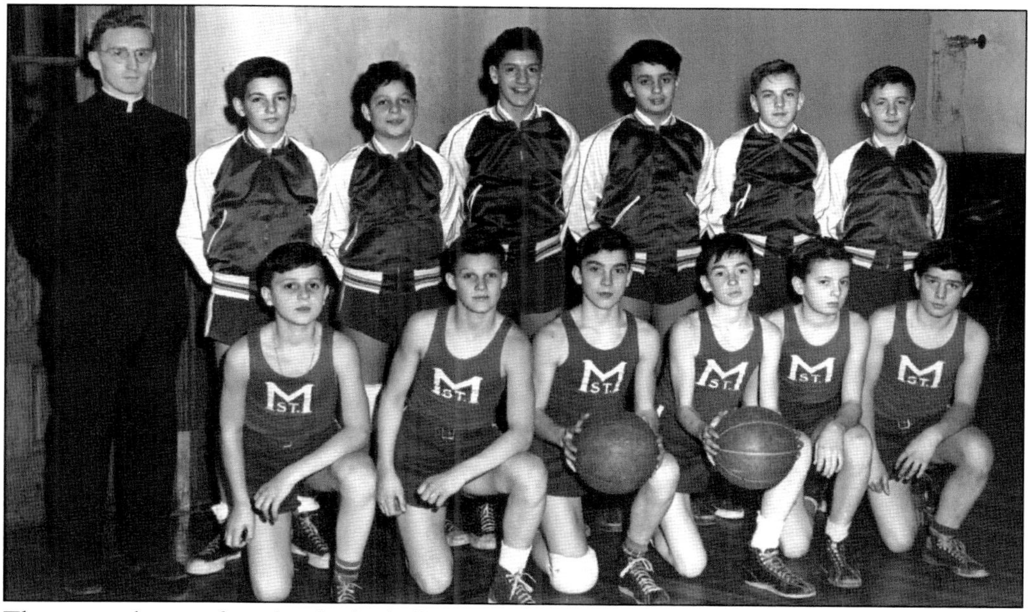

There was always a first-class basketball team at St. Mary's School under the guidance of coach and counselor Rev. Edward Ryan. The first floor of the elementary school at 212 Third Street was an auditorium/gymnasium. From left to right, the 1948 team includes (first row) John Bottillo, Anthony Cioffi, James Church, Donald Wilson, James Garrahan, and Maurice Germinario; (second row) Reverend Ryan, Carmen Casale, Francis Pratt, Louis DeMaria, Frank Bagarose, Lawrence Holmes, and Anthony Pasinella. (Courtesy of Rev. Edward Ryan.)

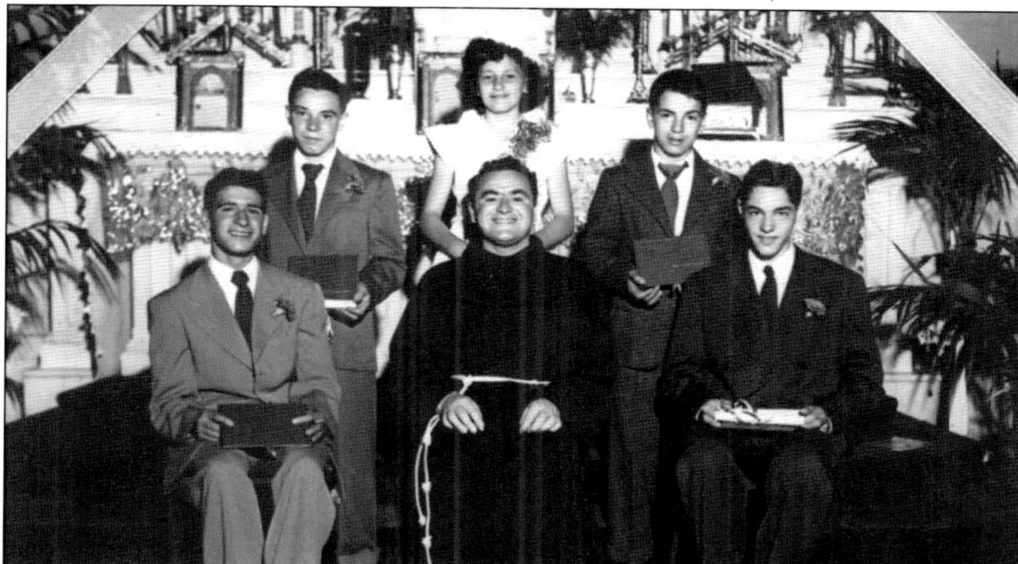

The St. Anthony's School class of 1949 is pictured with Rev. Augustine Ciuffo. From left to right are (first row) Michael Dinova, Reverend Ciuffo, and Peter Bonelli; (second row) Joseph Ryan, Nellie Salvaggio, and James Piscatella. The building at 1471 Fifth Avenue was demolished shortly after it closed in 1957. The Fourth Street school closed in the 1980s and is now the location of the Roarke Center, a facility serving inner-city residents. (Courtesy of Michael Dinova.)

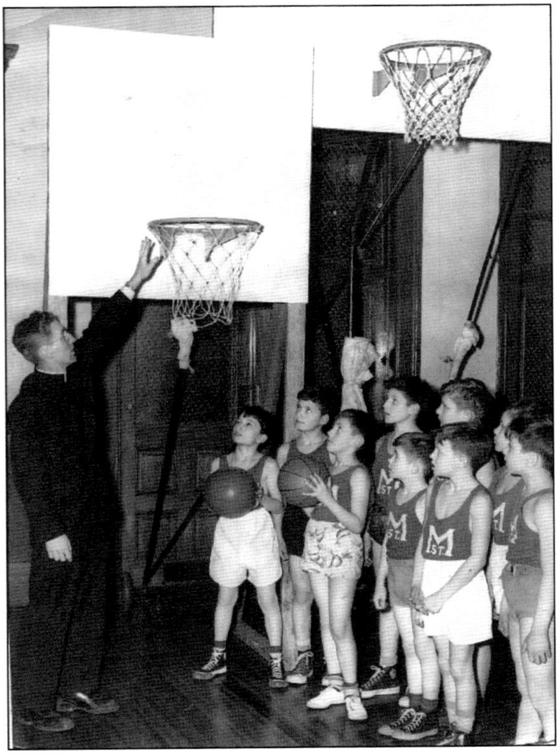

Playing basketball was a terrific outlet for young people. During his years as assistant pastor of St. Mary's parish, Rev. Edward Ryan coached many champion teams. From left to right are (first row) Dom Marro, Dom Bizzarro, Nick Marchese, Jack Huyck, and Angelo Bucciero. The boys in the second row are unidentified. (Courtesy of Rev. Edward Ryan.)

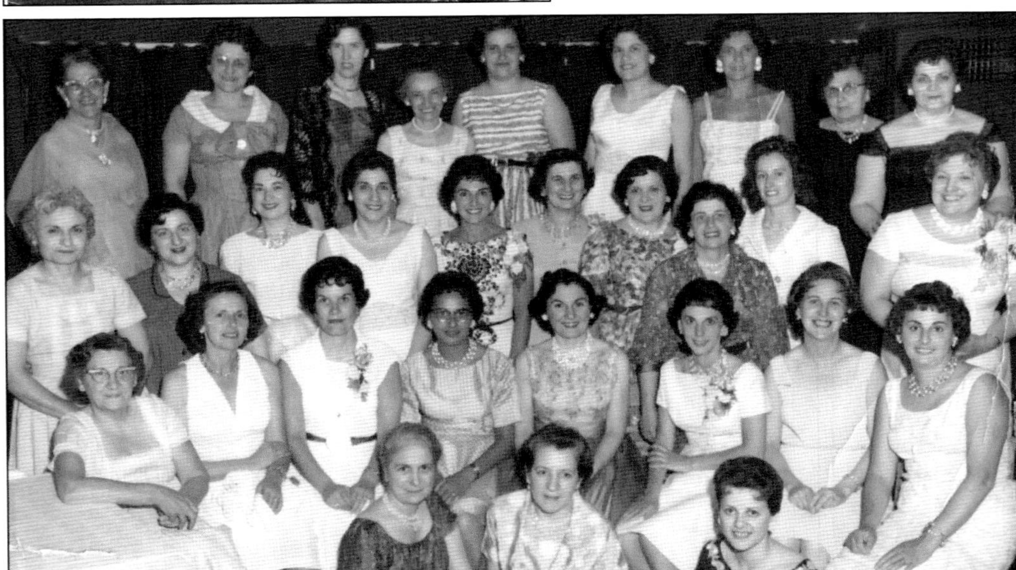

Steadfast supporters of St. Anthony's parish school, its Parent Teacher Association gathers for a group photograph in 1954. Among those who can be identified are Josie Ciarlone, Josephine Pascarell, Toni Celucci (president), Rose Julian (vice president), Jane Bendetti, Frances Margo, Marie Salvaggio, Elaine Valente, Mary Capano, Louise Desso, Jo Russo, Kay Clemente, Phil Martone, Antoinette Cioffi, Louise DeBonis, Mae Ciarlone, Mary Jean Debboli, Phil Riley, Kay Esposito, and Jo Oswald. (Courtesy of Rose Julian.)

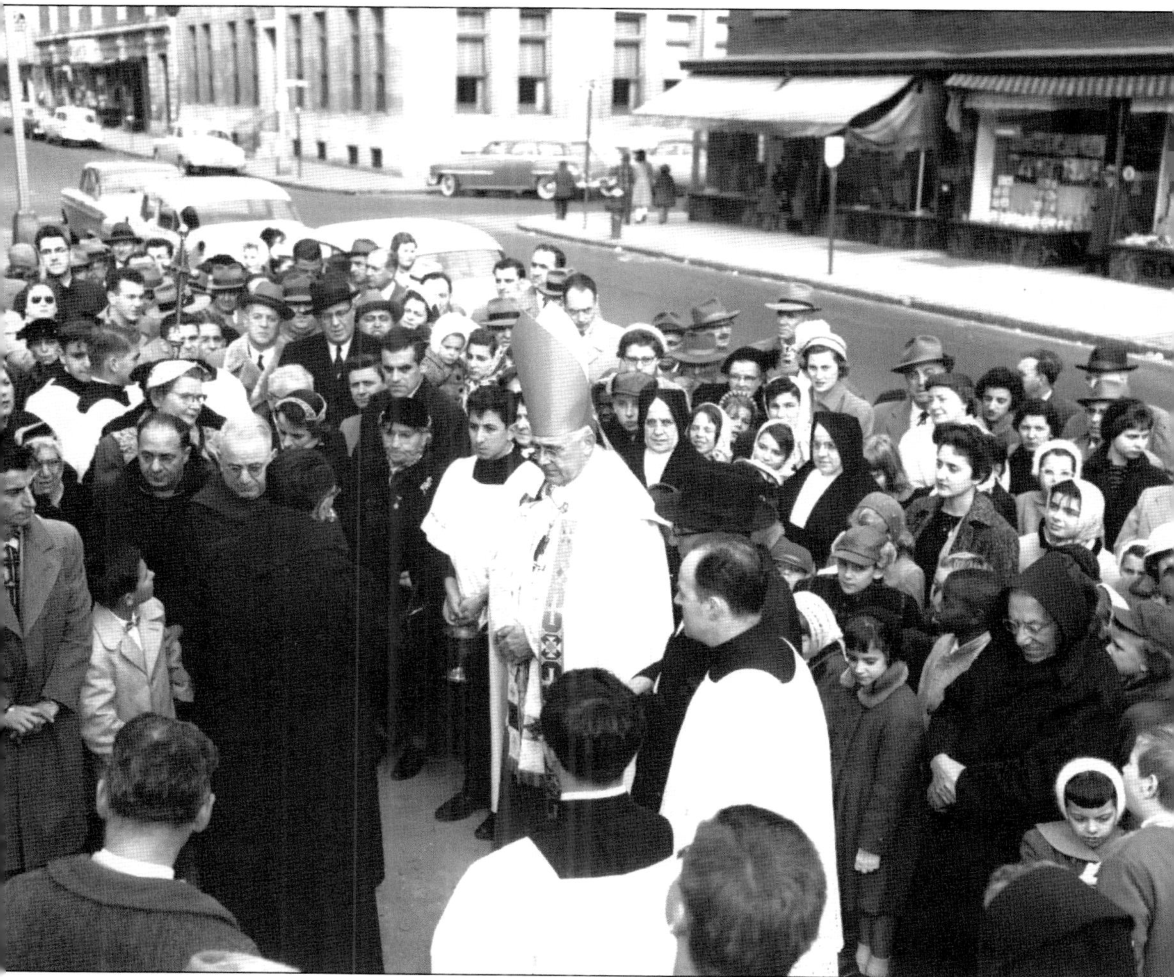

Bishop William A. Scully of the Albany Roman Catholic Diocese dedicates the cornerstone of St. Anthony's new parish school on November 11, 1956, amid a crowd of parishioners and onlookers. The school adjacent to the parish church at the corner of State and Fourth Streets was constructed at 107 Fourth Street and opened a year later. The dedication and blessing of the new school was on October 7, 1957. Bishop Scully was pastor of St. Mary's Church in Troy from 1945 to 1954. (Courtesy of the St. Anthony's Church Archives.)

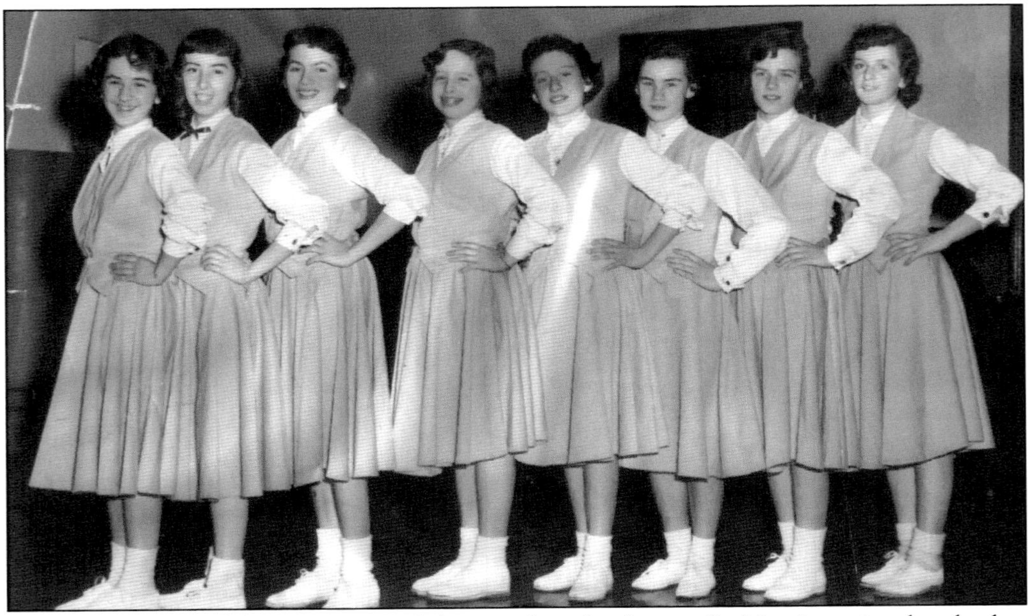

Always ready to lend their support and cheer to the school team, St. Mary's varsity cheerleaders prepare to begin one of their finely crafted maneuvers. From left to right are Caroline Pasinella, Judy Gerger, Maryann Bocketti, Patricia Burns, Liz Dolan, Jean Agostine, Mary Ann Piche, and Nicky Ann Casale. (Courtesy of Judy Gerger Brearton.)

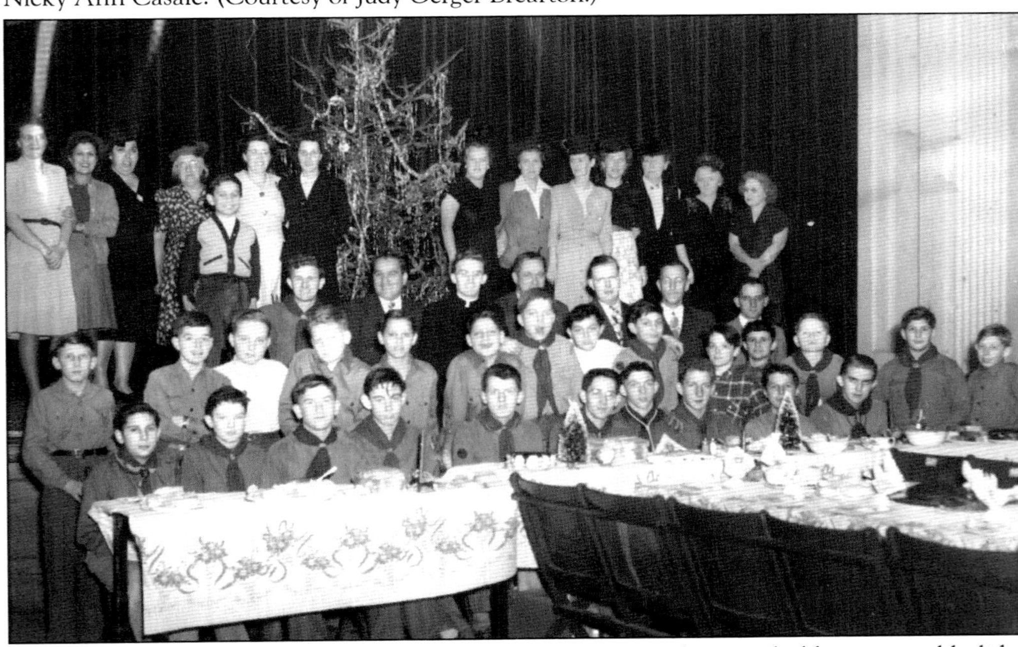

The St. Mary's parish Boy Scout Troop, with parents as invited guests, holds its annual holiday banquet in the school's auditorium/gymnasium. St. Mary's, like other parishes, often sponsored plays, concerts, suppers, and other events, sometimes to raise funds but most often to provide the community with wholesome entertainment. The auditorium contained a large stage as well as a kitchen. (Courtesy of Rev. Edward Ryan.)

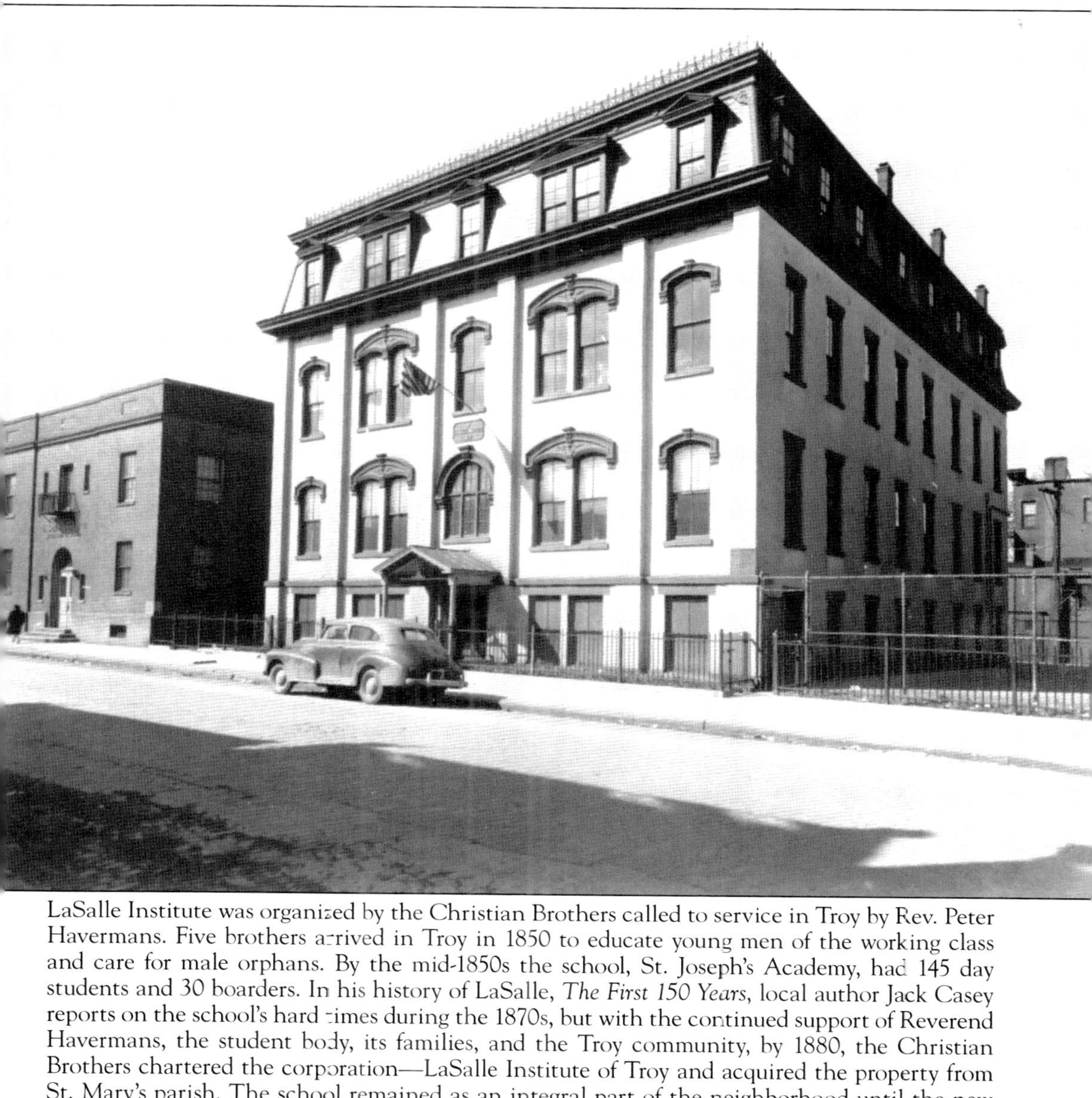

LaSalle Institute was organized by the Christian Brothers called to service in Troy by Rev. Peter Havermans. Five brothers arrived in Troy in 1850 to educate young men of the working class and care for male orphans. By the mid-1850s the school, St. Joseph's Academy, had 145 day students and 30 boarders. In his history of LaSalle, *The First 150 Years*, local author Jack Casey reports on the school's hard times during the 1870s, but with the continued support of Reverend Havermans, the student body, its families, and the Troy community, by 1880, the Christian Brothers chartered the corporation—LaSalle Institute of Troy and acquired the property from St. Mary's parish. The school remained as an integral part of the neighborhood until the new suburban campus was opened in 1966. (Courtesy of the LaSalle Institute Archives.)

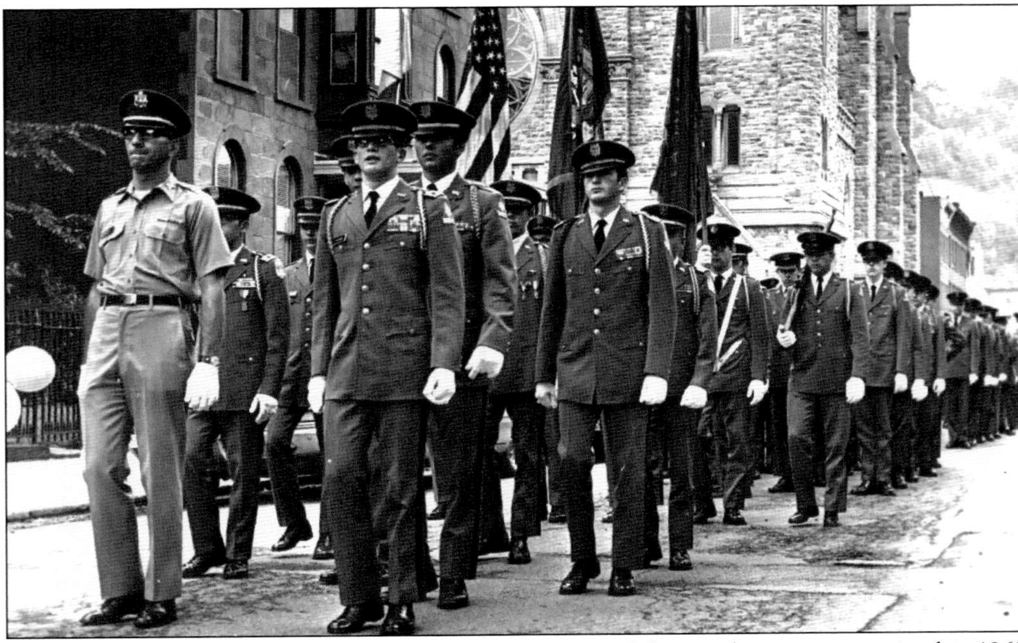

LaSalle Institute cadets are seen marching in memory of deceased war veterans in this 1969 photograph. More than 1,200 former cadets served in World War II, and 31 died in service. To this day, LaSalle honors Maj. William O'Donovan, a hero of the infamous Bataan Death March, by conducting its rifle team, named the O'Donovan Rifles. (Courtesy of the LaSalle Institute Archives.)

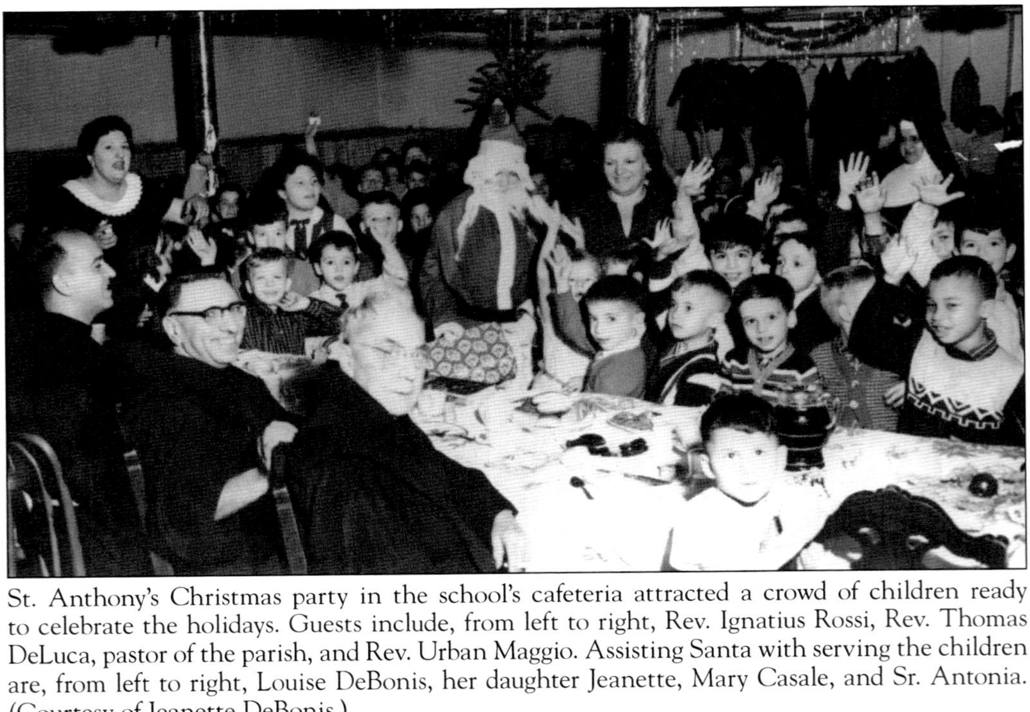

St. Anthony's Christmas party in the school's cafeteria attracted a crowd of children ready to celebrate the holidays. Guests include, from left to right, Rev. Ignatius Rossi, Rev. Thomas DeLuca, pastor of the parish, and Rev. Urban Maggio. Assisting Santa with serving the children are, from left to right, Louise DeBonis, her daughter Jeanette, Mary Casale, and Sr. Antonia. (Courtesy of Jeanette DeBonis.)

Four

Always Ready to Serve

The development of ethnic social clubs closely followed the establishment of the parish churches as gathering places for residents of the community. The Cristoforo Colombo Club, the Frosolone Club, the Cervinara Club, and the Pietro Gallese Club helped assimilate Italians and preserve their culture. Members volunteered their time, energy, and talents to sponsor and organize events from *festas* with music and food to dances, picnics, and sporting events. The Italian Welfare League, an early mutual-aid society, later sponsored the organization of the Italian Community Center (ICC). The Sons of Italy, the Knights of Columbus, and the Ciccarelli, Rea, Agars, Bevevino Garrison 1954 all continue to this day, along with the ICC, to have a positive impact on the community and its members. Groups also formed to address particular issues from Italian migration to saving homes when the government attempted to build a superhighway. Strong ties to the family and the neighborhood, and associations through their church and social organizations, helped maintain the value system that sustained the early immigrants and preserved *la via vecchia* (the old way). World War II and its aftermath would bring about significant changes to la via vecchia; but Little Italy neighborhoods throughout American communities continue to stand the test of time and flourish.

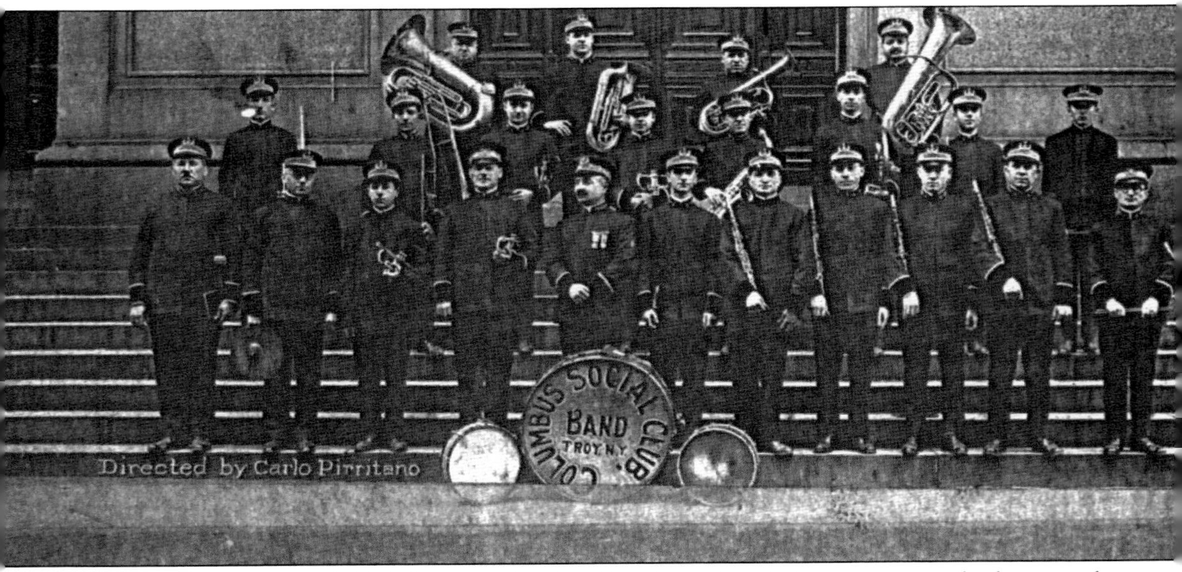

The Columbus Social Club Band, under the direction of Carlo Pirritano, marched in parades and performed at various community celebrations. Member volunteers included Troy tailors Anthony DeLucia on tuba and his first cousin Louis on clarinet. The club, originally called the Cristoforo Colombo Club and located at 86 Congress Street, was organized by attorney Philip Cirillo, a 1911 Albany Law School graduate and a founding member of the ICC and its president in 1939. Cirillo, corporation counsel for the City of Troy from 1948 to 1956, was active in several community organizations and St. Anthony of Padua parish. (Courtesy of Anthony DeLucia.)

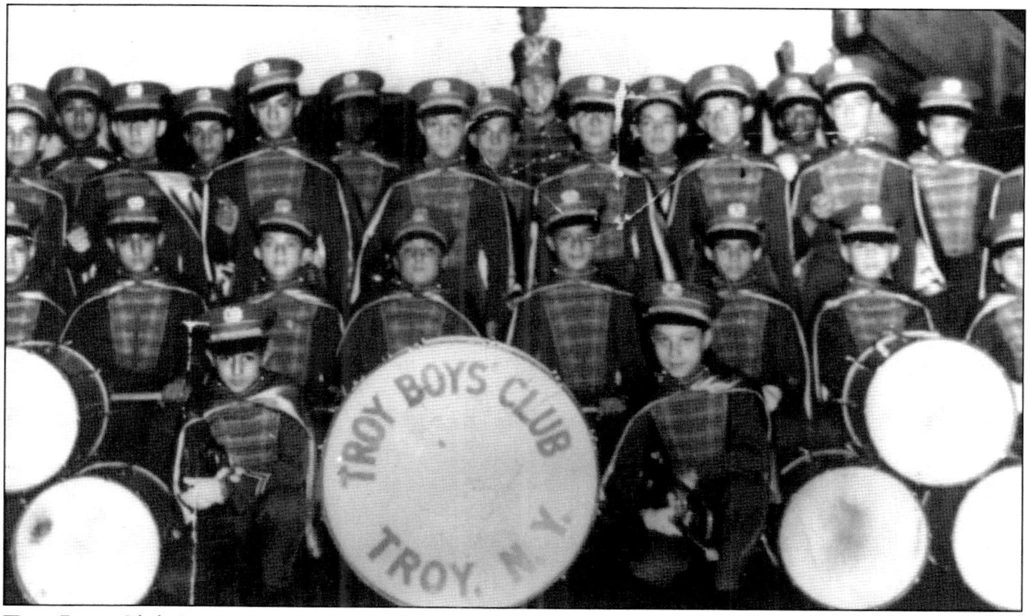

Troy Boys Club Drum and Bugle Corps was photographed in 1938, shortly before appearing at the 1939–1940 New York World's Fair. From left to right are (first row) Frank Melite and Frank Potenza; (second row) Edward McGovern, Joe Panza, John Milanese, Frank Marchese, Geno Ferretto, John Cardenuto, Nick Anthony, and Nick Furciniti; (third row) Emil Hug, Ed Verrillo, Guy Cardenuto, James Bevevino, Dom Brignola, George Collins, Nick Bevevino, Don Farina, Michael Zullo, Carlo Valenti, Frank Piscitella, James Gordon, Joseph Movana, Richard Gordon, and Edward Vigeant. (Courtesy of Louis DeLucia.)

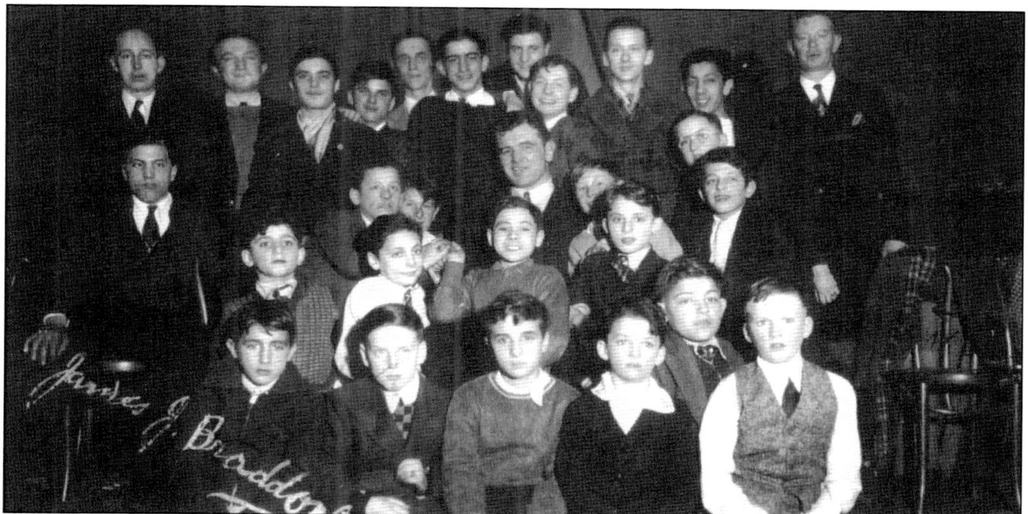

James J. Braddock, heavyweight champion of the world from 1935 to 1937, visits the Troy Boys Club. Among the excited young people who can be identified are Joseph and Nicholas Campese, Carlo Valenti, John Potenza, John Romeo, Jim Madden, Dominic Pafundi, John and Michael Milanese, and Charles McCade. Braddock was the subject of Hollywood producer Ron Howard's 2005 film biography *Cinderella Man*, with Russell Crowe in the role of Braddock, a depression-era boxing sensation. (Courtesy of Mickey Visk.)

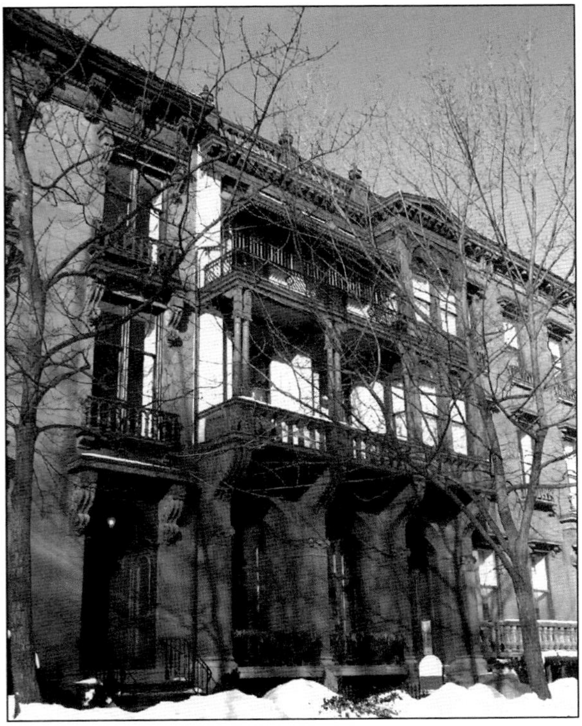

The ICC was established in 1935 and, for more than 50 years, occupied the exquisite 19th-century mansion of Troy journalist and diplomat John Morgan Francis at 191 Second Street. Francis was the founder and editor of the *Troy Daily Times* and envoy to Greece and other European nations. As a member of the Washington Park Association, the ICC was permitted to hold events in the beautiful private two-acre ornamental park across the street from its building. (Photograph by Dan Lennon.)

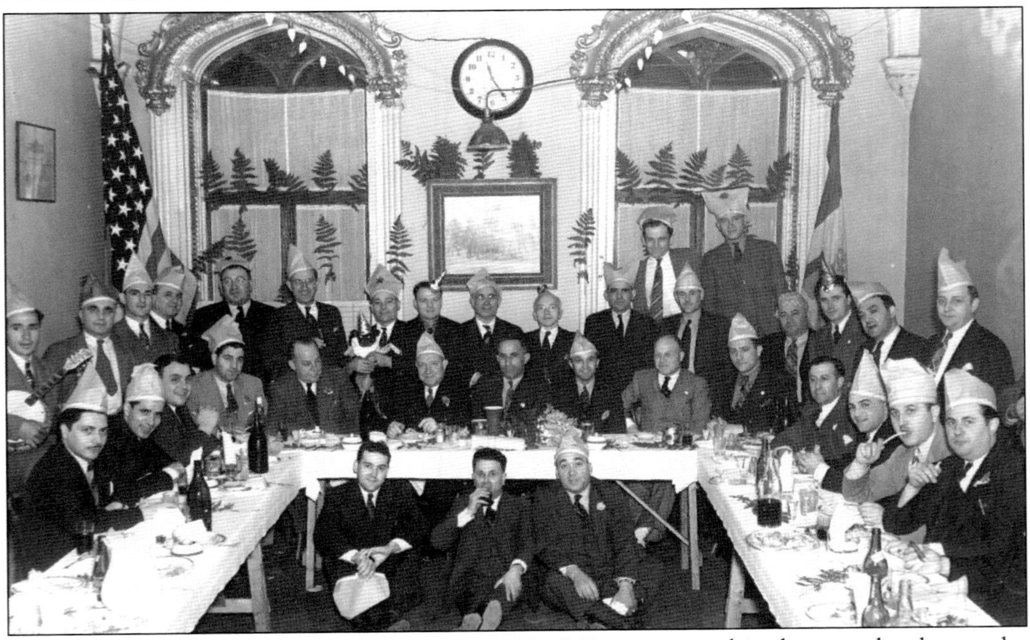

Members of the ICC socialize at the 1940 New Year's Eve party in this photograph taken at the center's 191 Second Street home. Among those who can be identified are Angelo Valente, Frank DeLucia, Pasquale Zucaro, Angelo Patette, Frank Marchese, Jerry Esposito, Eugene Bizzarro, and Michael Terribile. The establishment of the ICC was a significant achievement for the growing Italian community. (Author's collection.)

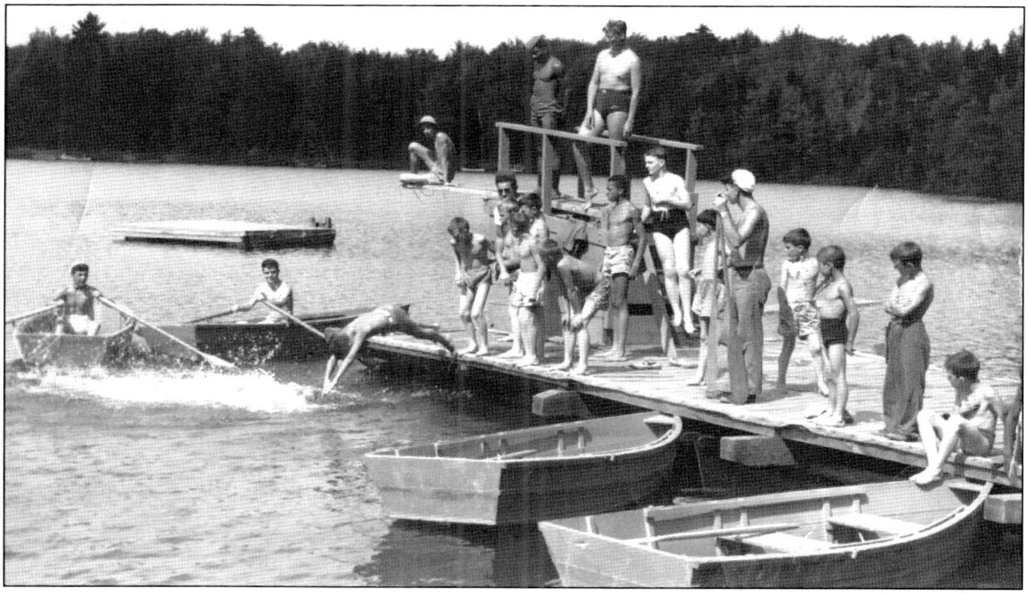

Camp Barker is an 85-acre summer camp on Forest Lake in Rensselaer County given to the Troy Boys Club in 1923 by C. W. Tillinghast. Among those who can be identified in this 1947 photograph are counselors Anthony DeBonis, Sam Turriglio, Carlo Valenti, Larry Johnson, and Ted Potenza. Campers learned to swim and could qualify for advanced swimming by taking junior and senior lifesaving courses. Inner-city children flock to the club. (Courtesy of Carlo Valenti.)

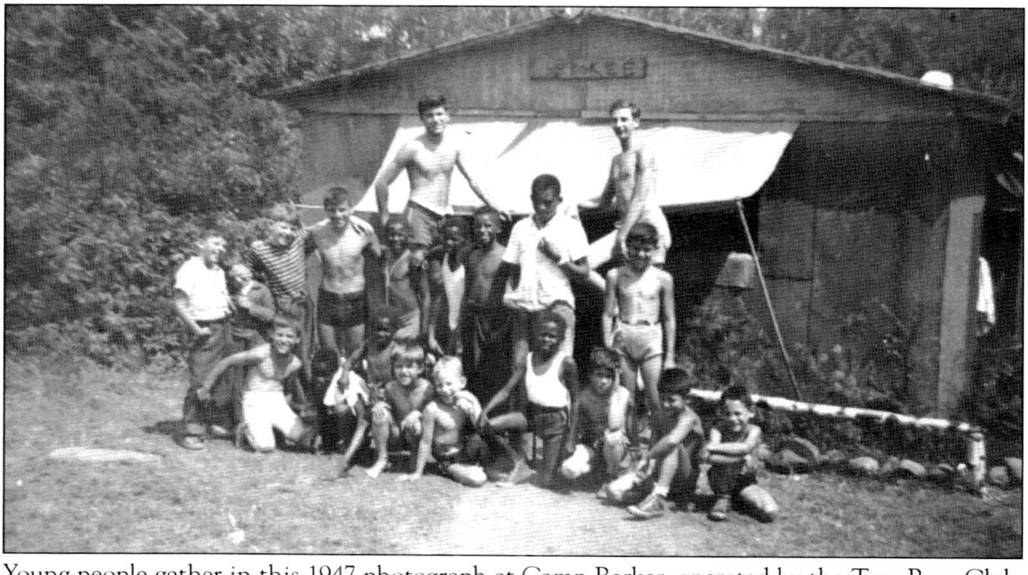

Young people gather in this 1947 photograph at Camp Barker, operated by the Troy Boys Club. Since 1923, the club has offered a popular summer program providing supervised recreation, arts and crafts, sports, and counseling for city children. Returning World War II veterans, using donated lumber and equipment from a variety of groups, including the Watervliet Arsenal and the Troy Fire Department, constructed cabins, docks, and other facilities at the camp and served as counselors and instructors. (Courtesy of Carlo Valenti.)

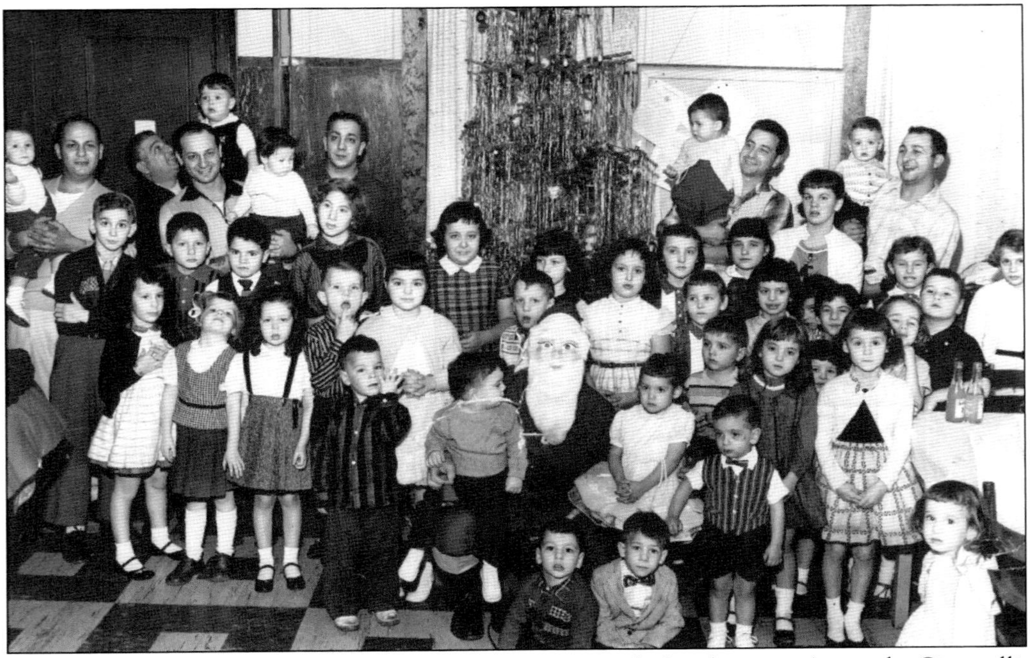

Neighborhood children are treated to a Christmas party at the local veterans' post, the Ciccarelli, Rea, Agars, Bevevino Garrison 1954, located at Liberty Street and St. Mary's Avenue. The post sponsors several annual family-friendly events and contributes generously to local charities but recognizes its priority to honor their fallen brothers. On duty for the holiday party are, from left to right, club members Joseph Bevevino, Vito Furciniti, James Bevevino, Peter Minetti, Vito Ciccarelli, and Dominick Bevevino, along with Santa. (Courtesy of the Ciccarelli, Rea, Agars, Bevevino Garrison 1954.)

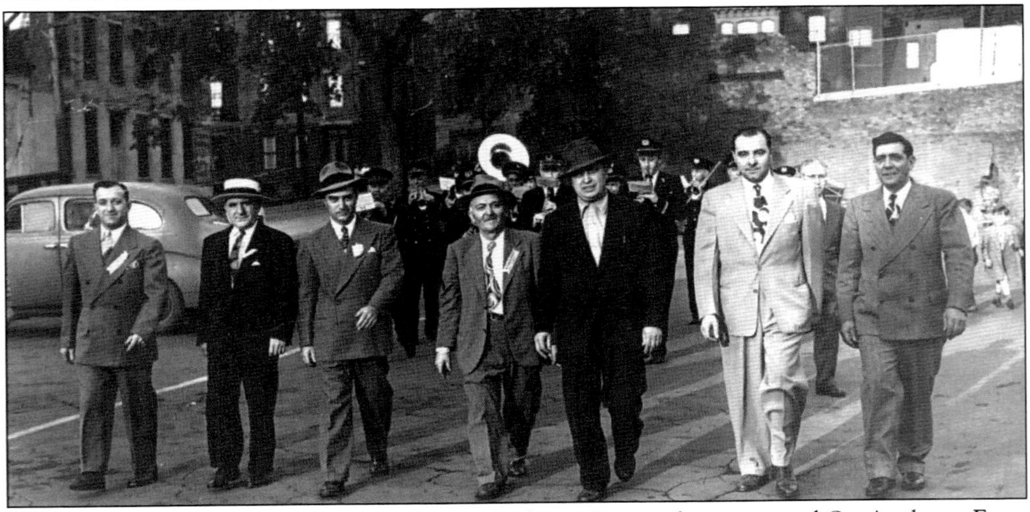

Stepping off at the public market at Hill and Liberty Streets for an annual St. Anthony Festa are, from left to right, Luciano Tornincasa, Luigi Bottillo, Anthony DeFazio, Louis Marchese, James Visk, Louis Rizzo, and John Rea. They are being followed by the ICC band. The first Festa of St. Anthony held in Troy was on June 11, 1906. Francipane's Italian Band of New York City marched in the parade through several miles of city streets. (Courtesy of Mickey Visk.)

The ICC, an early sponsor of Troy's annual Flag Day parade, regularly decorates a float and marches proudly through the Little Italy neighborhood, the parade route for the event, which attracts tens of thousands to honor the nation's flag. A color guard consists of several members dressed in the traditional uniforms of the carabinieri. The center also frequently sponsors a nationally known marching band. (Courtesy of the Italian Community Center Archives.)

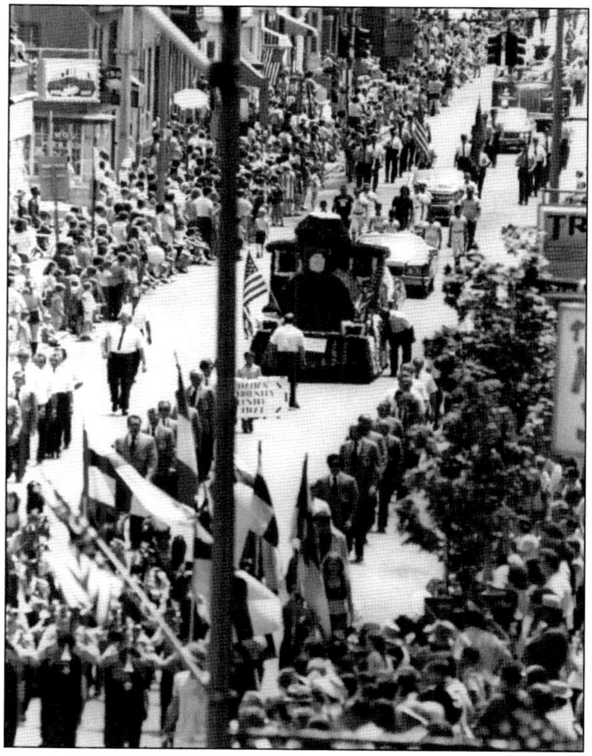

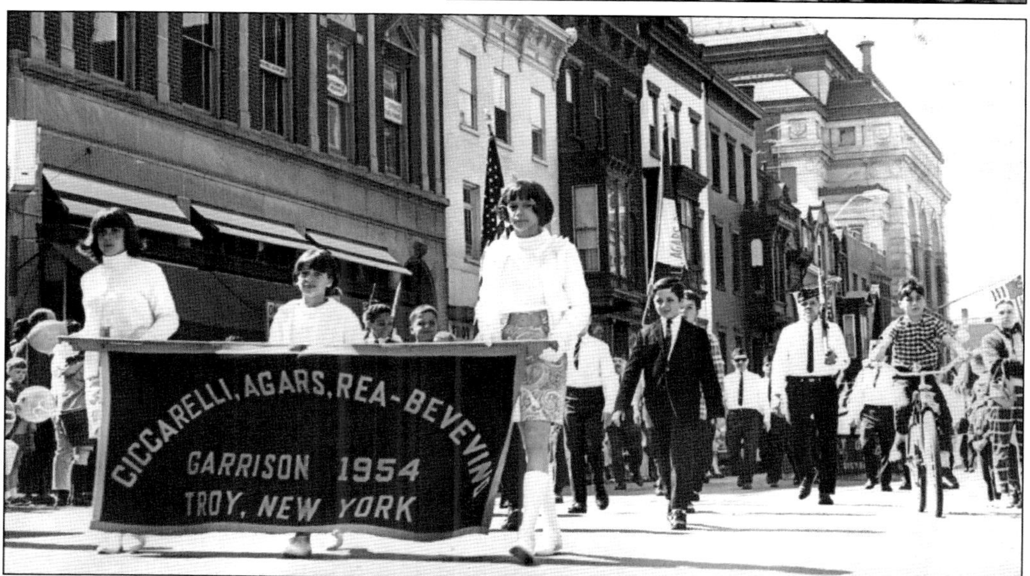

Troy's annual Flag Day parade is joined by a contingent from the Ciccarelli, Rea, Agars, Bevevino Garrison 1954. Holding the banner (under the post's earlier name) are, from left to right, Ann Marie Pascarella, Donna Mantello, and Josephine Esposito, followed by Joseph Cavallo Jr. and members of the veterans' post. The neighborhood post and the ICC were among the earliest supporters of the parade, first held on June 14, 1970. It is the largest such parade in the country. (Courtesy of the Ciccarelli, Rea, Agars, Bevevino Garrison 1954.)

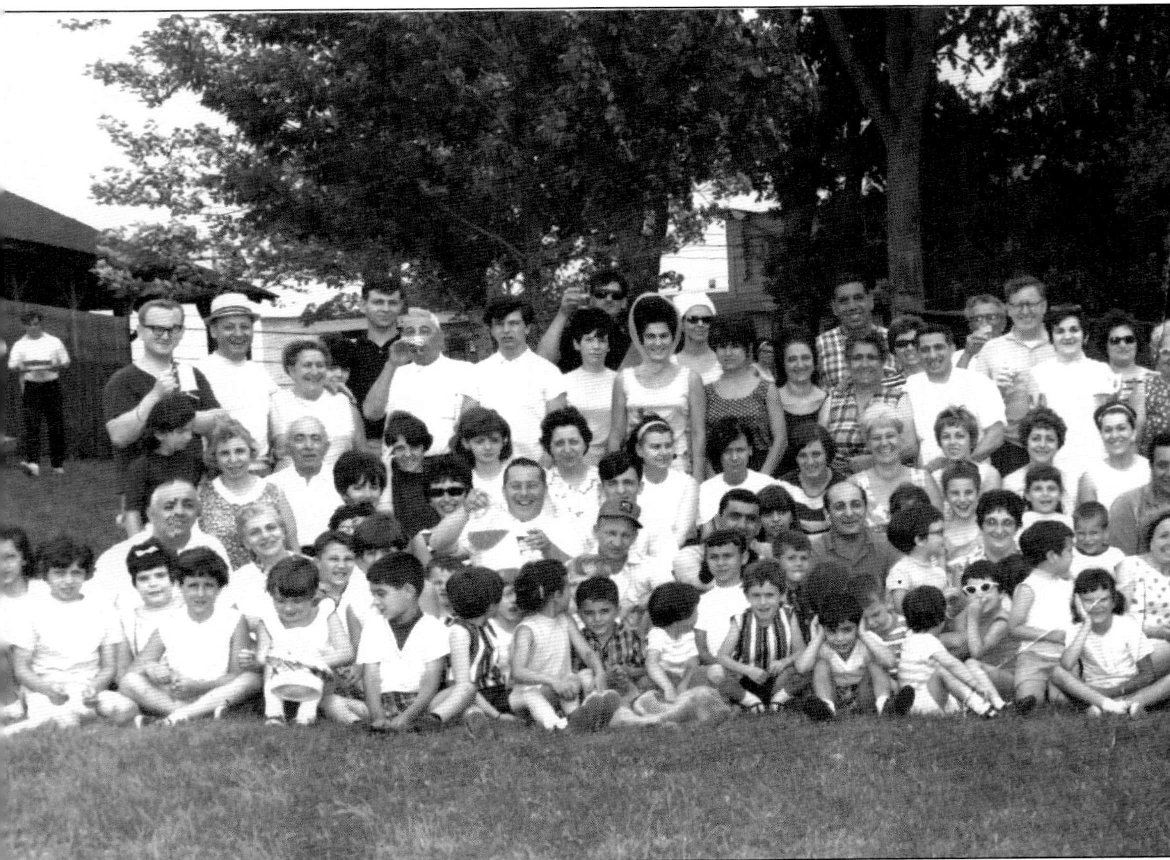

More than 140 neighbors attended the 1967 summer outing sponsored by the Ciccarelli, Rea, Agars, Bevevino Garrison 1954 held at the Country Grove picnic area. Most people attending were from the area of Havermans and St. Mary's Avenues, a historic part of Little Italy that contained more than 90 buildings, most of them modest two-story brick residences constructed after 1860 on streets nestled along the western slope of Mount Ida. As immigrants from southern

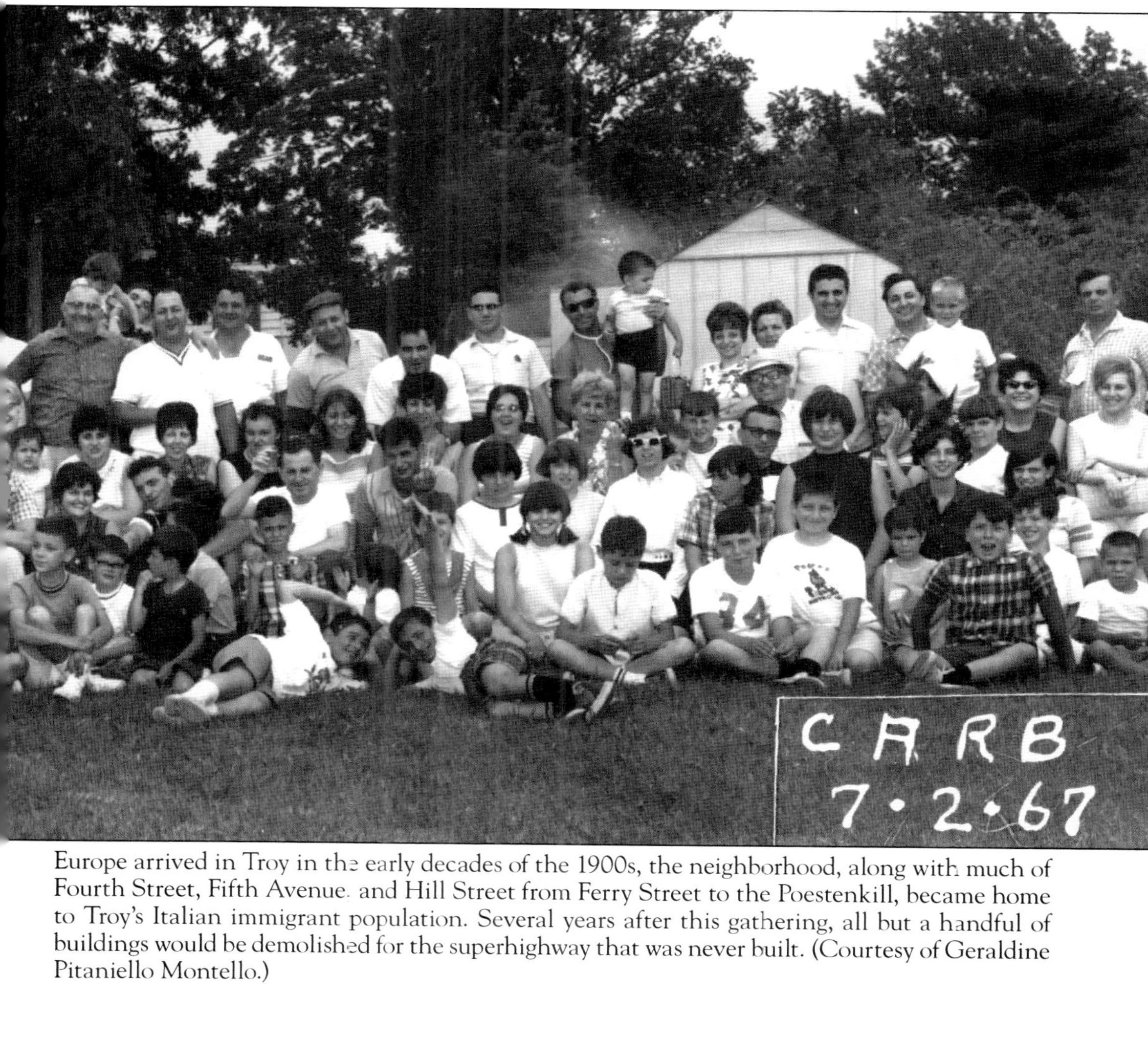

Europe arrived in Troy in the early decades of the 1900s, the neighborhood, along with much of Fourth Street, Fifth Avenue, and Hill Street from Ferry Street to the Poestenkill, became home to Troy's Italian immigrant population. Several years after this gathering, all but a handful of buildings would be demolished for the superhighway that was never built. (Courtesy of Geraldine Pitaniello Montello.)

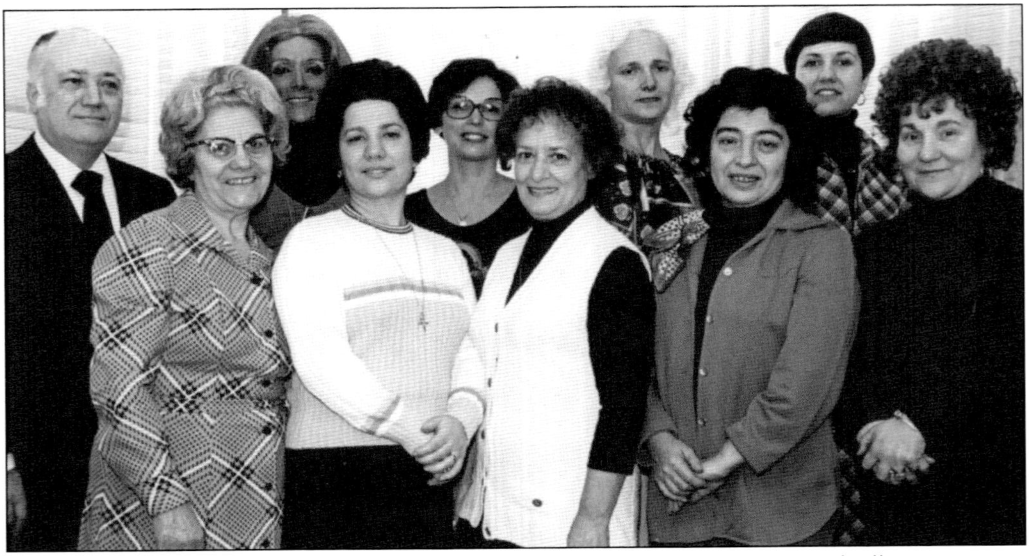

Members of the American Committee on Italian Migration of the Diocese of Albany organize for the second annual Italian Carnival Dinner Dance in January 1977. From left to right are (first row) Josephine DeFazio, Laura Safara, Ann Mantello, Theresa Mariano, and Rose Morini; (second row) Anthony DeFazio (diocesan chairman), Theresa Bove, Helen Farnam, Mary Blair, and Barbara Mamone. The committee, founded in 1952, was instrumental in the passage of measures to increase the numbers of Italians to enter America. (Courtesy of the DeFazio family.)

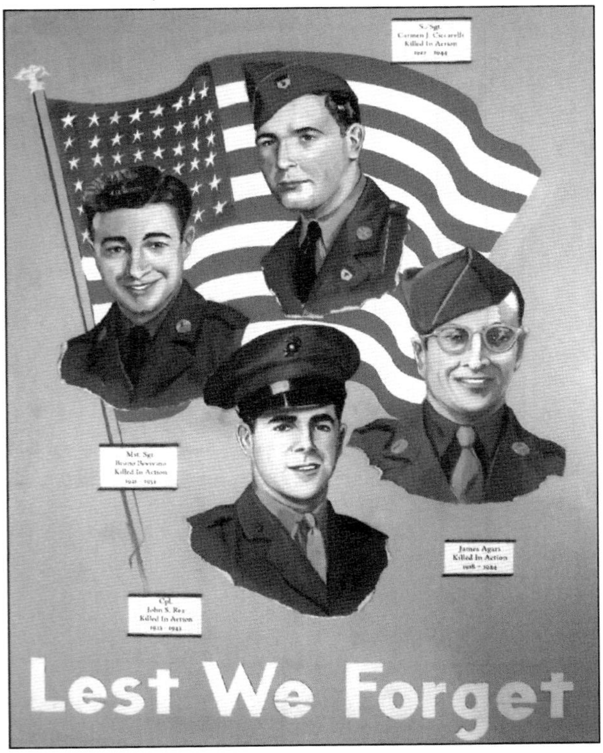

The neighborhood veterans' post is named for the honored brothers pictured here: S.Sgt. Carmine J. Ciccarelli (1922–1944), killed in action on August 7, 1944; James Agars (1918–1944), killed in action on July 6, 1944; Cpl. John S. Rea (1923–1943), killed in action on June 9, 1943; and M.Sgt. Bruno Bevevino (1921–1953), missing in action in Korea. (Courtesy of the Ciccarelli, Rea, Agars, Bevevino Garrison 1954.)

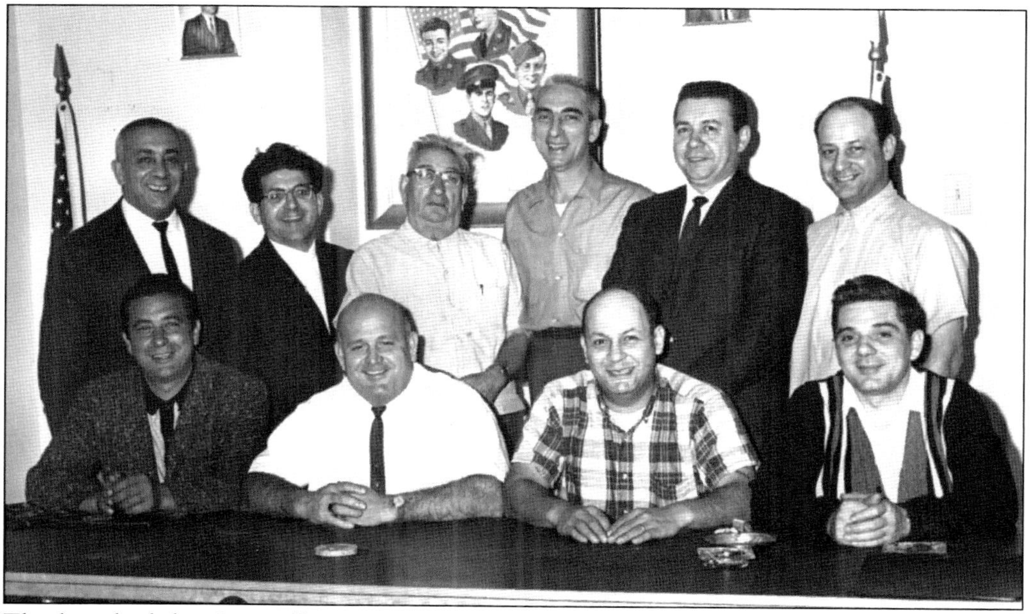

The board of the Ciccarelli, Rea, Agars, Bevevino Garrison 1954 is pictured at a meeting. From left to right are (first row) Vito Ciccarelli Sr., Jerry Agostine, Joseph Bevevino, and Pat Pascarella; (second row) Peter Minetti, Nick Furciniti, Caesar Montello, Paul Esposito, Rocco DeMeo, and James Bevevino. The post sponsors a Little League team, raises funds for those in need, and offers its facility for fund-raisers for worthy causes—all with the support of its member volunteers. (Courtesy of the Ciccarelli, Rea, Agars, Bevevino Garrison 1954.)

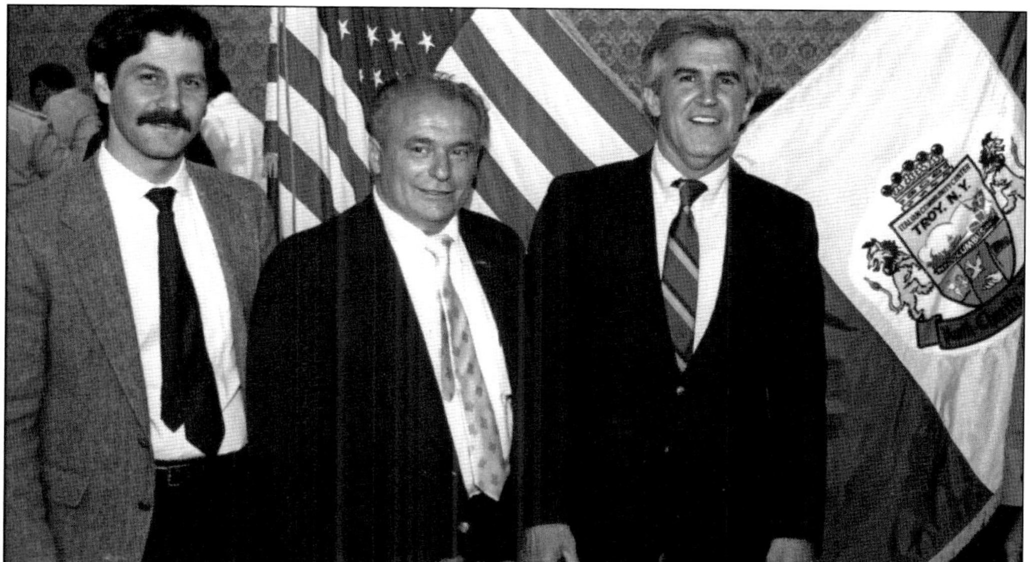

The ICC prepares for its new home as, from left to right, architect Vincent Lepera and contractor Louis Bianchi show plans for the project to center member New York State senator Joseph L. Bruno. The site of the new center, located at 1450 Fifth Avenue, was formerly the John Stanton Brewery, demolished after a major fire engulfed the building in 1963. The ICC continues its long tradition of charitable works in the community. (Courtesy of Carmela Bianchi.)

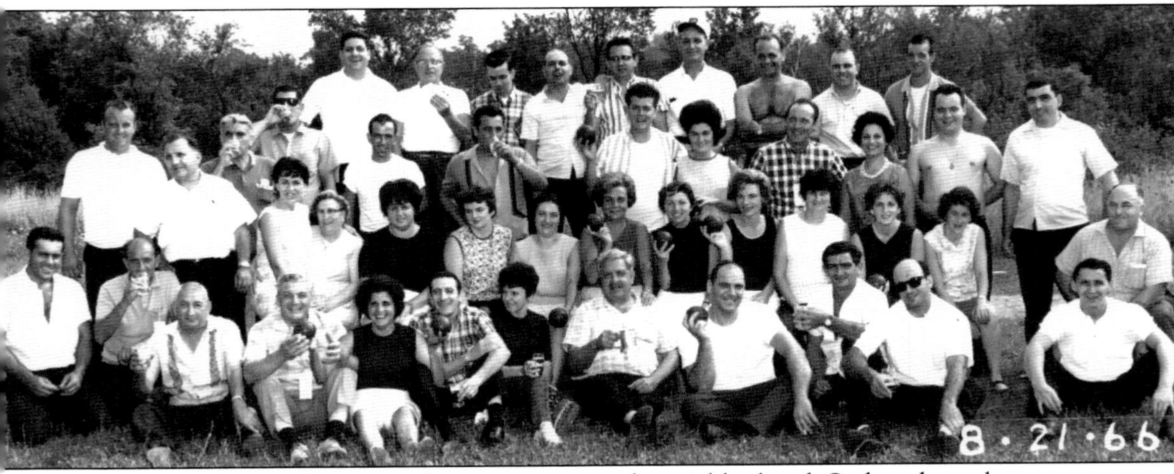

The age-old sport of bocce is a favorite pastime in the neighborhood. Gathered together are some of the most enthusiastic players, members, and guests of the Ciccarelli, Rea, Agars, Bevevino Garrison 1954, at one of its popular summer outings. This outing was held at the Country Grove picnic area in 1966. For several years, the veterans' post maintained an outdoor bocce court. In November 2005, the Friends of Little Italy celebrated the opening of its two bocce courts at the former public market on Hill Street. In attendance was seven-time United States National Bocce Tournament champion Michael Nicosia of San Jose, California. The ICC has an indoor bocce court in its building at 1450 Fifth Avenue. (Courtesy of Geraldine Montello.)

Five

Open for Business

Bell foundries, iron and stove works, garment shops, lumberyards, railroad freight yards, breweries, and gasworks provided employment and were close enough for many people to be able to walk to work. Small shops sold groceries, baked goods, fruits and vegetables, meats and poultry, and provided personal services—from barbershops to beauty salons, dry cleaners, tailors, and shoe repairs—for the convenience of those who lived within a few blocks. For more than 50 years, there were as many as 60 mom-and-pop stores on Fourth Street from Ferry Street south to Ida Street. Many of the shop owners lived in apartments above the shops. Many businesses had a life expectancy of 30 to 50 years as they were passed down from one family member to another. Among the longtime neighborhood businesses were Mangione's Locksmith, DeFazio's Import Store, Lomaestro's Quick Shoe Repair, Bottillo's Barbershop, Mercla's Bakery, DeMaria's Gulf gas station, Pusatere Brothers Fruits and Vegetables, the Volcano Restaurant, and the Red Front Restaurant and Tavern. People also bought from the peddlers who sold their goods from house to house. Local residents referred to Troy's business district as Uptown, though its amenities were only a few blocks' walk from the neighborhood. Throughout American cities, Little Italy neighborhoods continue to inspire a sense of community and pride.

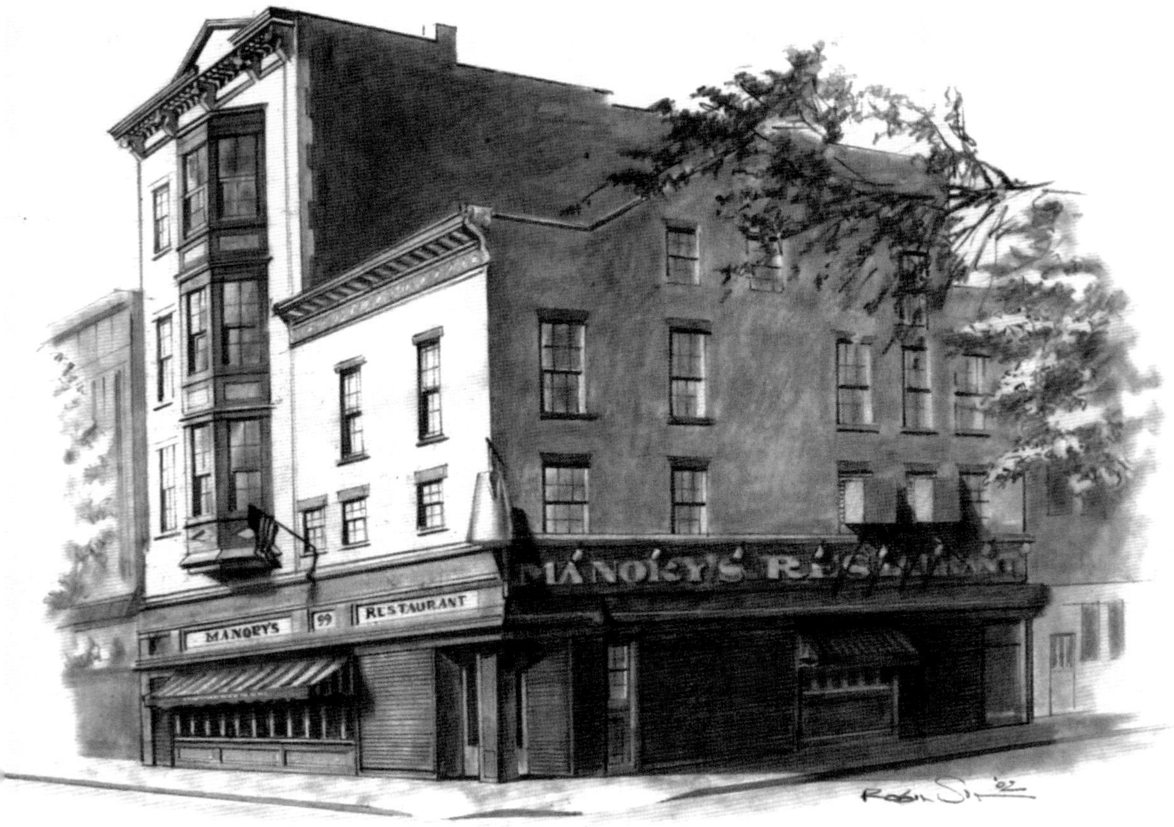

Manory's Restaurant is one of the earliest Italian-owned businesses in Troy, established in 1930 at the corner of Fourth and Congress Streets by Joseph Manori, one of the founders of the ICC and a prominent Italian businessman. Over the years, the business has been continued by members of the Lombardo and Marchese families and is not only one of the oldest businesses on Fourth Street but also Troy's oldest continuously run restaurant. (Courtesy of Louis Marchese.)

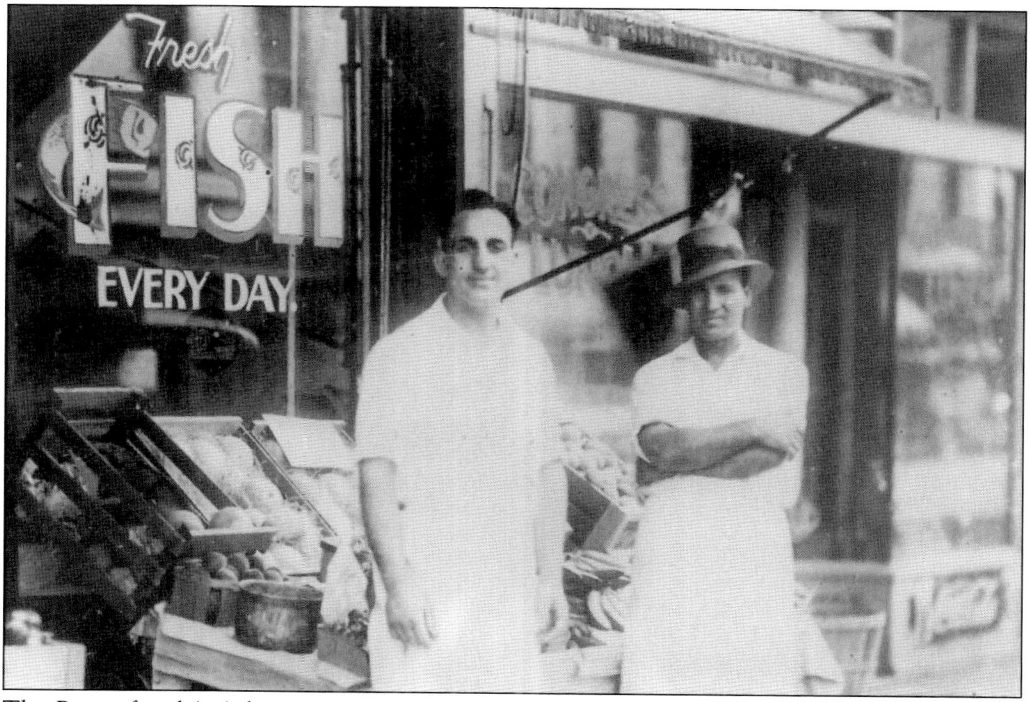

The Prezio family's Atlantic Fruit and Fish Market was located on the south side of Congress Street between Fifth Avenue and William Street. Until the advent of the supermarket, each store had its specialty. Any given block in a neighborhood might contain a dozen such stores. (Courtesy of the Prezio family.)

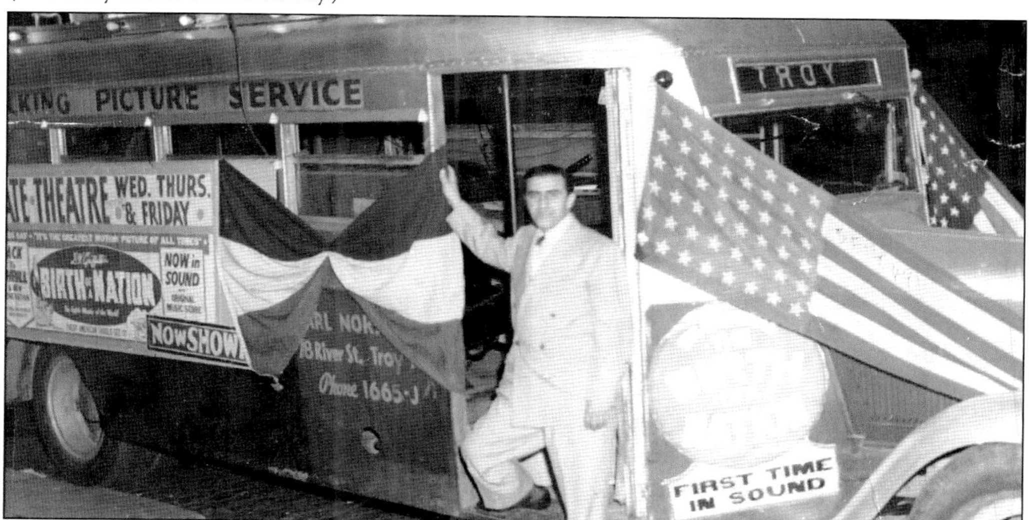

John Capano, owner of the State Theatre at 143 Fourth Street, rented a promotional tour bus in September 1949 to advertise D. W. Griffith's epic film *Birth of a Nation*. For many years, the neighborhood movie theater, originally called the Rose, featured Italian-language films on Monday and Tuesday evenings, as well as the ever-popular serial adventures and cartoons on Saturday mornings. During the 1940s and 1950s, Troy had 11 movie theaters. (Courtesy of John Capano Jr.)

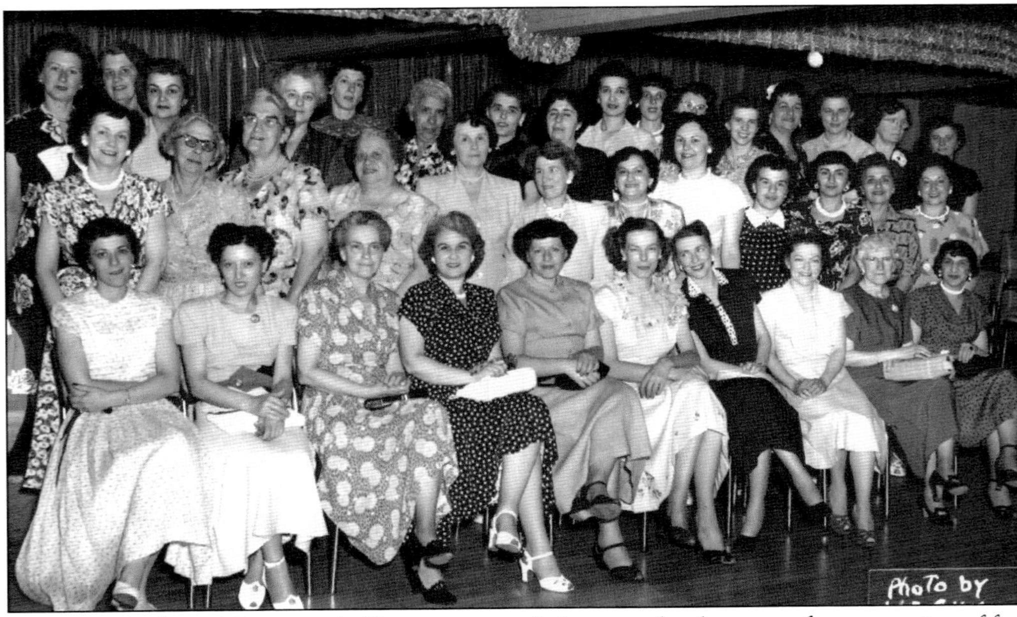

Cluett, Peabody and Company's Christmas party brings out the shop crew for an evening of fun and socializing. Troy's garment industry, which once employed 15,000 women (particularly for the manufacture of shirts and collars), earned the city one of its nicknames, "the Collar City." Among those who can be identified in this photograph are Beatrice Piazza (first row, right); Carmen Pastore (second row, fourth from left); Ann Dinova (second row, ninth from left); and Louise DiSalvatore (third row, right). (Courtesy of Philomena Bizzarro DiSalvatore.)

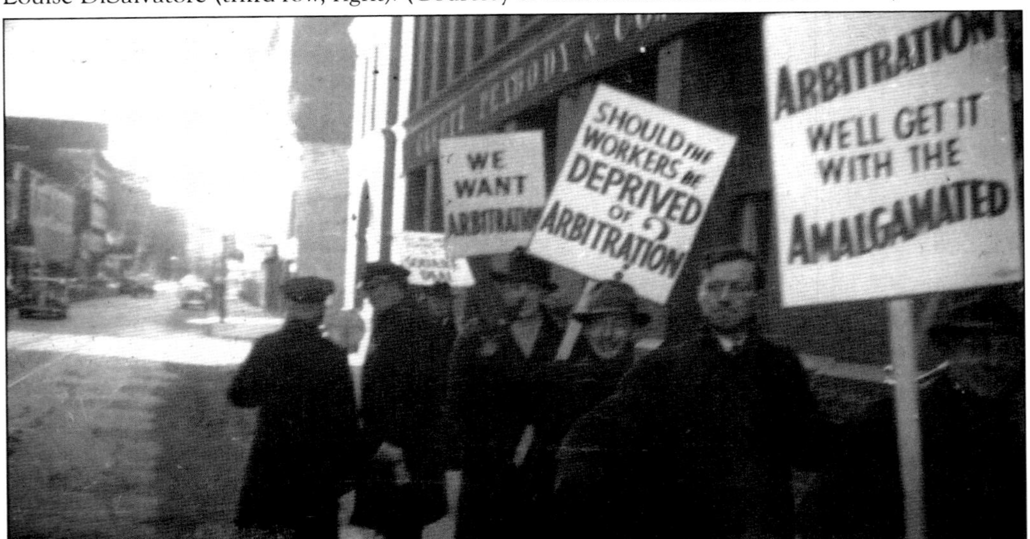

Workers gather to picket the Cluett, Peabody and Company building during a wage demonstration. Troy's garment workers were without union representation for many years. Those who worked in shops manufacturing men's apparel were eventually represented by the Amalgamated Clothing Workers of America. Workers in the women's-wear industry joined the International Ladies Garment Workers of America. Both unions had thousands of members among Troy's working class. (Courtesy of the Visk family.)

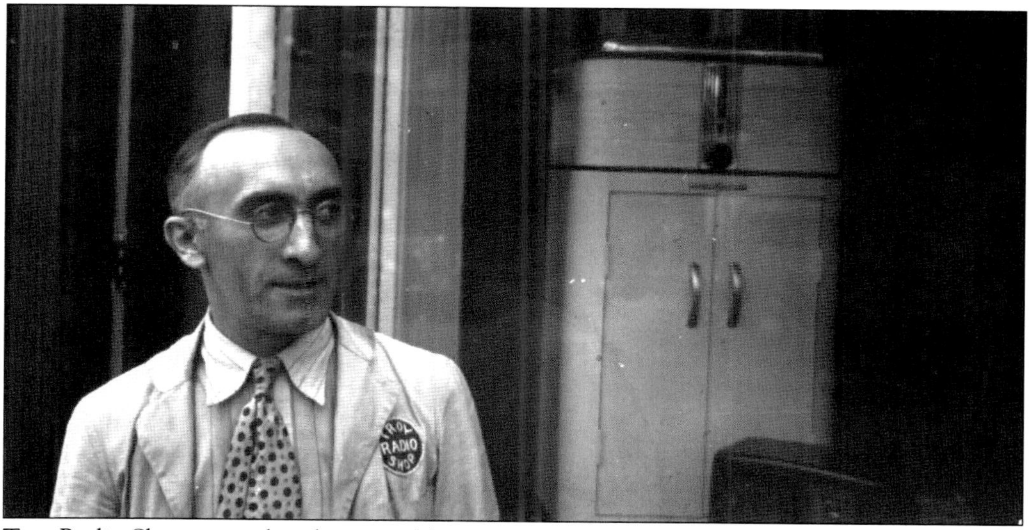

Troy Radio Shop, owned and operated by Donato (Dan) Palladino, was one of many specialty businesses on Fourth Street. Palladino's expertise was radio repair, but he would also sell reconditioned radios. When television became popular in the 1950s, he sold and serviced some of the first black-and-white sets in the community. Boxing matches were one of television's early attractions, and occasionally Palladino would invite friends and family to watch in the store. (Courtesy of Marie Palladino Cairns.)

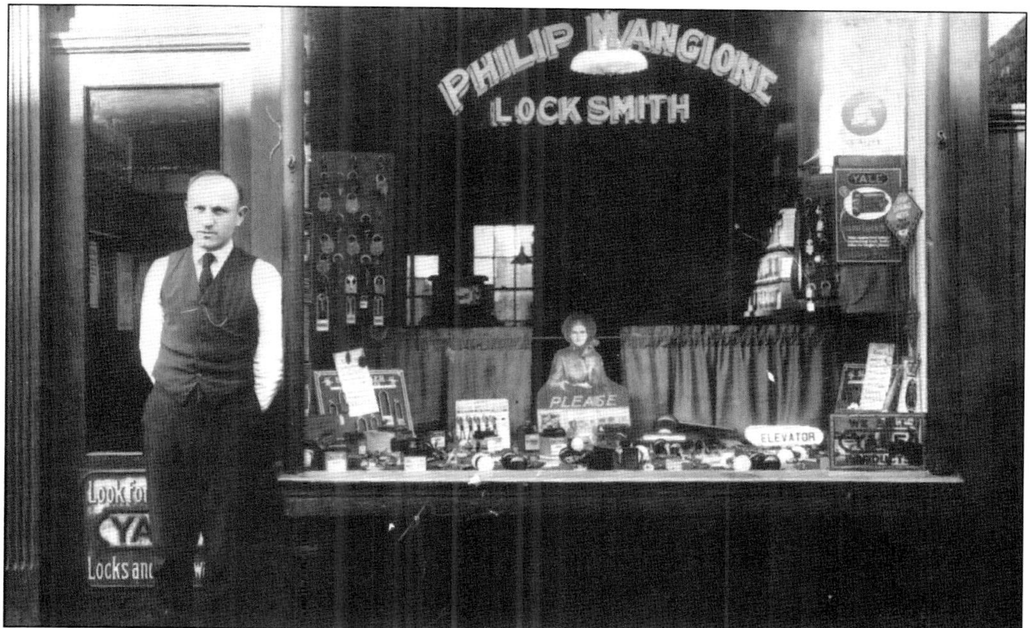

Phillip O. Mangione arrived in Troy in the early 1880s from Frosolone. Since 1885, four generations of Mangiones have operated the family business. This 1921 photograph shows son William in front of the shop when it was located at 189 Fourth Street. The present shop displays an exhibit case with photographs, various locks, and other equipment sold over the years. The Mangione family first lived in a small brick residence on William Street. (Courtesy of the Mangione family.)

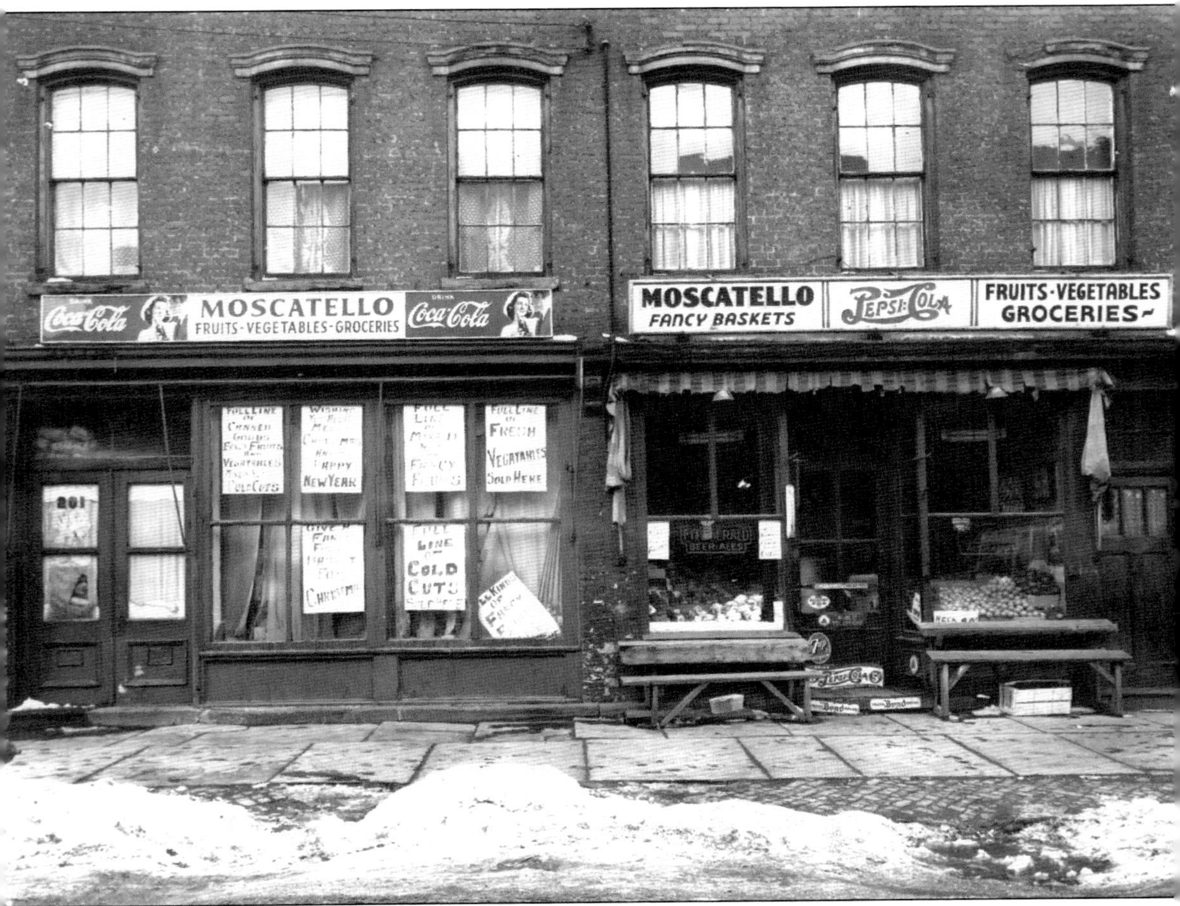

Anthony Moscatello, Dominic Patti, and Joseph Masher were longtime produce men on Fourth Street who would later expand their inventory to include grocery items. Moscatello's store, shown in this 1920 photograph, was located in the first-floor storefronts of two three-story brick buildings at the corner of Fourth and Division Streets and remained in business for almost 40 years. For many years, teams of brothers were thought to corner the market in Little Italy's produce business. The names Sgarlata, Pusatere, Battaglia, Speciale, Schillaci, and Laiacona represent the core of a group of men whose lifework was in fruits and vegetables. In the early years, Italian immigrant men used pushcarts, then sheds, and finally storefronts to sell their fresh produce. (Courtesy of Josie Moscatello Biski.)

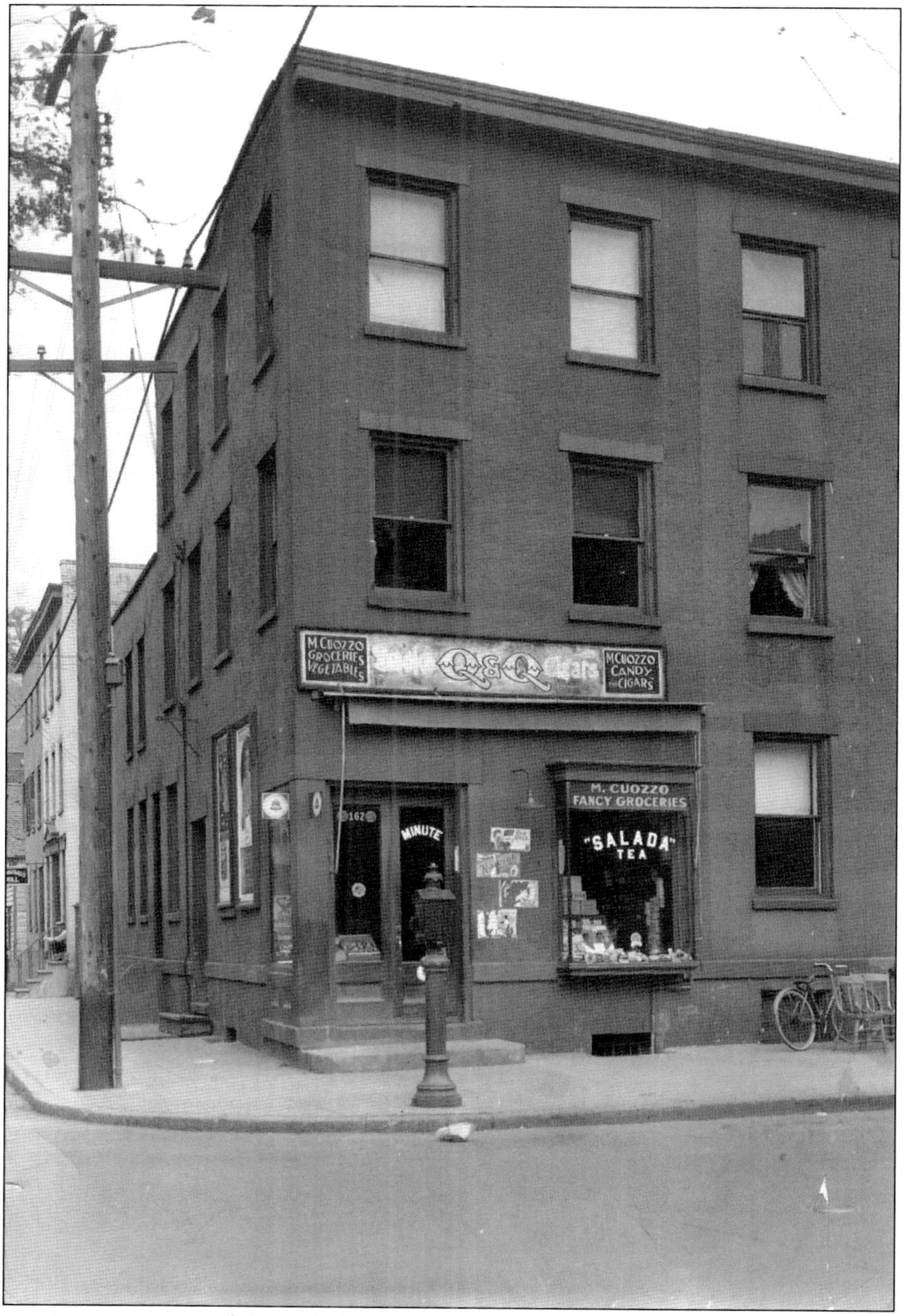

The exterior appearance of Cuozzo's Grocery Store, located at the corner of Third and Division Streets, has not changed much since this 1938 photograph. The family-owned store was purchased by Michael Cuozzo Sr. in June 1925 from the Flaugherty sisters, Irish immigrants. Cuozzo was from Avelino, Campania. His wife, Josephine, was from Candela, Apulia. Members of the family have lived in the apartments above the store for more than 80 years. (Courtesy of Nicholas Cristiano.)

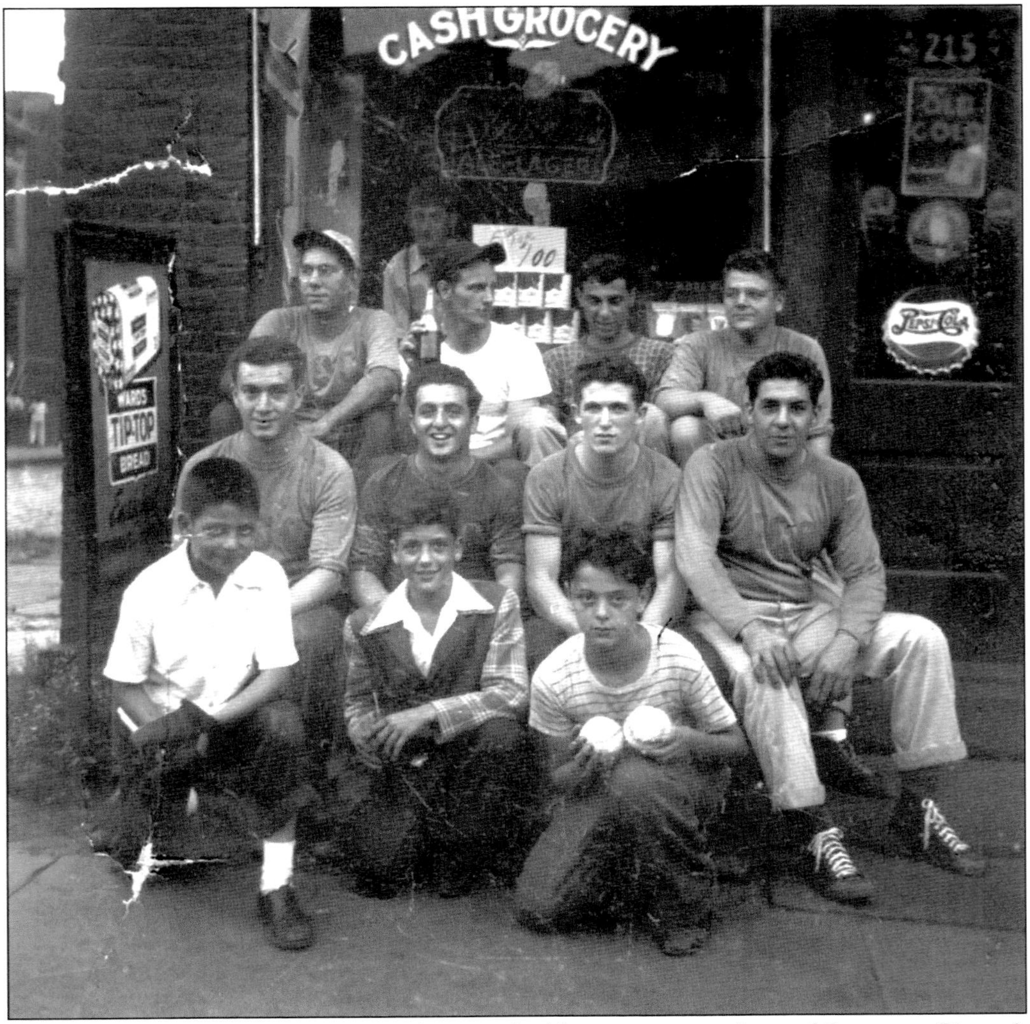

One of many local softball teams is photographed hanging out in front of Francesco Bianco's Grocery at the corner of Washington and Hill Streets after a game at the public market. From left to right are (first row) two unidentified and Patrick "Buster" Martone (batboy); (second row) Marco Zucaro, unidentified, Charles Abrunza, and unidentified; (third row) Hank Merola, Louis Cioffi, Anthony Lanzillo, and Charles Testo. Bianco opened a grocery in 1919 at 55 Hill Street. (Courtesy of John Merola.)

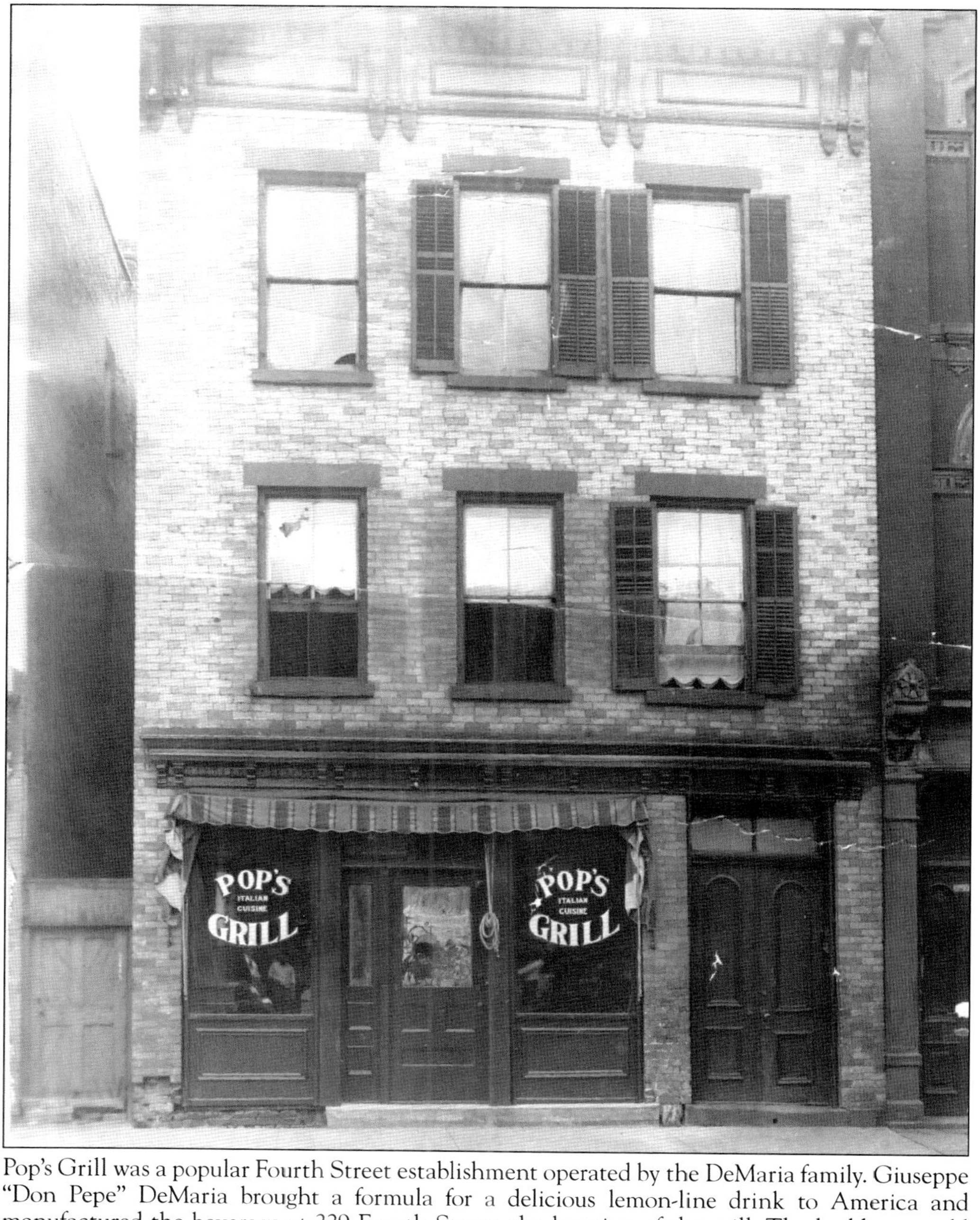

Pop's Grill was a popular Fourth Street establishment operated by the DeMaria family. Giuseppe "Don Pepe" DeMaria brought a formula for a delicious lemon-line drink to America and manufactured the beverage at 229 Fourth Street, the location of the grill. The building would later be the site of DeMaria's Meat Market for more than 30 years. Don Pepe, a skilled butcher, learned his trade as a young man in Cervinara, Italy. The establishment was typical of the early businesses along Fourth Street, owned by immigrants who usually lived in an apartment above their place of business. Within a few years of their arrival, the bustling street became home to hundreds of Italian immigrant families. (Courtesy of the DeMaria family.)

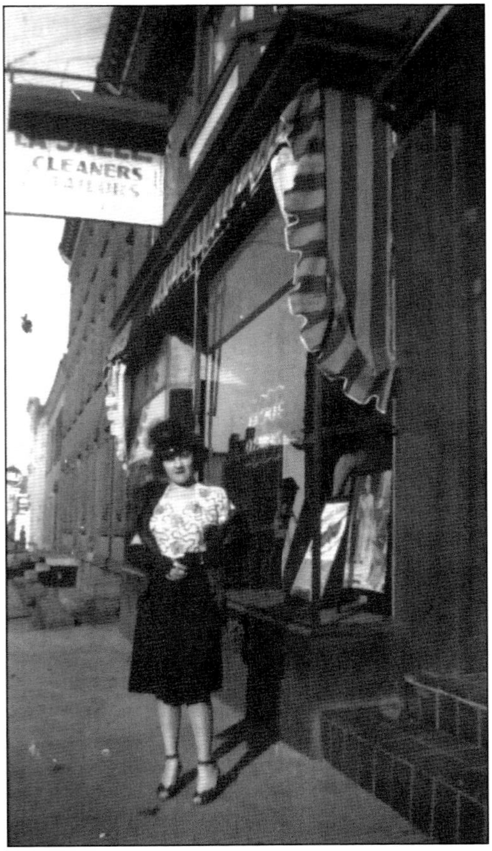

A stylish Lucille DeMaria stands in front of Anthony "Soaker" Santora's LaSalle Cleaners and Tailors, a longtime family-owned business at 228 Fourth Street. The two three-story brick buildings to the left of the dry cleaner's were demolished within a few years of this 1946 photograph. They were replaced by a large one-story commercial building that became the site of several businesses, including Masher and Company Prepackaged Vegetables, Detroit Supply Company, and Vanilla Bean Bakery. (Courtesy of Lucille DeMaria Salerno.)

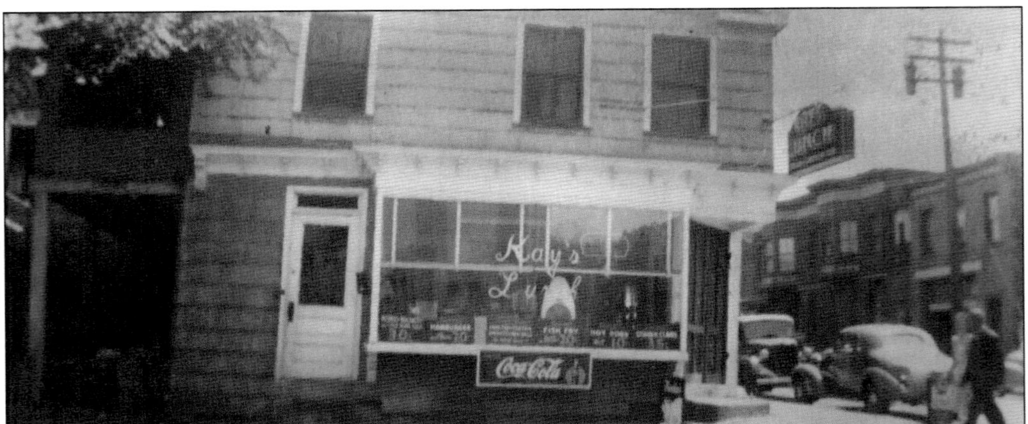

Over the years, the southeast corner of Fourth and Washington Streets was home to several neighborhood luncheonettes, including Kay's Lunch, operated by Kay Clemente Bruno. The site was later Americo Simpson's Fish and Chips, and Rocky's Luncheonette, owned and operated by Rocco DeScanio. The combination of a friendly, casual atmosphere and home-style cooking, always appreciated, made small neighborhood businesses successful. (Courtesy of Karen Bruno Chiera.)

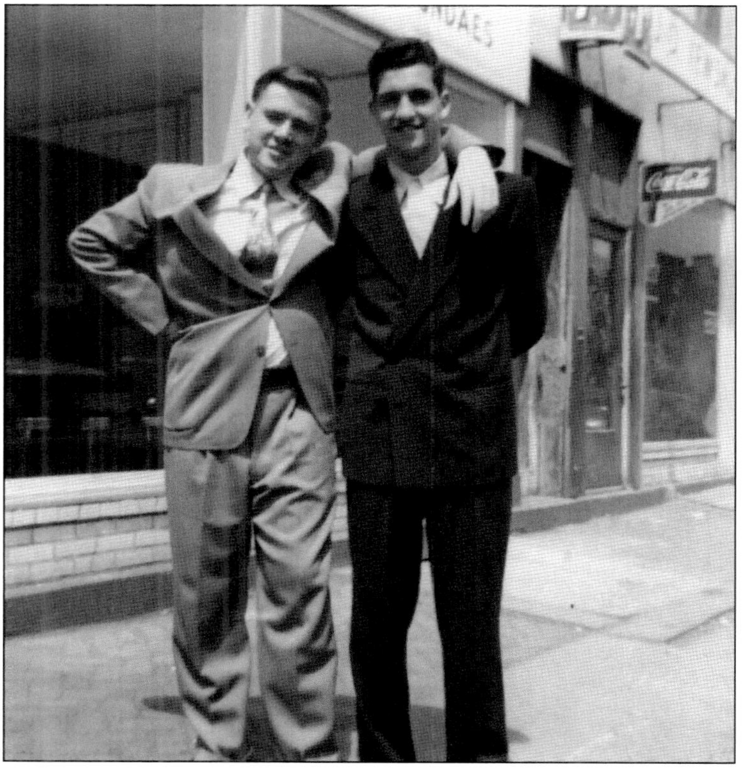

Daniel Bayly (left) and Louis DeMaria Jr., in their Sunday best, are in front of 233 Fourth Street, the home of Stewart's Ice Cream Shop (notice the counter and stools in the window). The popular ice-cream parlor, which opened in Troy in 1950 and remained at that location until 1971, was the company's first store to locate outside Saratoga Springs, the company's home base. Its most popular feature was a make-your-own sundae. (Courtesy of Marion Church Field.)

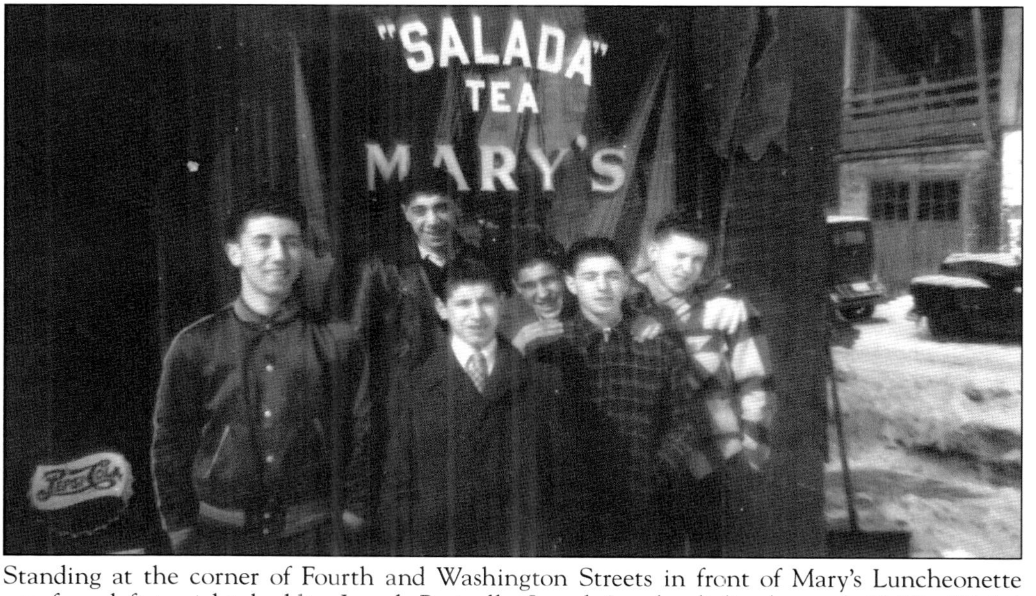

Standing at the corner of Fourth and Washington Streets in front of Mary's Luncheonette are, from left to right, buddies Joseph Pasinella, Joseph Lombardi (in the rear), Phillip (Philo) Germano, Anthony Ragosta, Joseph "Chico" Cavallo, and Lawrence (Larry) Reigert. This corner site was also the locale of luncheonettes later owned by Tony Testo and Rocco DiScanio. Until 1965, its next-door neighbor was LaSalle Institute, which provided a steady customer base for the corner business. (Courtesy of Jean Turriglio Cavallo.)

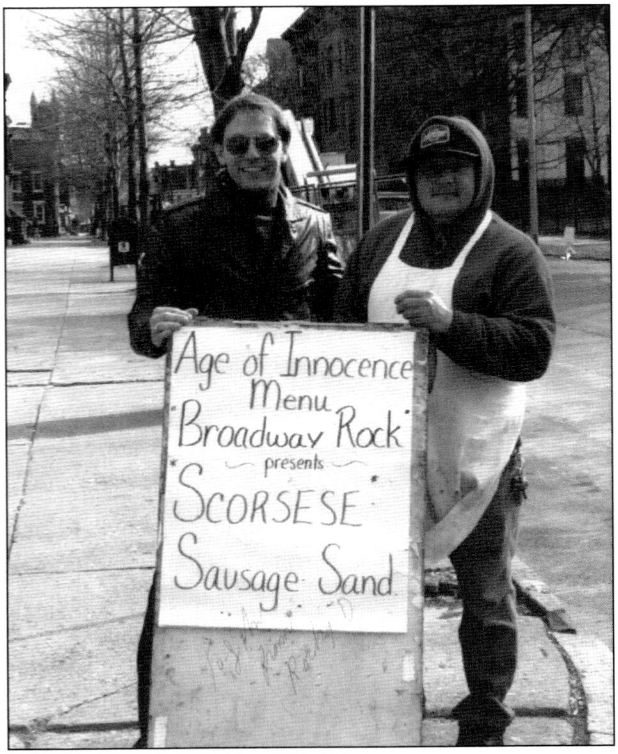

John Oswald joins friend Rocco DiScanio of Rocky's Luncheonette. During the filming of *The Age of Innocence* in Troy's Washington Park neighborhood, DiScanio set up his sandwich cart along Third Street to provide the Scorsese Steak Sandwich, named in honor of director Martin Scorsese. Troy's Victorian architecture has attracted several major film crews to the city. Rocky's cart was a popular amenity at many community events. (Courtesy of John Oswald.)

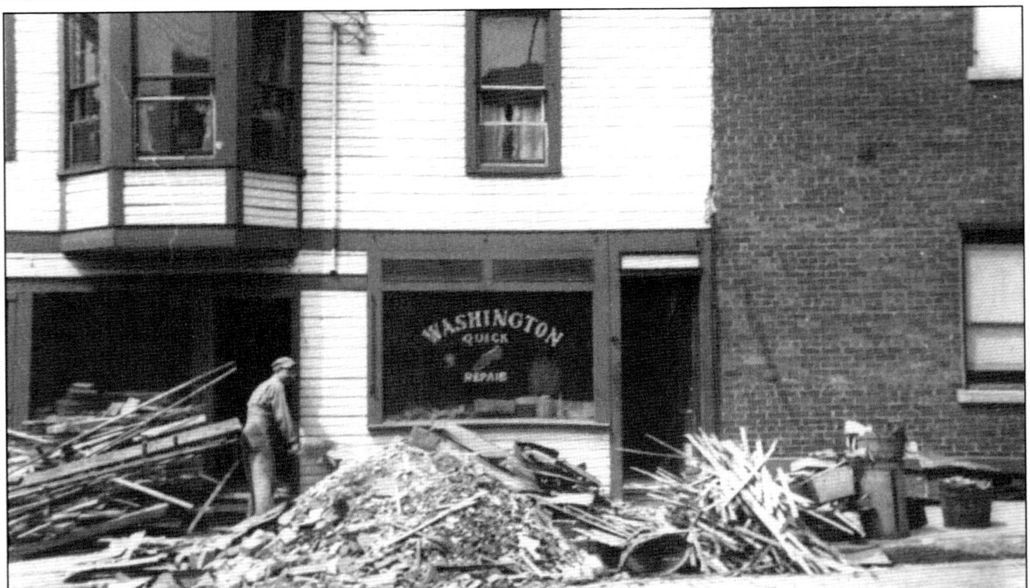

Elizabeth "Bettina" Lomaestro and her husband, Benevenuto, were early neighborhood business owners working from the modest two-story building they owned at 408 Washington Street. Bettina operated a confectionery and Benevenuto repaired shoes. When the confectionery closed in the 1930s, they decided to expand the space for the shoe-repair shop. The family resided in an apartment on the second floor. (Courtesy of Bonnie Lomaestro Walsh.)

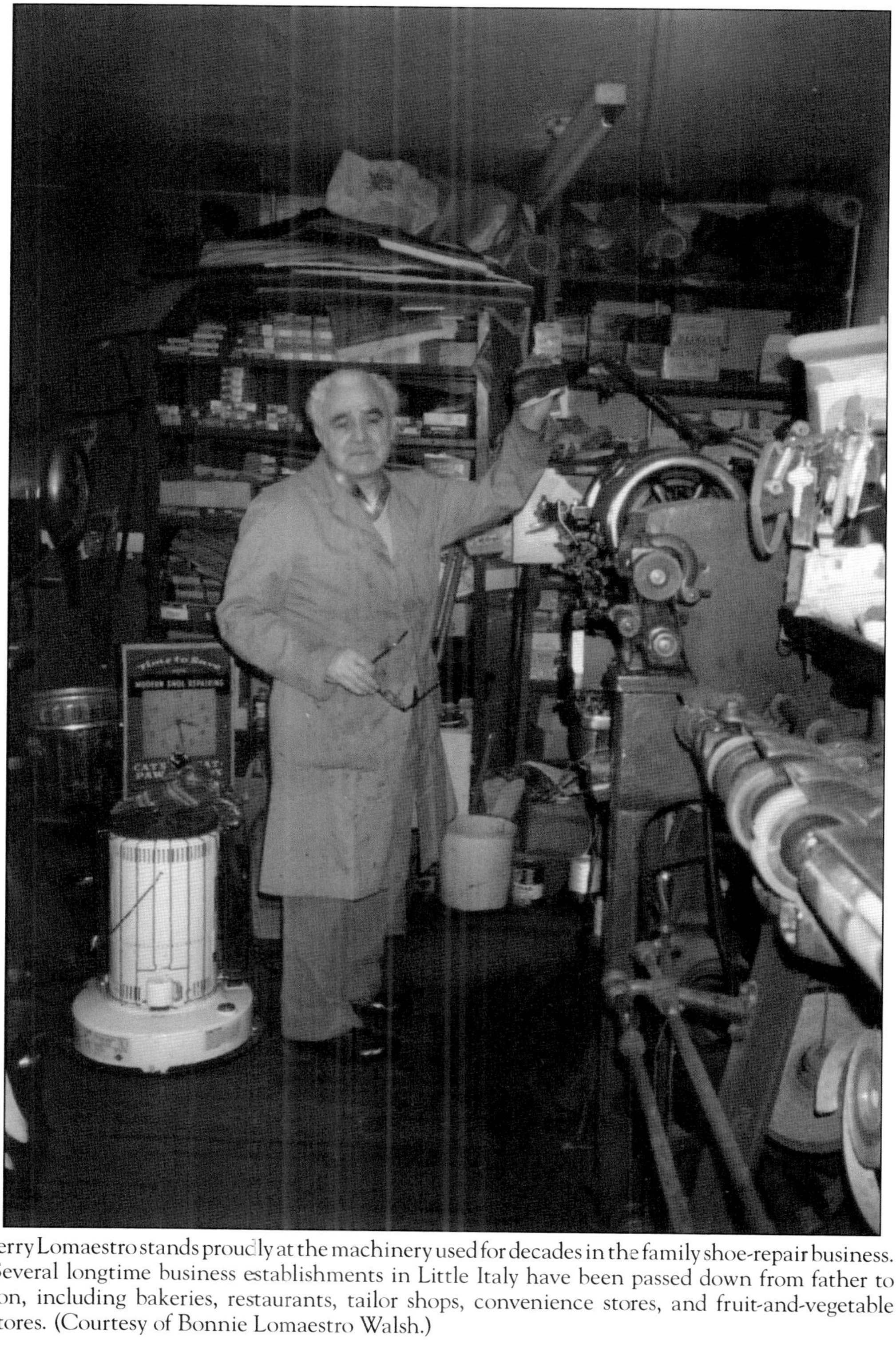

Jerry Lomaestro stands proudly at the machinery used for decades in the family shoe-repair business. Several longtime business establishments in Little Italy have been passed down from father to son, including bakeries, restaurants, tailor shops, convenience stores, and fruit-and-vegetable stores. (Courtesy of Bonnie Lomaestro Walsh.)

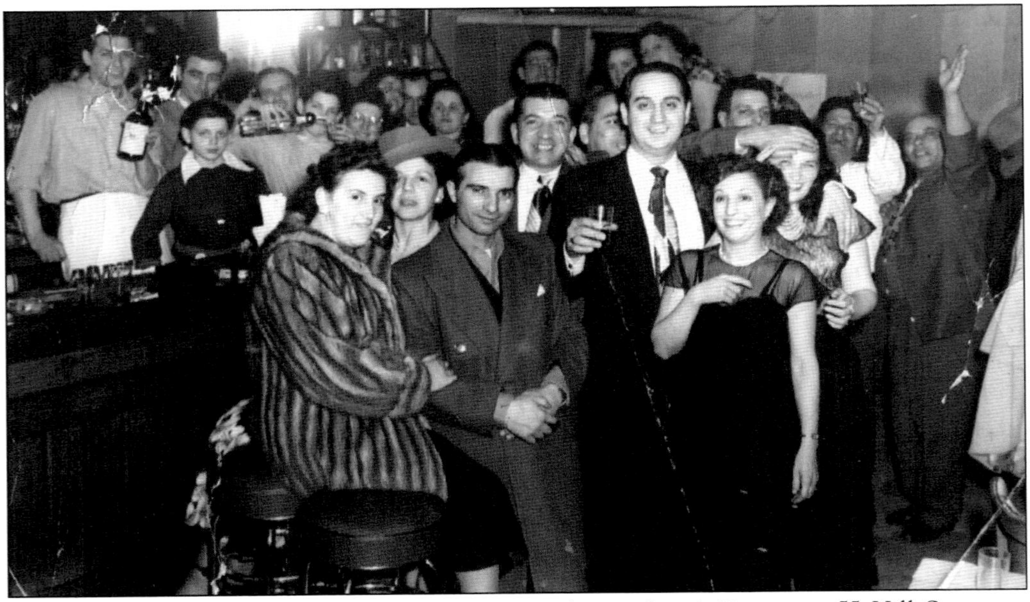

Family and friends of Mildred Riggione Ionata gather at Jerry's Tavern at 55 Hill Street on February 16, 1949, to celebrate her birthday. In the foreground are, from left to right, Lucy Casale, Viola DeMaria, Nicholas Casale, Louis DeMaria, Dr. James Testo, and Eva Lamiano. For many years, the tavern was a social center for people in the neighborhood and was available as a popular place to hold bridal showers, banquets, and family celebrations. (Courtesy of Marie Casale Santora.)

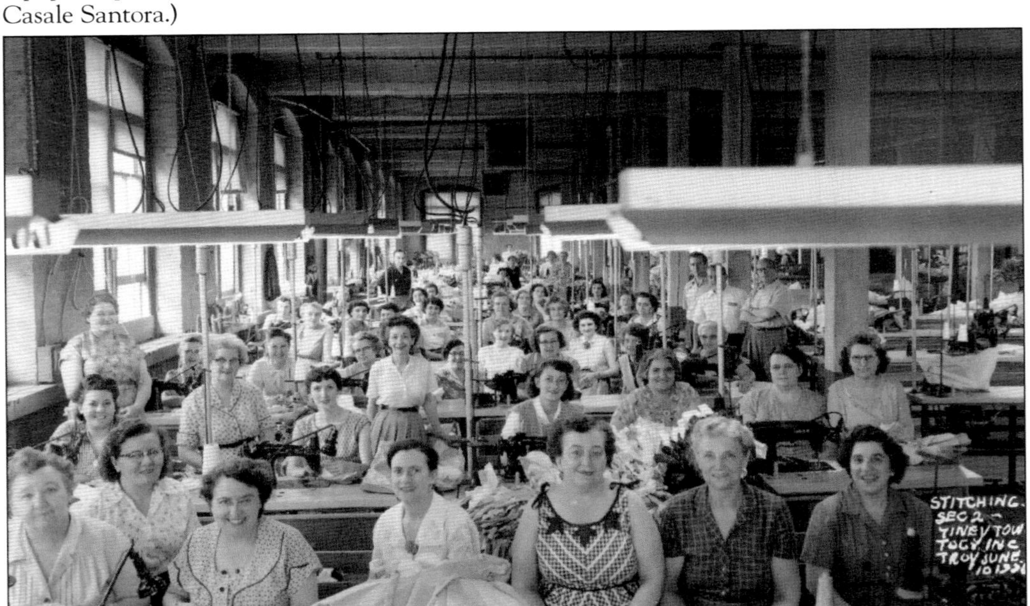

The Stitching Department of Tiny Town Togs included among its employees Ann Comerfort, Stella Lombardi, Betty Turriglio, and her mother, Lena Turriglio, in this June 1950 photograph. Fifty workers of the New York City–based company moved to the dressmaking shop at 2 River Street in 1935. Once the total operation had moved to Troy, 250 employees were hired. (Courtesy of Jean Turriglio Cavallo.)

Anthony DeFazio is photographed amid his stock of grocery products inside his Italian import store on Fourth Street. DeFazio opened the business with the help of his father, Giuseppe, in 1951 in the basement of a small two-story building, eventually relocating to a larger space across the street, which also provided a residence above the store. DeFazio and his wife, Josie, immigrated to the United States in the 1930s. (Courtesy of the DeFazio family.)

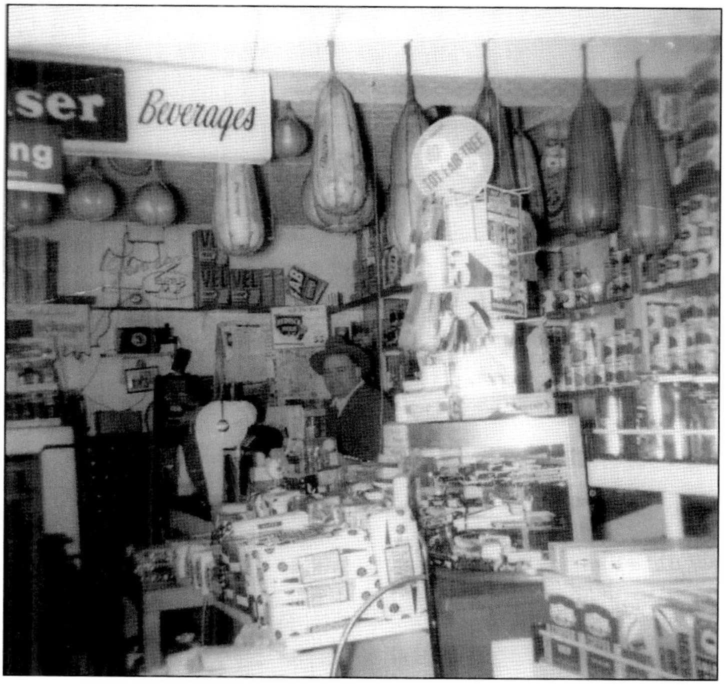

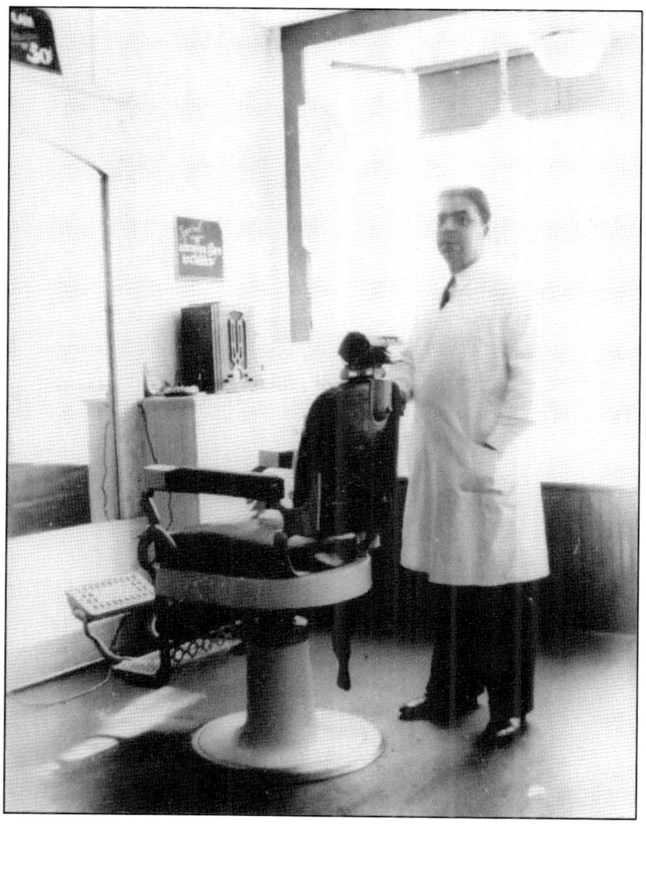

Peter J. Padalino stands beside his chair at his barbershop at 314 Fourth Street. The first-floor commercial space in the two-story brick building at the corner of Fourth and Jefferson Streets has had a long and diverse history as a confectionery, a pharmacy, and a hair-styling salon. The second floor contained an apartment, sometimes for the owner of the business on the ground floor, sometimes as an income apartment. (Courtesy of the Marchese family.)

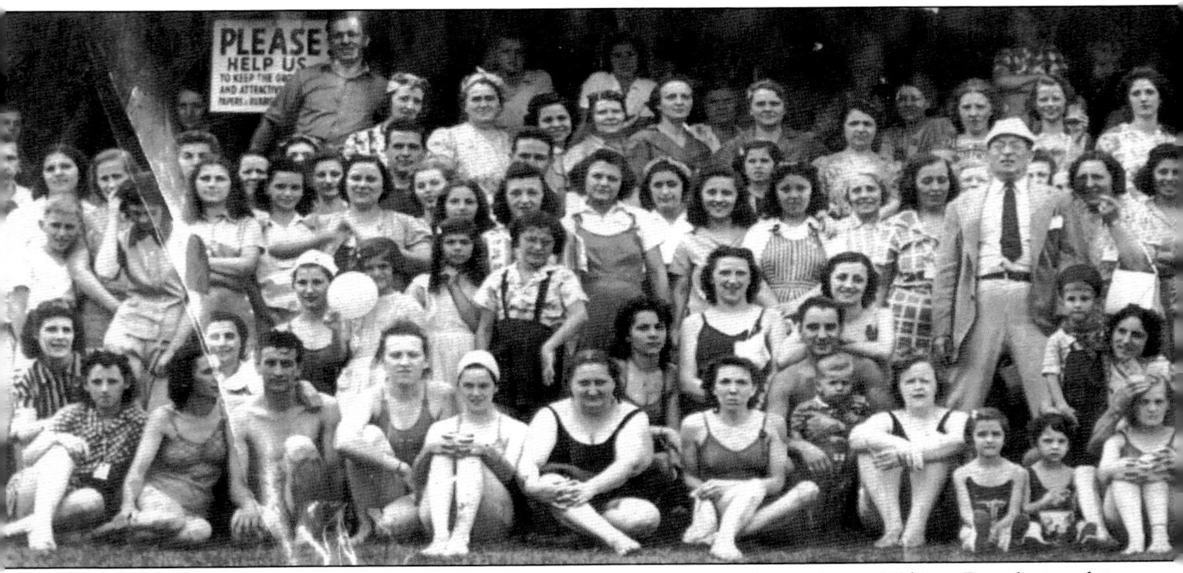

Employees of Tiny Town Togs enjoy a company-sponsored picnic at White Beach in this 1939 photograph. The company was one of the largest manufacturers of children's dresses in the country and, during its 40 years in Troy, a major employer of hundreds of neighborhood residents, many of them Italian immigrants. The city's reputation as a center of experienced garment workers may have been a major reason for the firm's relocation from New York City in

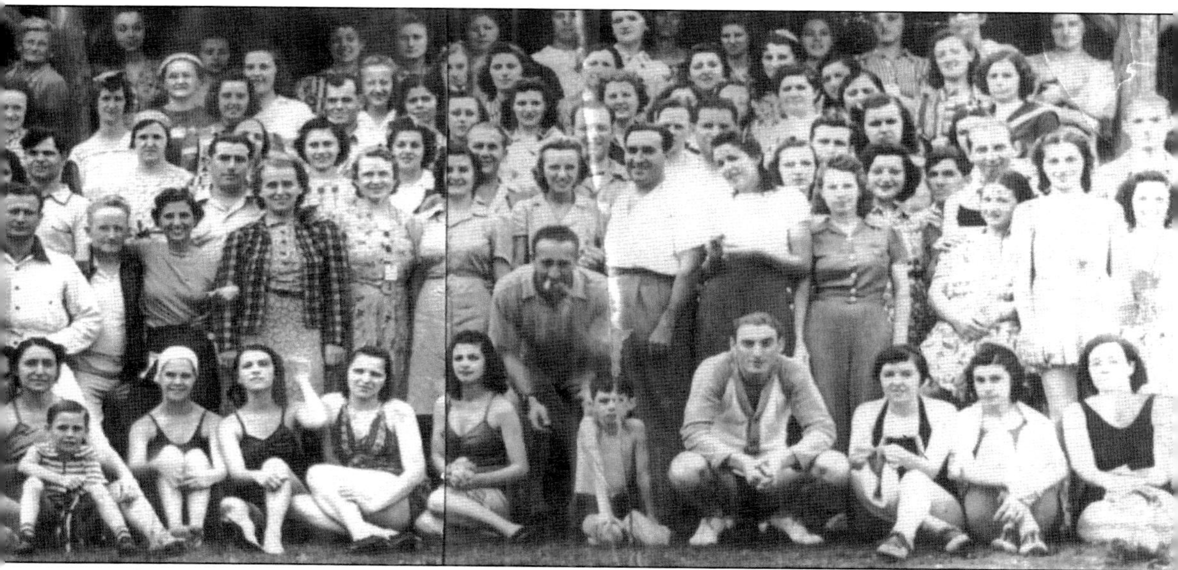

1935. The city of Troy, eager to obtain the children's dress manufacturer, agreed to pay $2,500 of the estimated $10,000 cost of moving the manufacturing equipment to the city. The relocations coming in the midst of the Great Depression must have been a significant boost for employment in Troy. (Courtesy of Frank Lamiano Jr.)

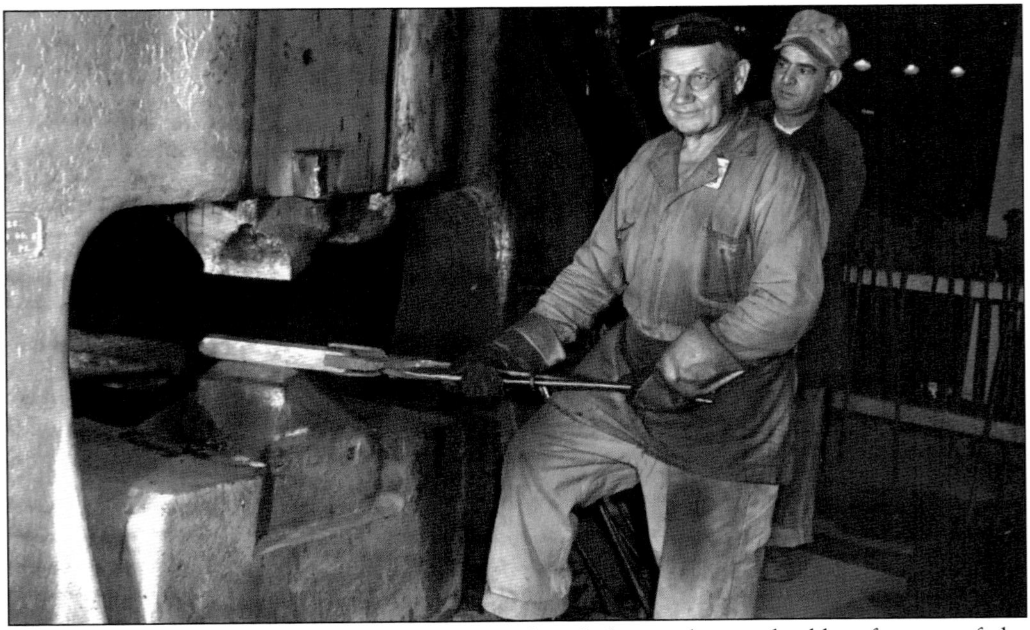

Michela (Mike) Terribile works behind an unidentified coworker at the blast furnace of the Watervliet plant of Allegheny Ludlum Steel. Each worker was issued a numbered photograph identification card with basic descriptive information, including the signature of the employee. Over the years, several major steel mills in the area, beginning with the Burden Iron Works and Republic Steel, employed many men from the neighborhood. (Author's collection.)

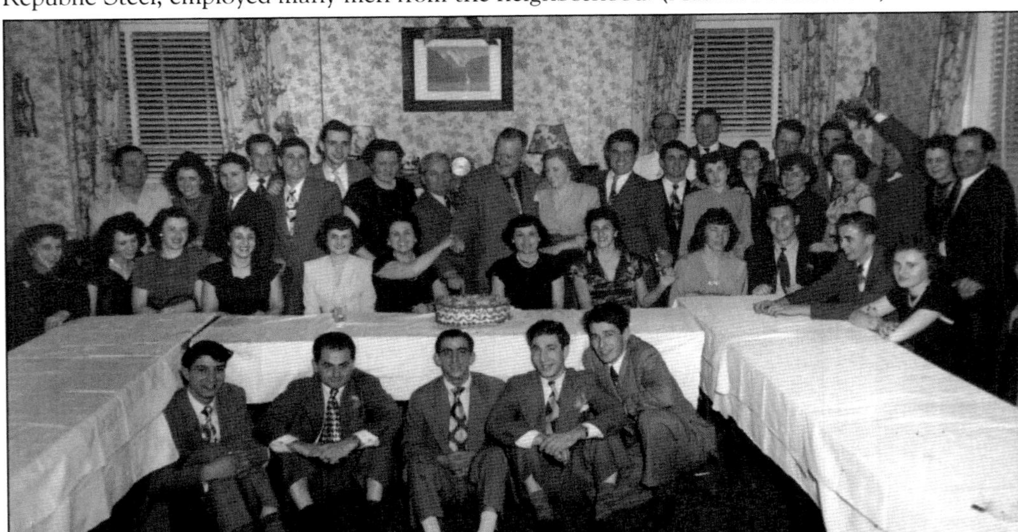

Owners and employees of Clemente Sand and Gravel gather for this holiday photograph taken in 1949. At the time, almost everyone in the photograph, including members of the Clemente and Albarelli families, as well as Nick Cavallo, Anthony "Stretch" Valente, Joe Marchese, Joe Marano, and Patrick Fucci, lived in Little Italy. The firm, established in 1915 by Salvatore and Orazio Clemente, has been involved in major construction projects in the Capital Region for more than 90 years. (Courtesy of Anthony Clemente.)

Six

The Neighborhood

Little Italy consists of half of the 40 blocks of South Central Troy, which is located directly south of the city's downtown business district, an easily identified neighborhood because three of its boundaries—the Hudson River to the west, the slopes of Mount Ida to the east, and the canal to the south—are natural geographic features. Ferry Street, its northern boundary, separates the city's commercial hub from South Central, but the proximity to downtown places many amenities within walking distance.

There are noticeable differences between the two major residential areas of the South Central neighborhood. The area from the campus of Russell Sage College east to Third Street and south to Washington Place contains Washington Park, the private ornamental park that is the geographic center of South Central, and many handsome, stately mansions built prior to 1850 by early prosperous Troy residents. Little Italy is the location of hundreds of two- and three-story 19th-century brick buildings, a mix of row houses and freestanding homes, most built to the front lot line, some still with shops and storefront businesses on the street level. The area is nestled along the western slope of Mount Ida: Fourth Street, Fifth Avenue, Hill Street, and side streets from Ferry south to the Poestenkill, the eastern half of South Central.

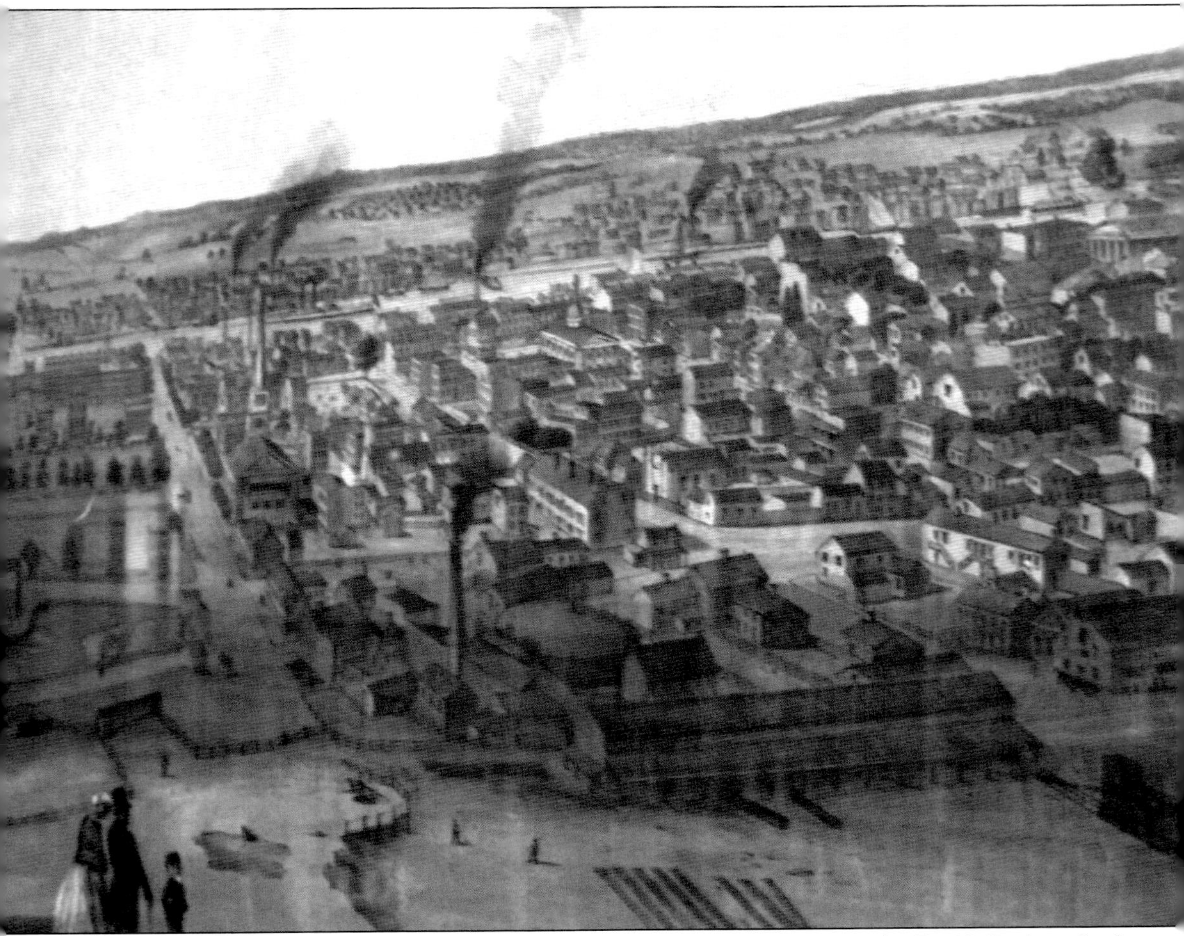

Troy is shown in an 1848 lithograph, in a westward view from Mount Ida. By 1848, there had been several disastrous landslides along its western slope. Washington Park and the row houses along Washington Place, developed between 1835 and 1842, are located on the left in a sparsely populated area. The area to the right is a fully developed business district. At the base of Mount Ida is the stoneware factory. The use of clay from Mount Ida is reported in early histories of the city. The population of Troy in 1848 was approximately 21,000. (*Troy's One Hundred Years: 1789–1889*, by Arthur James Weise.)

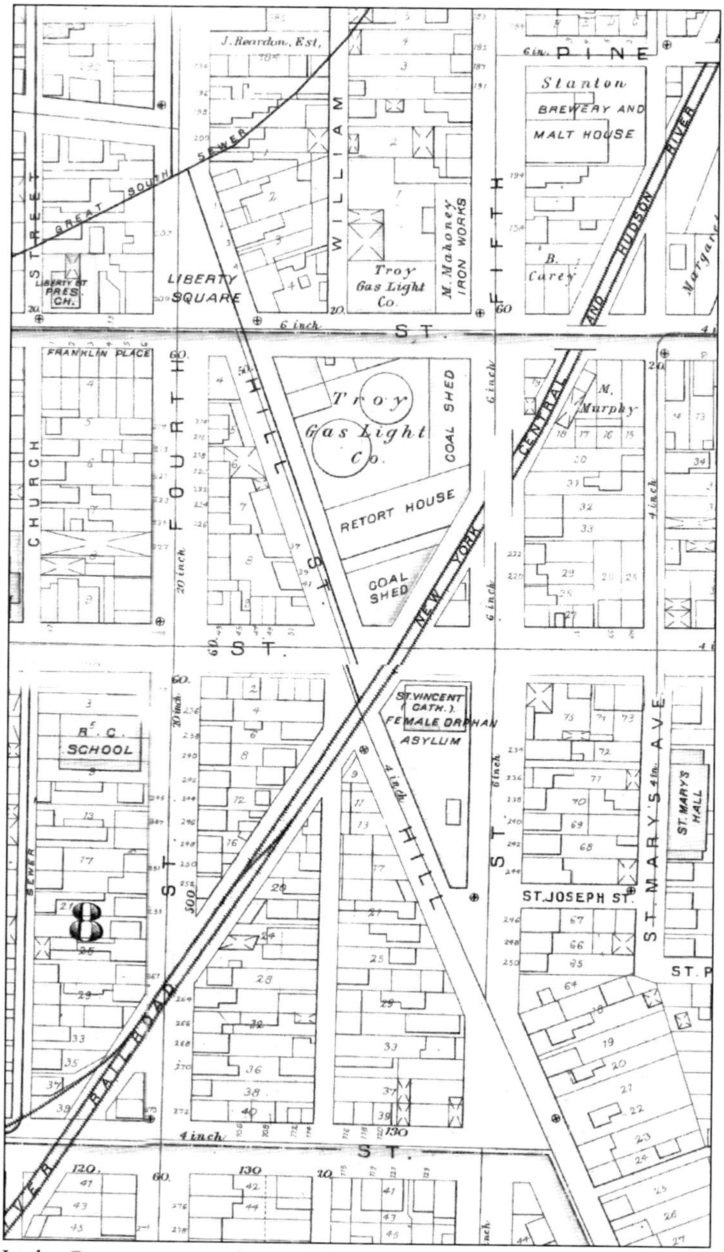

The Troy Gas Light Company complex and the surrounding neighborhood are shown from the *City Atlas of Troy*, published by G. M. Hopkins in 1881. The map shows a representation of the neighborhood now referred to as Troy's Little Italy. Most of the buildings were constructed of brick. The lots were small and narrow. Most of the neighborhood consisted of Irish immigrants. The only green space was the private two-acre ornamental Washington Park. It was not until 1902 that 80 acres of land purchased by the city from the Warren and Vail estates located on Mount Ida were converted to parkland and opened to the public. This is what the neighborhood looked like to the early Italian immigrants arriving in Troy in the 1880s. (*City Atlas of Troy*, by G. M. Hopkins.)

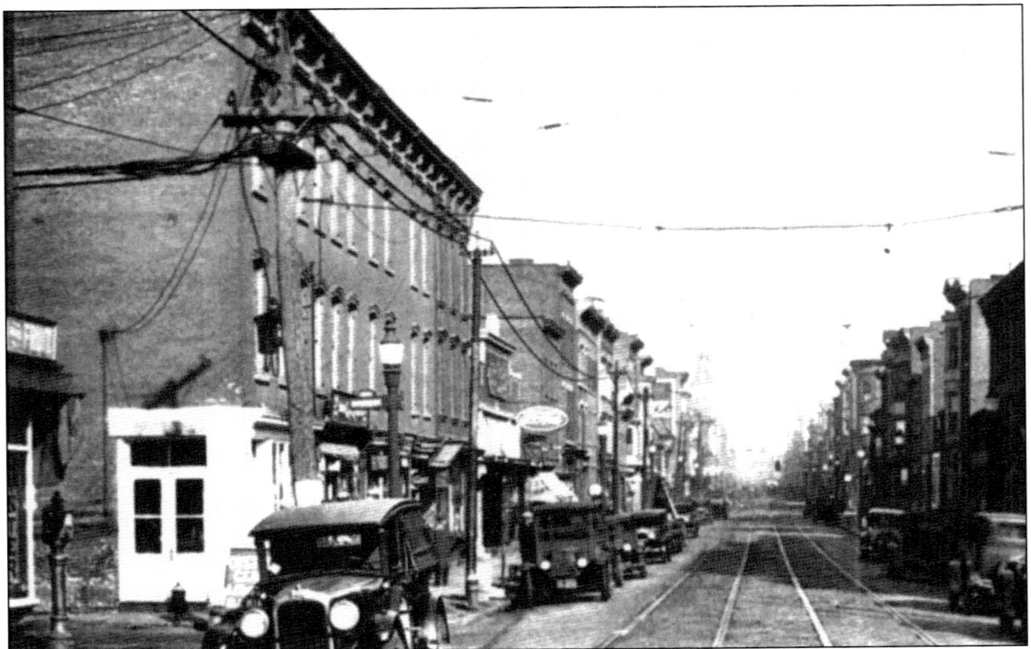

Fourth Street, Little Italy's main street, is pictured in this 1928 photograph. The block, looking north between Division and Ferry Streets, is typical of the two- and three-story 19th-century brick buildings, a mix of row houses and freestanding structures. Dozens of buildings contained shops on the first level, with apartments on the upper floors. (Courtesy of the Rensselaer County Historical Society.)

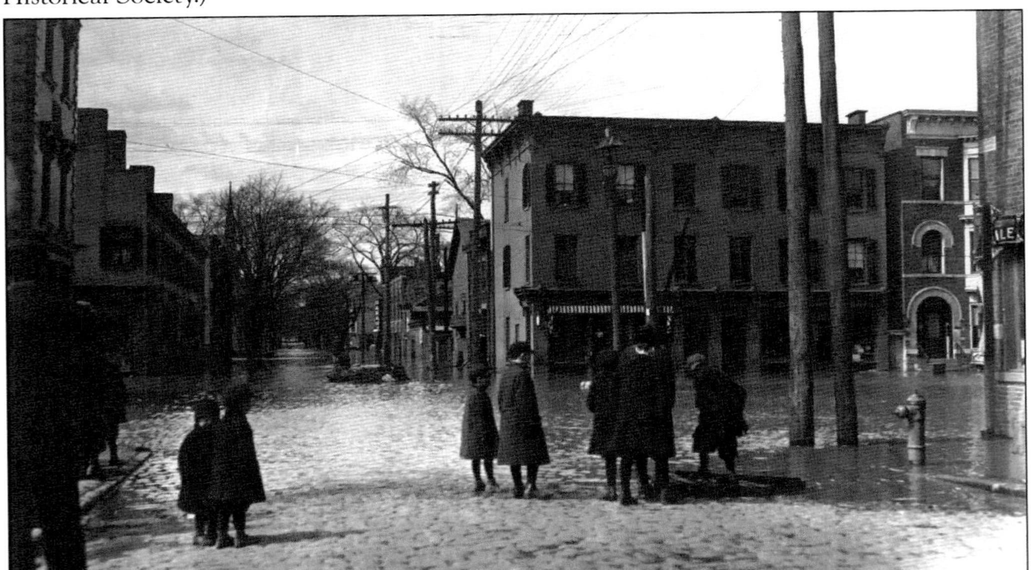

A 1936 photograph taken during one of Troy's major floods shows the intersection of Fourth, Liberty, and Hill Streets. Partially shown on the left is the three-story Liberty Square Hotel. On the right behind the two three-story buildings on Fourth Street is the historic Liberty Street Presbyterian Church, a two-story frame building. (Courtesy of Mayor Harry Tutunjian.)

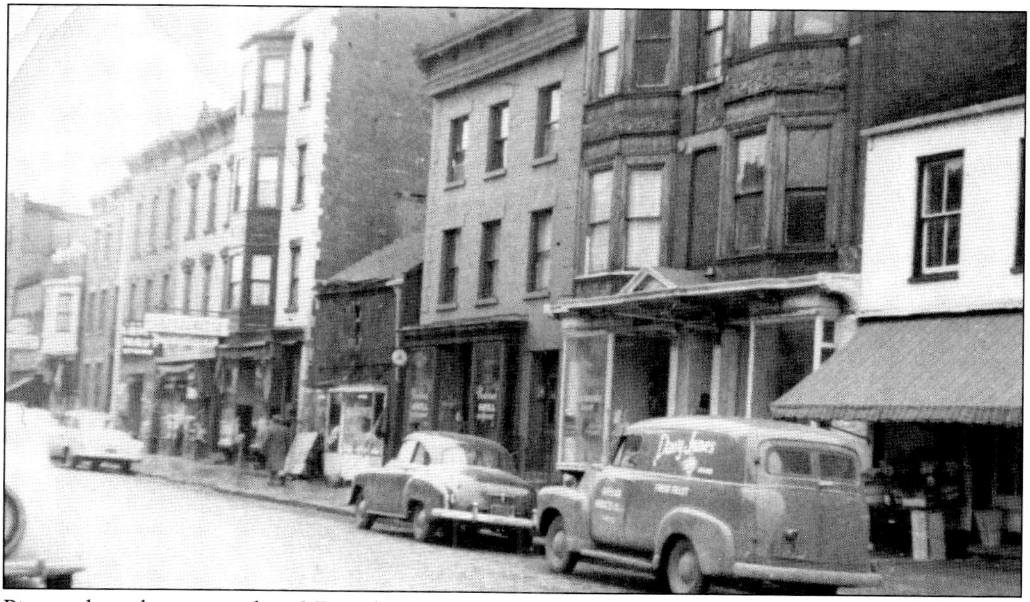

Pictured is the east side of Fourth Street between Ferry and Congress Streets. Half of the buildings shown, beginning with the small one-story frame unit in the center of the photograph, have since been demolished. At the time of the photograph, businesses on the block included a pharmacy, a fish market, a restaurant, a men's apparel store, a newsstand, a bakery, a shoe store, a beauty salon, a barbershop, and a tavern. (Courtesy of Anna Cuozzo.)

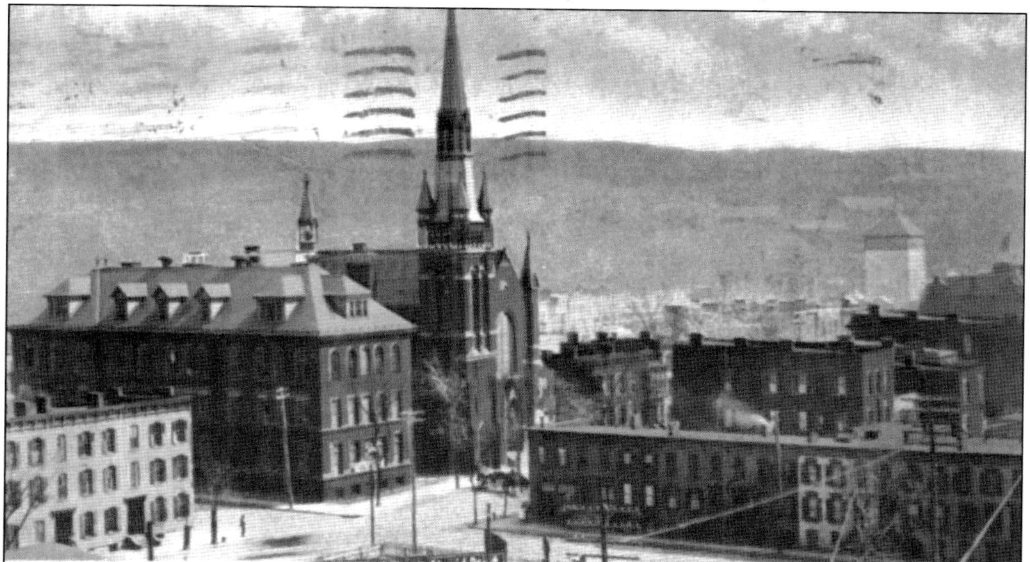

St. Lawrence Church Academy, which opened in 1890 on the northeast corner of Jefferson and Third Streets, is adjacent to St. Lawrence Church, Troy's first German congregation, formed in 1860. The brick edifice pictured was consecrated in 1884 and was directly south of a wooden church constructed in 1870. Some time after the school closed, the building was converted to apartments. Many of the neighborhood buildings remain. (Courtesy of the Joe Connors postcard collection.)

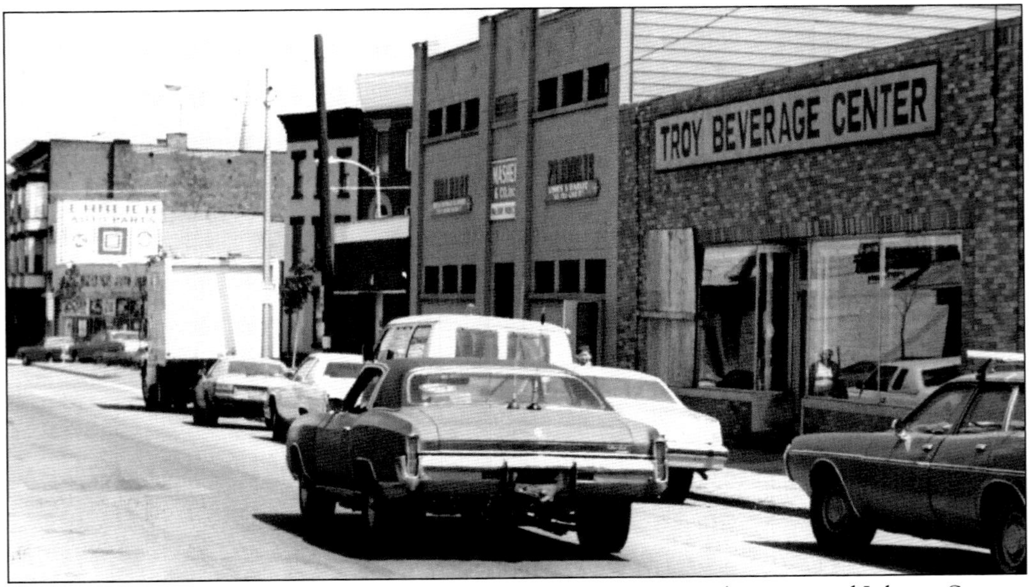

Shown on this page are two pictures of Fourth Street between Washington and Liberty Streets. Pictured looking north from Masher and Company, located at numbers 214–216 for more than 35 years, is the Troy Beverage Center at numbers 218–226, and, for more than 50 years, Ehrlich Supply Company Auto Parts at number 200. The Vanilla Bean Bakery was located in the buildings from 214 to 226 Fourth Street for almost 20 years, until August 2007. (Courtesy of the City of Troy.)

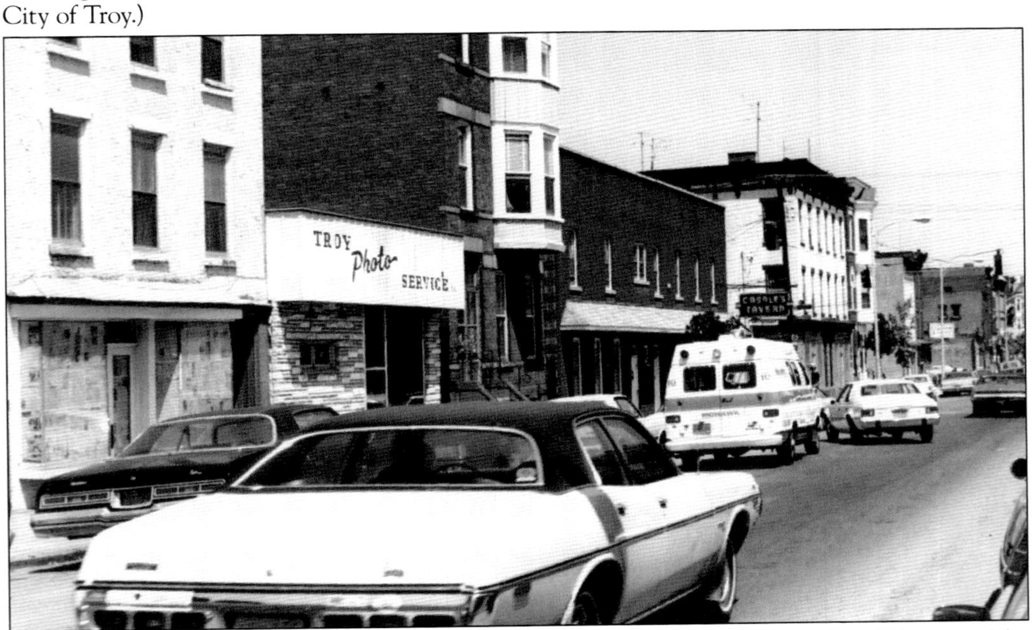

Businesses along the west side of Fourth Street, included groceries at number 221, owned by the Rubino and later the Testo families, a dry-cleaning establishment, Paul's Barber Shop, and eventually Margie's Tavern. Troy Photo Service was located at number 219 for more than 25 years. Casale's Tavern, on the corner of Fourth and Liberty Streets, was in business for more than 30 years. (Courtesy of the City of Troy.)

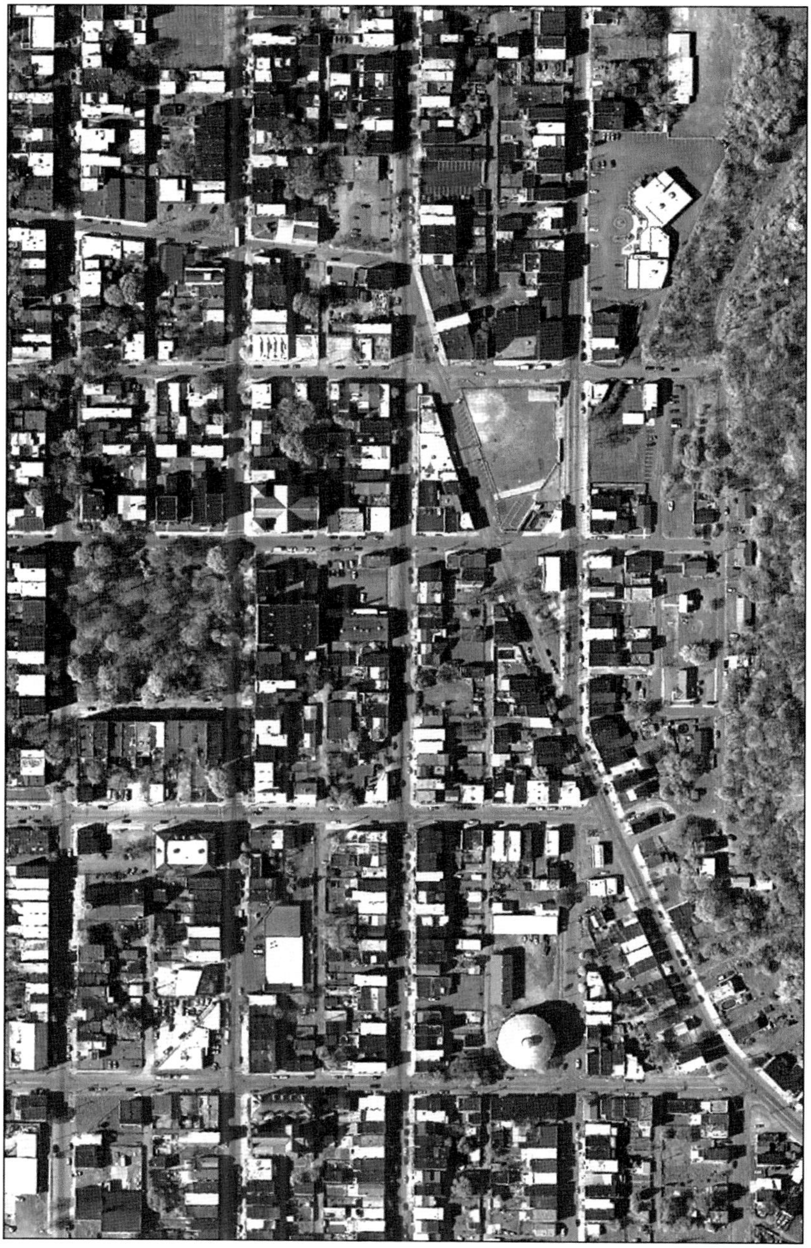

Pictured is a recent aerial view of a portion of South Central Troy, a neighborhood that consists of 40 city blocks, located south of the central business district from Ferry Street to the Poestenkill and from the Hudson River to Prospect Park. The geographic center of the neighborhood is the beautiful privately owned two-acre Washington Park. The area is home to several active neighborhood groups—Think First (for First Street), Historic Second Street, the Washington Park area, and the Pottery District. Little Italy is the section stretching along the slope of Prospect Park from Ferry Street to the Poestenkill. Prospect Park, located on Mount Ida, is a backdrop for the crowded neighborhood and provides a pleasant view that each of the seasons brings to its landscape. (Courtesy of the New York State Geographic Information Systems.)

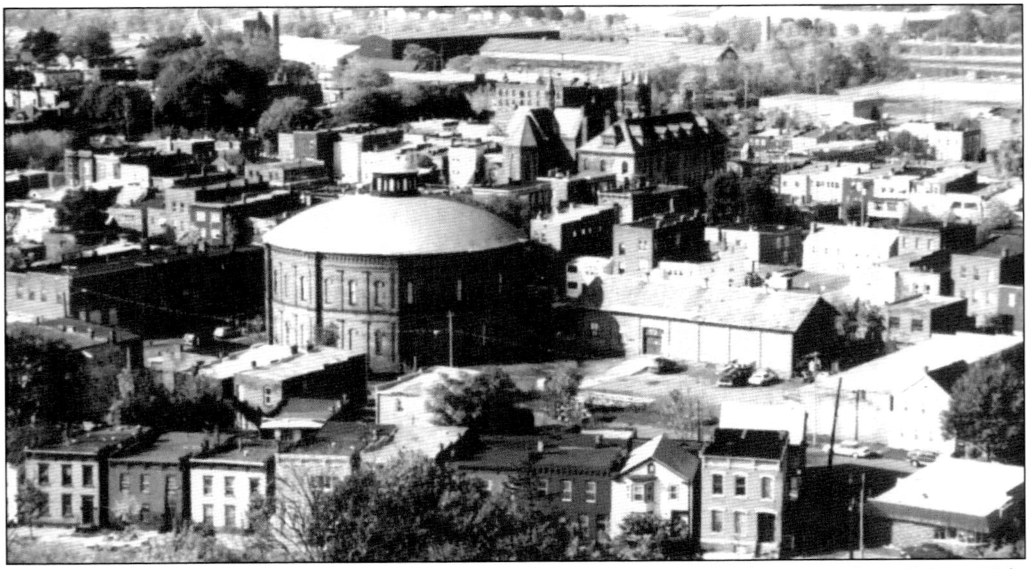

Photographer Joe Connors captures a part of the neighborhood with a view from Mount Ida overlooking a section of Little Italy. Troy's historic Gasholder House is surrounded by the neighborhood's modest two-story brick buildings. The Gasholder House, added to the National Register of Historic Places in 1971, is owned and carefully tended by Sage Brothers Paint Company. (Courtesy of the Joe Connors postcard collection.)

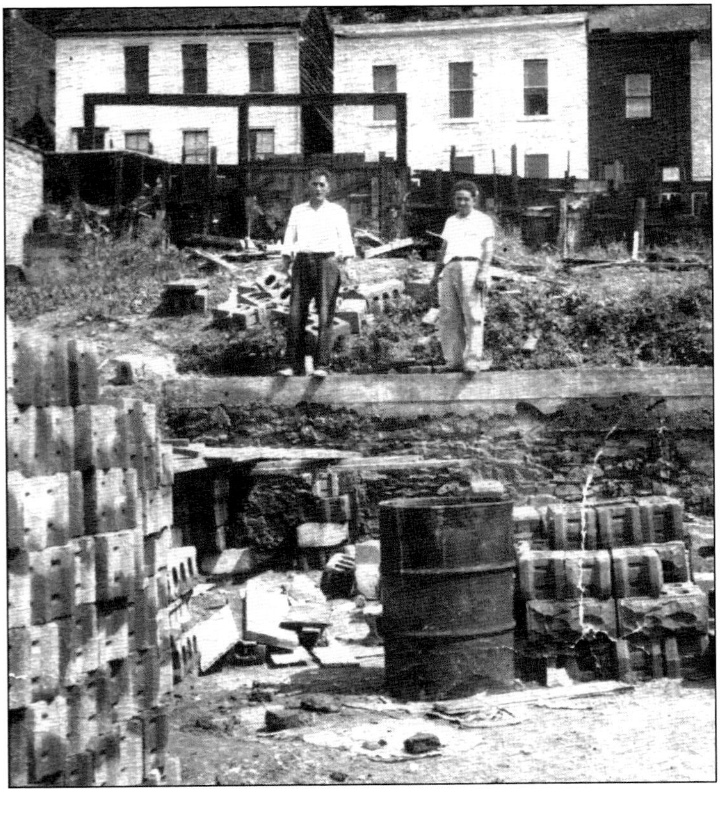

Giuseppe Esposito is seen with his son Michael Esposito Sr. on the site of a garage construction at Michael's newly purchased St. Mary's Avenue property. The site, the original location in 1859 of St. Mary's Hall built by Rev. Peter Havermans for St. Mary's School, was purchased in 1945 from James Foley. The property, along with the row houses in the background of the photograph, was among many that would be demolished in 1970 for an arterial that was never built. (Author's collection.)

Seven

The People of Little Italy

Little Italy was a stereotypical blue-collar neighborhood—stable, peaceful, and clean. Almost all homes were owner occupied. While backyards were relatively small, many homeowners found room for a fruit tree or a grape arbor and a vegetable garden. Most women who worked outside the home were employed in Troy's garment industry at such shops as Tiny Town Togs and Cluett, Peabody and Company. Men worked as laborers in the steel mills, or at the Ford Motor Company, or the Watervliet Arsenal. Others were tradesmen—tailors, shoe repairmen, or masons. Children played along the slopes of Mount Ida's Prospect Park, in the public market on Hill Street, and on the streets of the closely knit neighborhood. The most dramatic change in the neighborhood occurred in the late 1960s. Residents organized to fight against the plans for a superhighway through the neighborhood. The government's use of eminent domain won out. Hundreds of people were forced to move. More than 100 homes were demolished. In a short period of time, a treasured part of Little Italy was lost, but the memories remain. People continue to gather at reunions and community events held in the neighborhood: the conversation about the old neighborhood continues even as plans for future projects and events develop. It is a neighborhood that is proud of its past and has faith in its future.

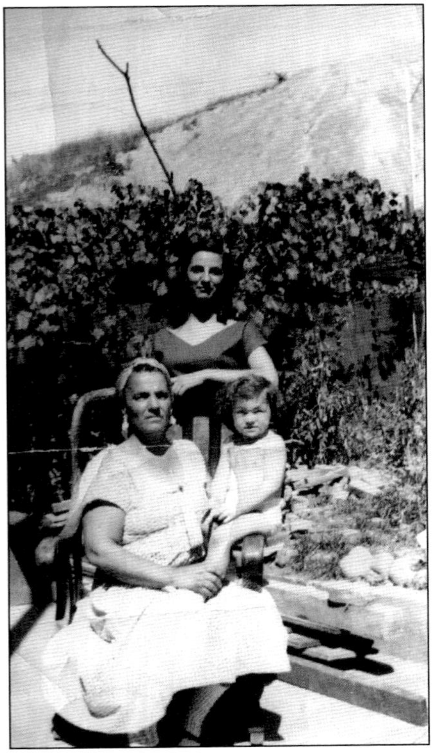

From left to right, Pasqulina "Beatrice" Del Giacco, Marietta DePaoli, and Antoinette Del Giacco relax in their backyard at 75 Havermans Avenue. Residential lots on the street were barely large enough for walkways—referred to as gangways—separating buildings. The privileged few were property owners on the east side of the street along the western slope of Mount Ida's Prospect Park. Many of these residents extended their gardens by terracing part of the park slope for vegetable gardens and trees. (Courtesy of Marietta DePaoli.)

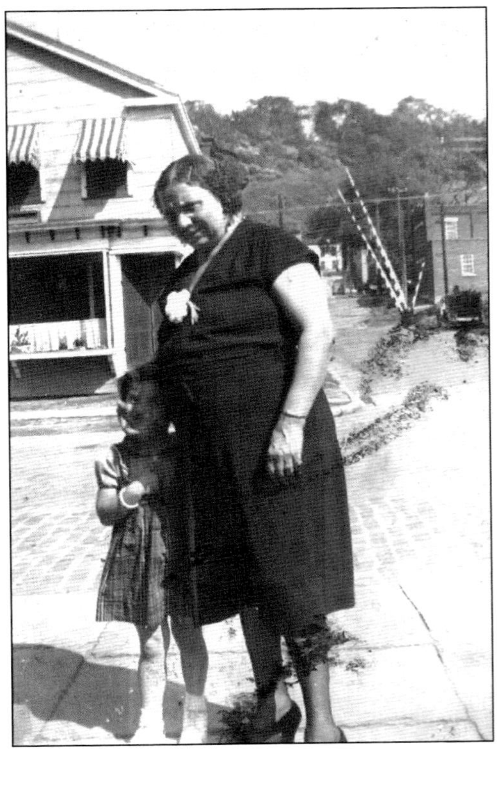

Mary DeMaria and her granddaughter Marion Church stand on the corner of Fourth and Washington Streets, Little Italy's busiest intersection was a place one could expect to see neighbors. Within a block, there were clusters of small convenience stores catering to many of the daily needs of residents. Most blocks contained a grocery, a newsstand, a tavern, a barbershop, a bakery, and a luncheonette. (Courtesy of Marion Church Field.)

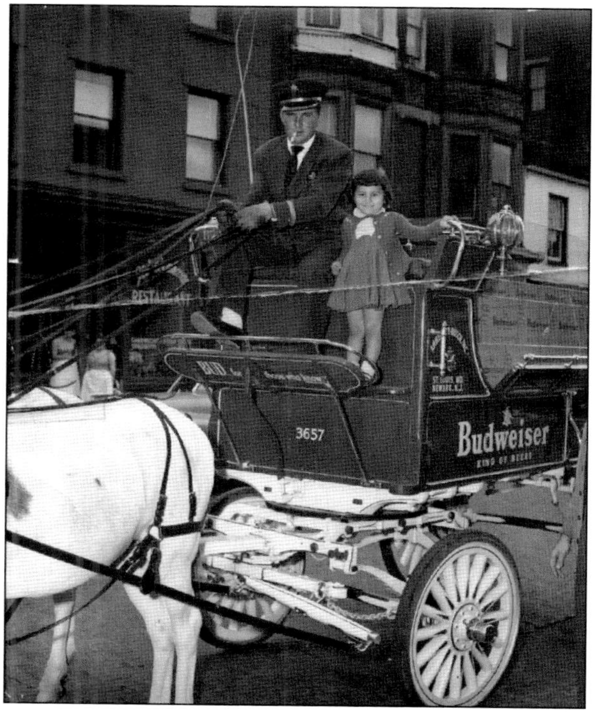

Four-year-old Jeannette DeBonis is riding in style on a promotional Budweiser wagon (without the Clydesdales), stopping temporarily at the 147 Fourth Street business owned by her father, James, in this 1952 photograph. The Woodchuck Grill, one of several neighborhood taverns "where everybody knows your name," was a popular local watering hole. The tavern was located across the street from the State Theatre, just below Congress Street. (Courtesy of the DeBonis family.)

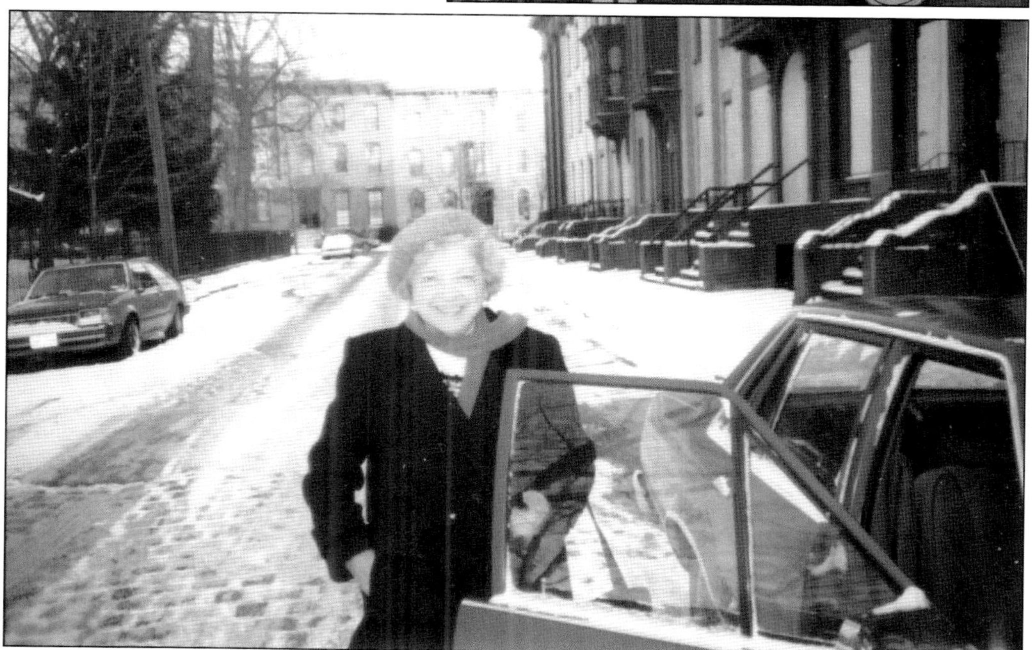

Celia DeMaria Church, longtime Little Italy resident and neighborhood volunteer, stands on Washington Place between the private ornamental park and the historic row of brownstones built in the 1840s. If there was a project to benefit the community, it was certain that Celia was an active member of the organizing group. Activities at St. Mary's parish and the ICC were especially high on her list of priorities. (Courtesy of Marion Church Field.)

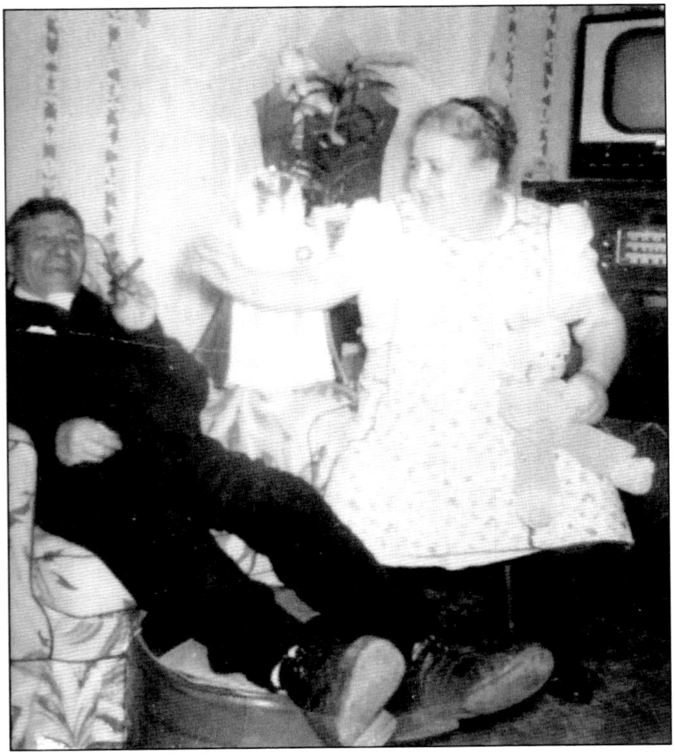

Vito and Erminia Furciniti, two beloved residents of the neighborhood, lived in a small framed cottage at the corner of St. Mary's Avenue and St. Joseph Street. Both were from the village of Candela in Apulia. They were the parents of eight children, including a son, Pvt. Gerald Furciniti, who was killed in action in World War II on November 6, 1944. (Courtesy of the Furciniti family.)

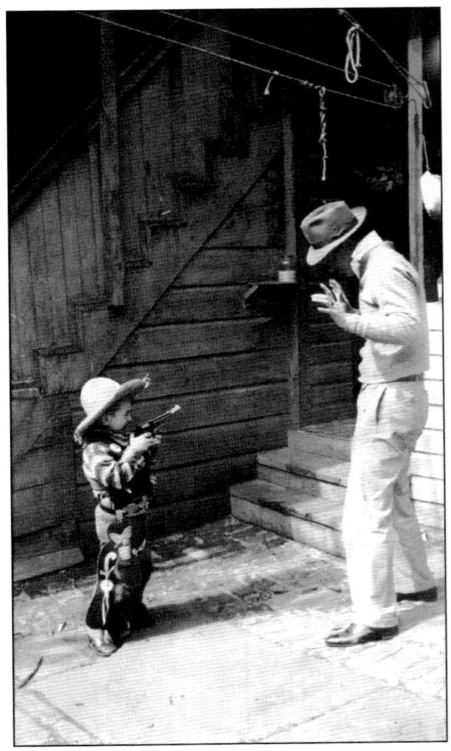

The movies had a lot to do with the Americanization of second- and third-generation Italian Americans. Toy guns and Western clothing helped reenactments such as this one, performed by the father-and-son team of Frank Visk Sr. and Jr. in their Liberty Street backyard in 1945. Ironically, in many of the "cowboy and Indian" pictures, the Native Americans were often portrayed by Italian American actors. (Courtesy of Frank LaPosta Visco.)

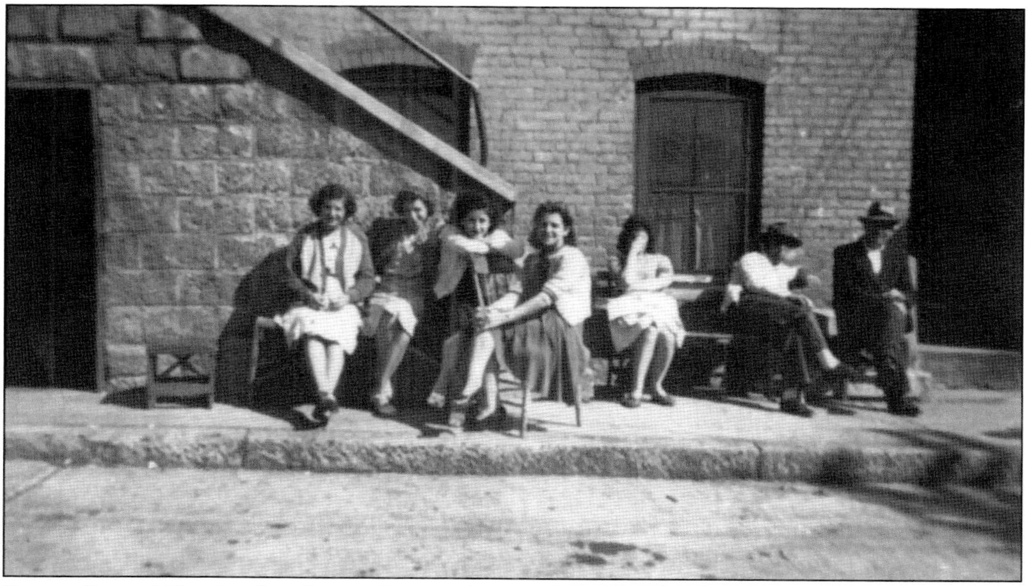

Consuello and Derrico family members gather to chat. Wooden benches were a common sight in front of homes in the neighborhood. Front stoops also provided seating for residents who would often gather to engage in friendly conversation. Italians enjoyed being out of doors, no doubt a reminder of sunny Italy. Backyards were generally small and usually devoted to vegetable gardens. Children played freely in the streets under the watchful eyes of residents. (Author's collection.)

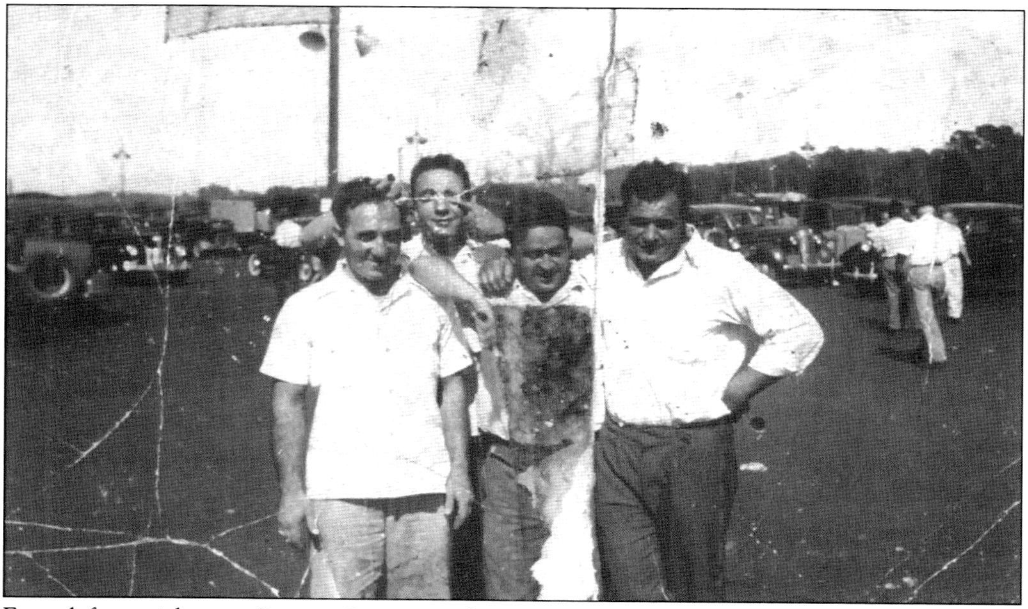

From left to right are Cosmo Pusatere, of Pusatere Brothers Fruits and Vegetables; Michael Laiacona, known locally as "the celery king"; Michael Esposito, fruit-and-vegetable peddler; and Jerry Pitaniello, who sold bushels, bags, and other containers, taking a break from their work routines in the Menands Regional Market. The central market was established in 1933 and is still an active wholesale market. (Courtesy of May Teta Pitaniello.)

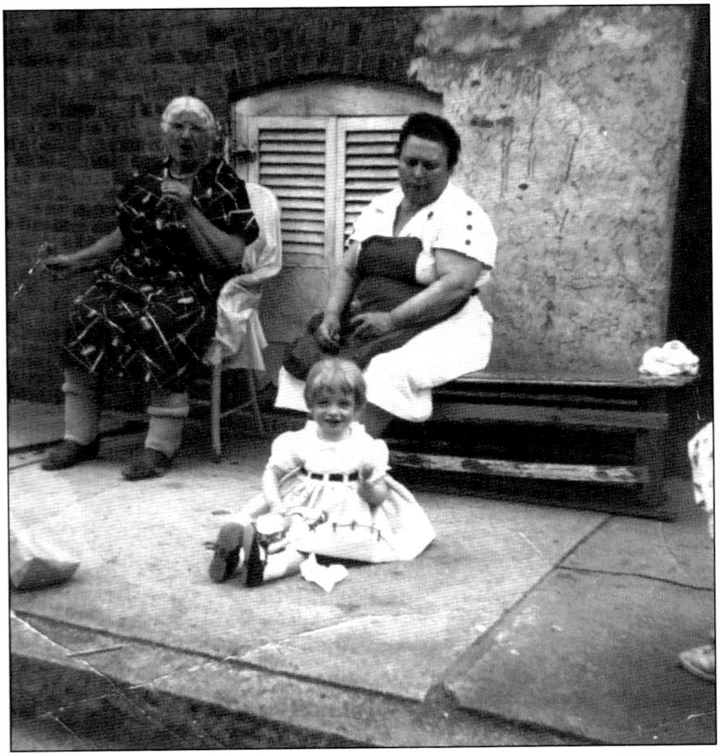

Neighbors Marguerite Donato and Josephine Pascarella chat and watch over three-year-old Phyllis Walsh (Donato's great-granddaughter). In her later years, Donato, affectionately regarded by many as "the first neighborhood watch," would sit for hours observing life in the neighborhood from the second-floor bay window of her residence at 45 Havermans Avenue, one of only three original buildings remaining on the street following major demolition in 1970. (Courtesy of Louise Donato Finelli.)

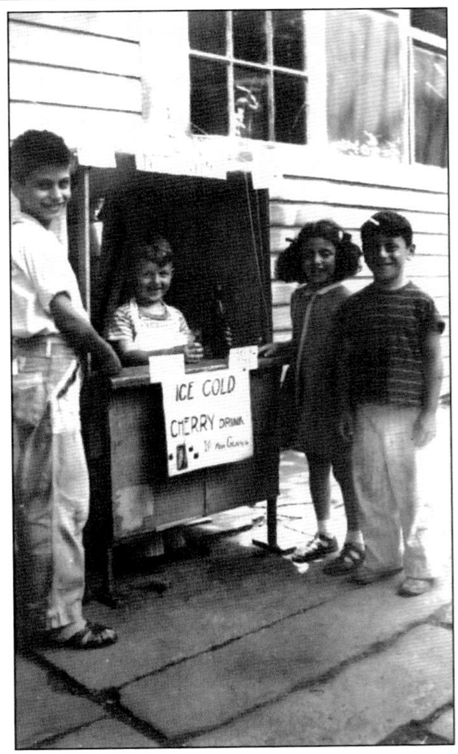

In the early 1940s, everyone participated in the war effort. On Tory Hill, children would put on backyard talent shows, conduct scrap drives, and find other ways to raise money for the USO. Standing to the left of the refreshment stand is Mickey Visk, whose father, Vincenzo "Jimmy," built the stand. Mary Ann Tornincasa and Louis Marchese are the first customers to plunk down a penny to proprietor Frank Visk Jr. (Courtesy of Mary Ann Tornincasa Grogan.)

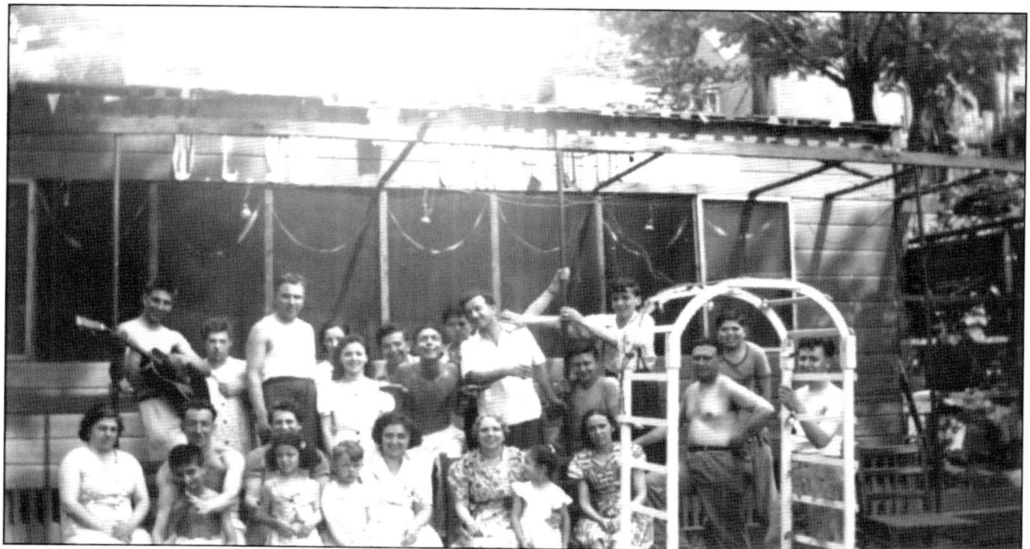

The second generation of the Visk (Visco) family in America numbered eight—four sons and four daughters. Their offspring were counted by tens. Weekend communal meals in their Liberty Street backyard were such an important ritual that the handyman of the clan, Vincenzo "Jimmy" constructed a foul-weather "banquet hall." He was not too pleased when the finished project was named for what it resembled: "the Barracks." (Courtesy of the Visk family.)

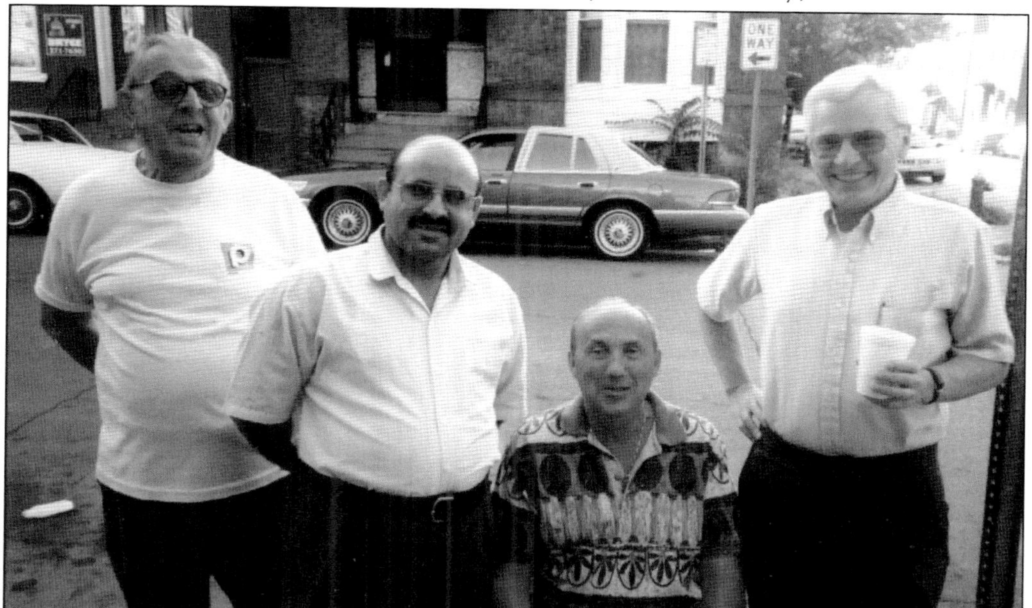

The Corner Coffee Club consisted of men of the neighborhood who met for early-morning coffee at the Santandra and Merola convenience store at Fourth and Adams Streets. The club continued after the store changed owners. Pictured are, from left to right, Frank Piscitella, who worked part time at the store; Mohamed Algahtiy, present store owner; Tony Carnevale, a local barber and part-time sexton at St. Mary's Church; and Rev. Harry Donaghy, pastor of St. Mary's Church. (Courtesy of Tony Carnevale.)

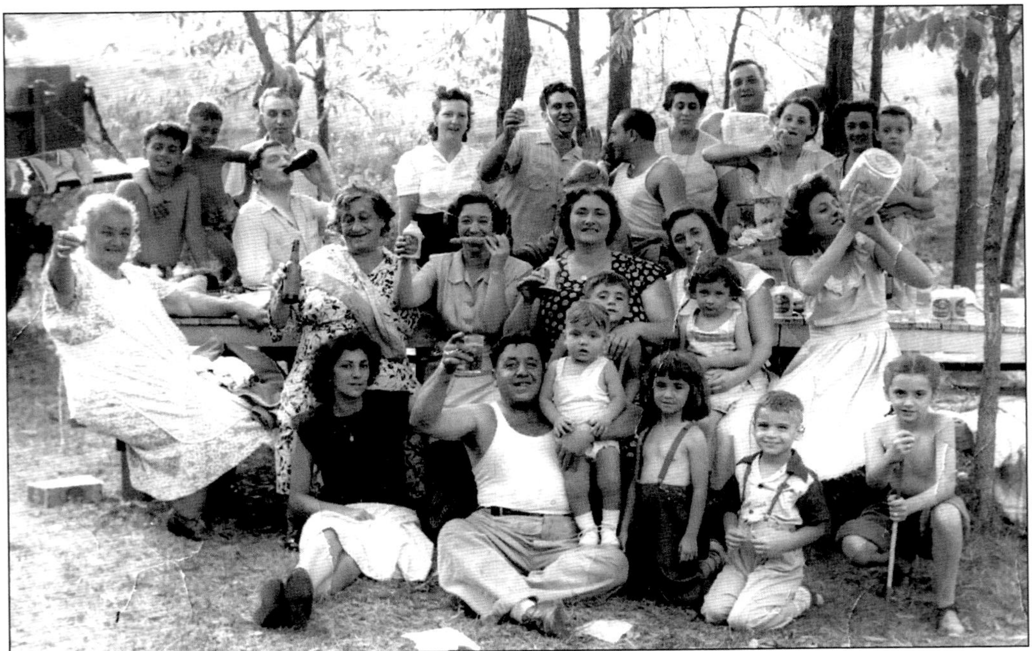

Several generations of the Pasinella, Merola, and Abrunza families of Fourth Street—from great-grandchildren to great-grandmother, with uncles, aunts, and cousins in between—enjoy a picnic. Picnics for Italians were not just sandwiches and salads. Often pots and pans were taken along for pasta and sauce, and sausage and meatballs. Lake Lorraine, Snyders Lake, Glass Lake, and Crystal Lake were favorite picnic areas. (Courtesy of the Pasinella family.)

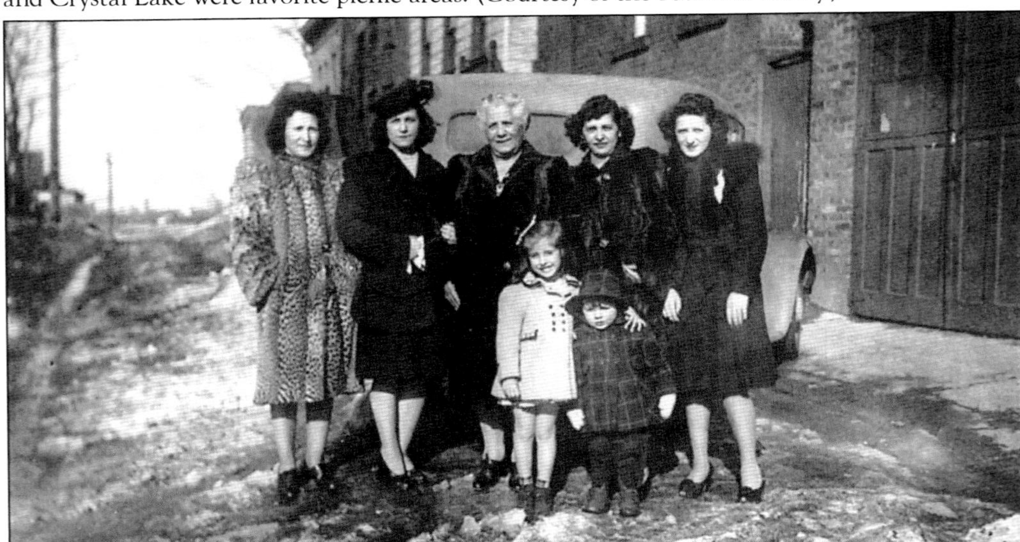

Children Joan Luckowitz and cousin Patrick Derrico visit their maternal grandmother, Maria Derrico, from left to right, with aunts Antoinette Chesney, Julia Wilkowicki, Susan Rinaldi, and Minnie Krill in front of their grandmother's home at 21 Havermans Avenue. The avenue was named for Rev. Peter Havermans, who made significant contributions to the city and to the neighborhood. (Courtesy of Joan Luckowitz O'Konski.)

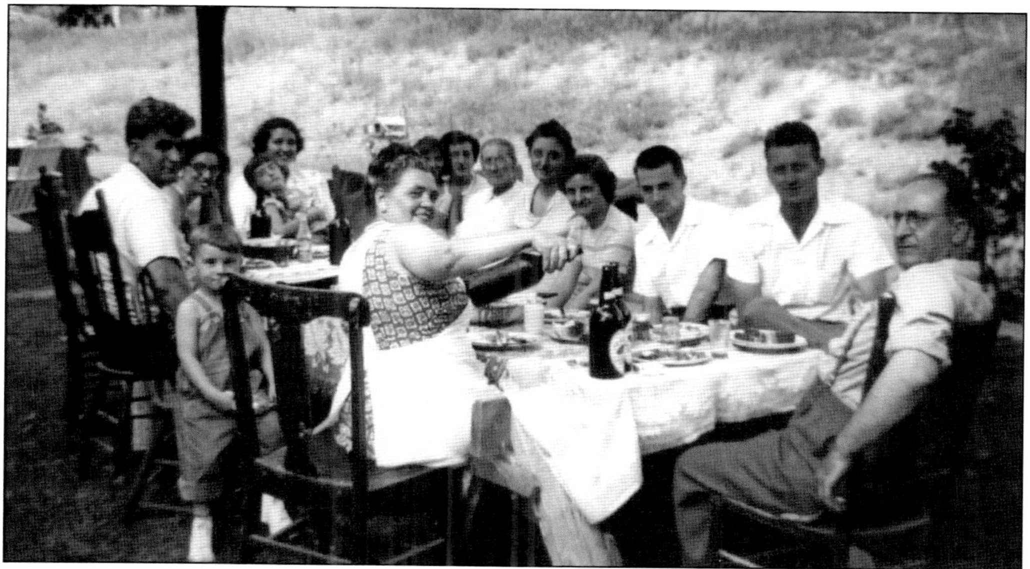

Jennie DeRubertis pours the wine as family and friends gather at the Colarusso farm in rural Tomhannock, Rensselaer County, not far from the huge city-owned reservoir. To her left are, from left to right, Tommy O'Brien, Philip Colarusso, Theresa Gentile, young Judy Gerger napping on the lap of Mary Genevive, Lita DeRubertis, Millie O'Brien, Carmina Gentile, Mary Gerger, Peg and Dan O'Conner, Joseph O'Brien, and John DeRubertis. (Courtesy of Judy Gerger Brearton.)

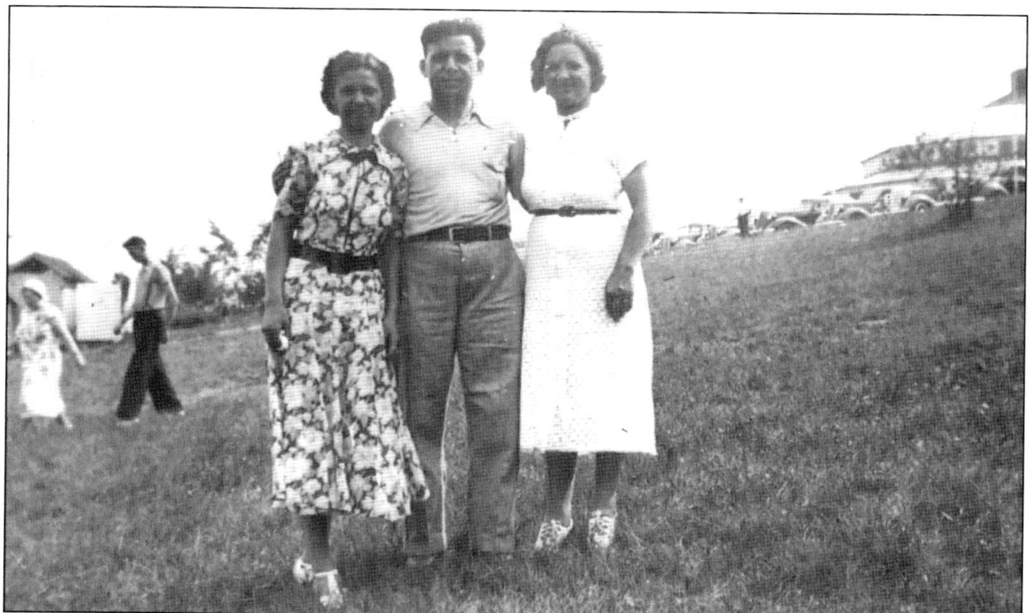

From left to right, Antoinette, Michael, and Carmella Terribile are photographed at the National Shrine of the North American Martyrs in Auriesville, New York. Catholics from various ethnic groups would attend an annual pilgrimage, complete with morning mass at the circular outdoor church (seen in the background) built in 1930. Later in the day, they would join in the Stations of the Cross and gather with friends for a picnic. (Author's collection.)

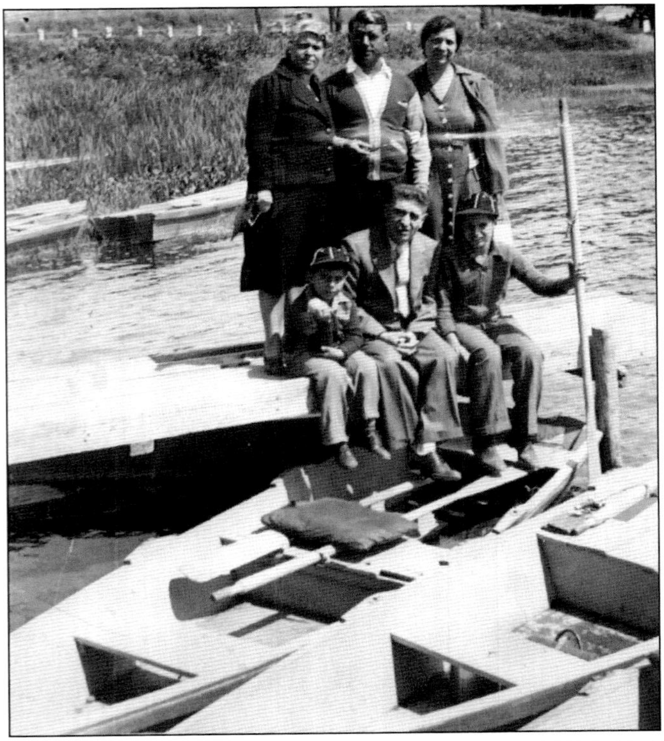

This 1938 photograph was taken at Cossayuna Lake in Rensselaer County, a popular summer retreat for city folk. From left to right are (sitting on the lakeside dock) Nicholas Cristiano, Michael Cuozzo Sr., and Gene Cuozzo; (standing) Josephine Cuozzo and Nicholas and Catherine Cristiano. Michael owned Cuozzo's Grocery at the corner of Third and Division Streets; the Cristiano family owned Christie's Grocery Store. (Courtesy of Nicholas Cristiano.)

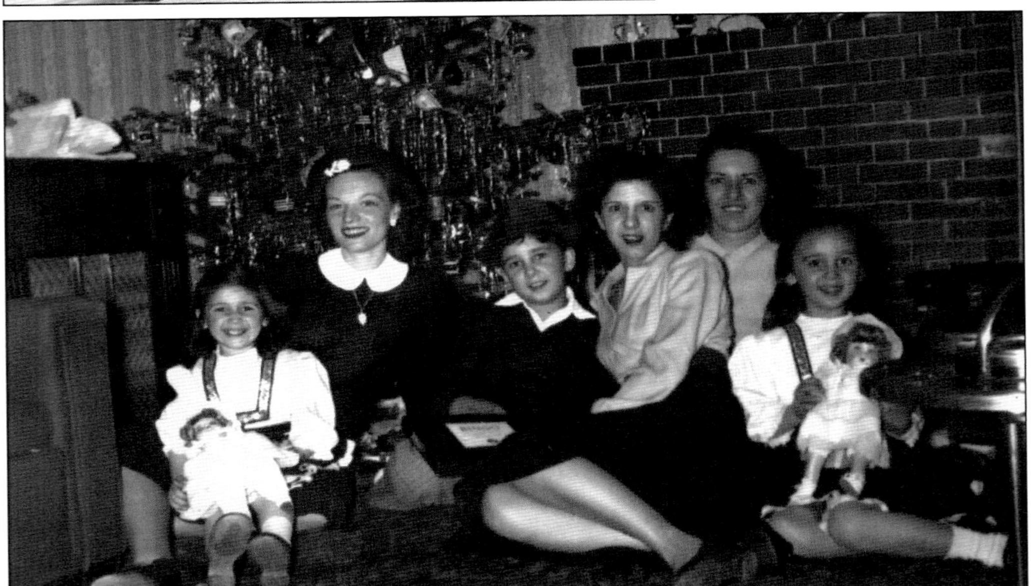

Christmas Day 1950, at 30 Havermans Avenue, is remembered as the first Christmas without their dad for the Esposito children. Michael Sr., known as "Espo," a produce peddler, died at the age of 35 earlier in the year. His wife, Antoinette, returned to work in the garment industry after his death to support her young family. Pictured in the photograph are, from left to right, Carmella Esposito, Donna Cavallo, Michael Esposito, Toni Terribile, Dorothy Terribile, and Nancy Esposito. (Author's collection.)

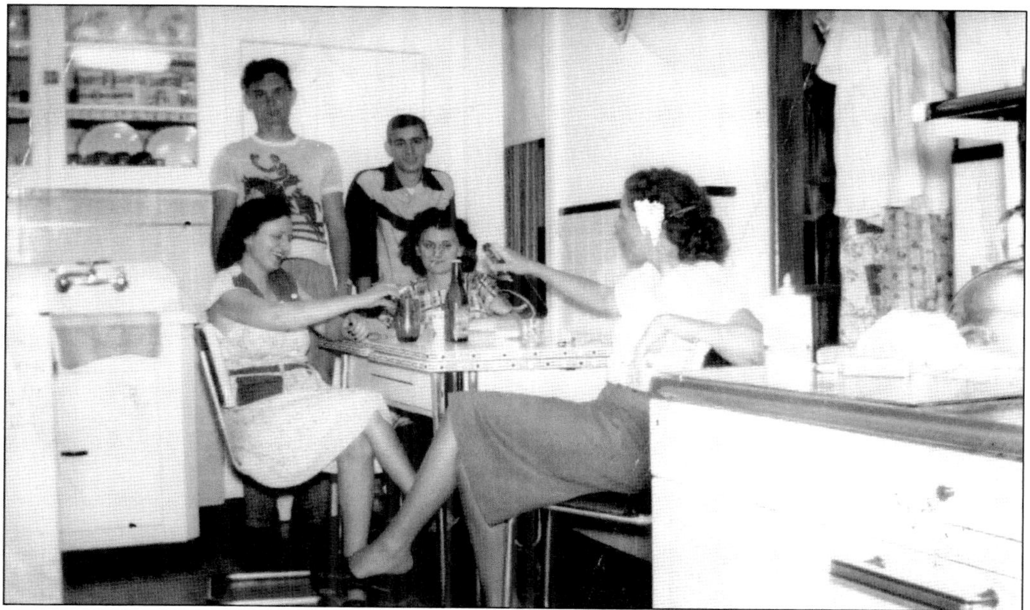

From left to right, the Teta sisters—Lucy Saracino, Mary Pitaniello, and Grace Gazelone—gather for morning coffee in Lucy's kitchen, with Grace's son Gabe and nephew Rocco Teta looking on. Lucy and her husband, Michael, owned the two-story brick residence and rented an apartment to Grace and her husband, Michael. Mary and her husband, Jerry, lived a block away. (Courtesy of Mary Teta Pitaniello.)

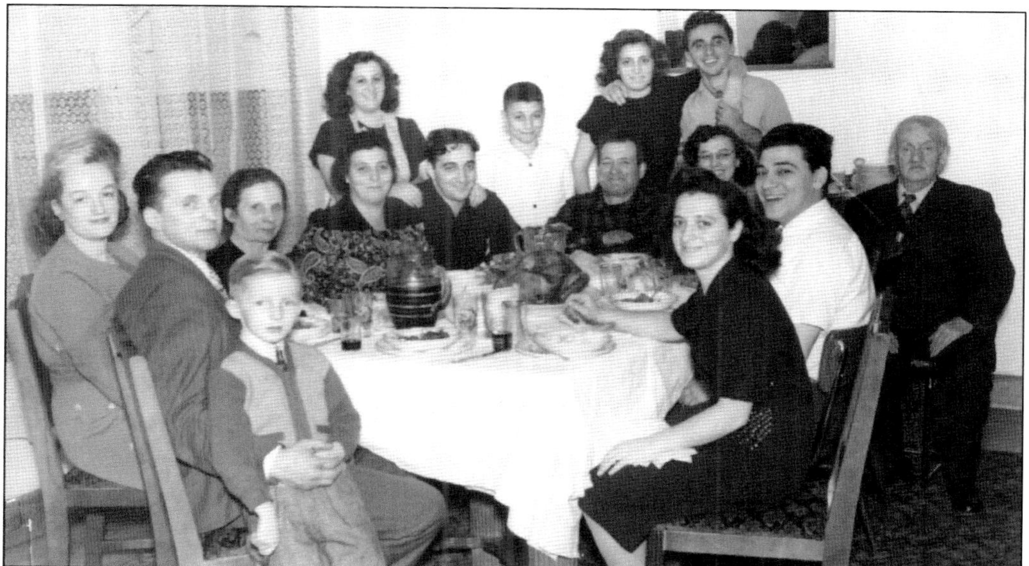

Thanksgiving Day dinner in 1947 is shared with family and friends at the home of Edith and Alex Novack. Clockwise from bottom left are (seated) Ronnie Crowley, John and Mary Krupa, Parosha Novack, Erminia Riggione, Ernest Marro, Luigi and Nicolina "Lee" Riggione, Christopher Emperor, and Charles and Mary Renna; (standing) Philomena Marro, Jerry Riggione, and Edith and Alex Novack. At the time, Alex Novack owned and operated the Tavern, a popular gathering place on Broadway in Troy. (Courtesy of Edith Riggione Novack.)

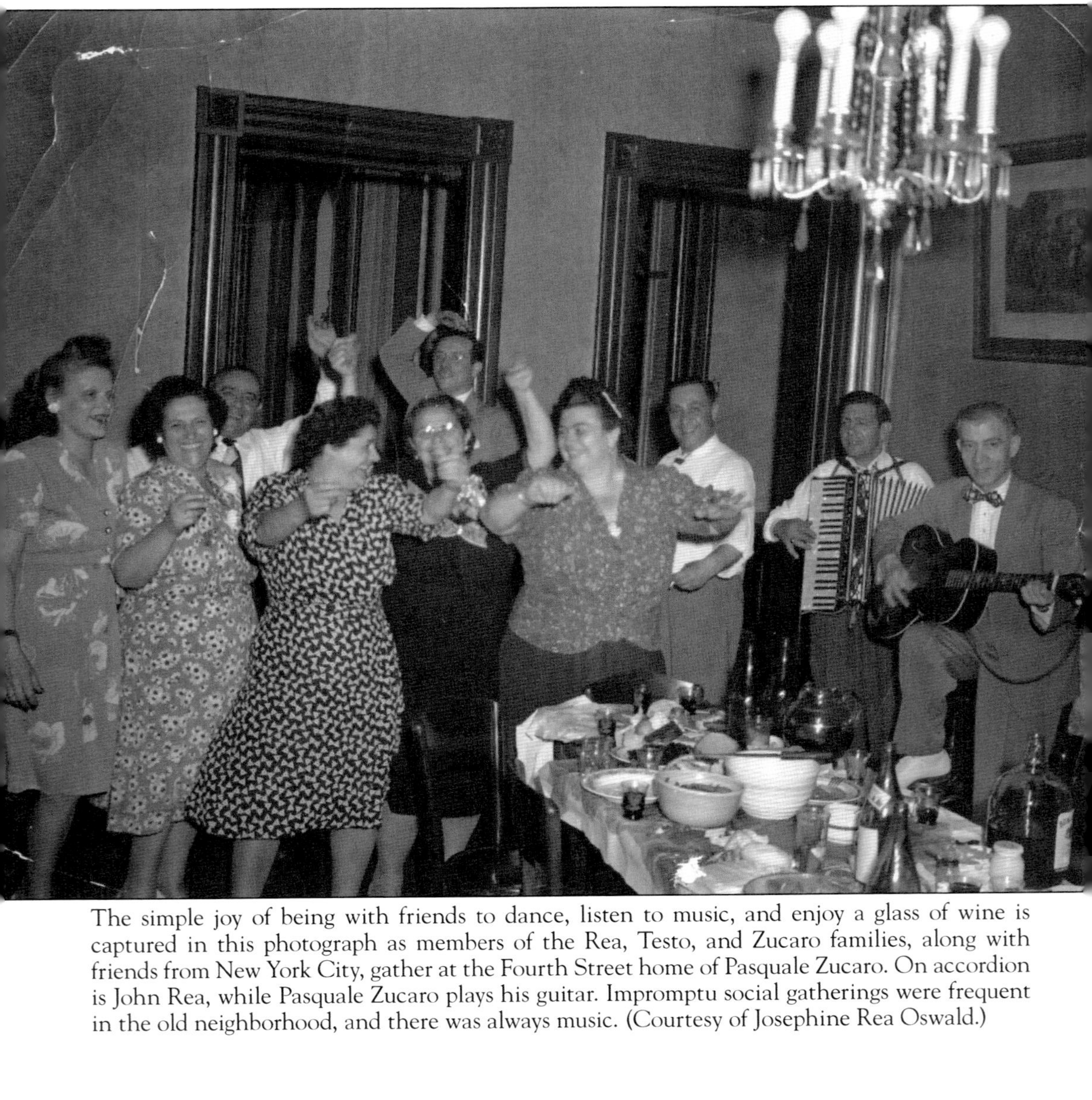

The simple joy of being with friends to dance, listen to music, and enjoy a glass of wine is captured in this photograph as members of the Rea, Testo, and Zucaro families, along with friends from New York City, gather at the Fourth Street home of Pasquale Zucaro. On accordion is John Rea, while Pasquale Zucaro plays his guitar. Impromptu social gatherings were frequent in the old neighborhood, and there was always music. (Courtesy of Josephine Rea Oswald.)

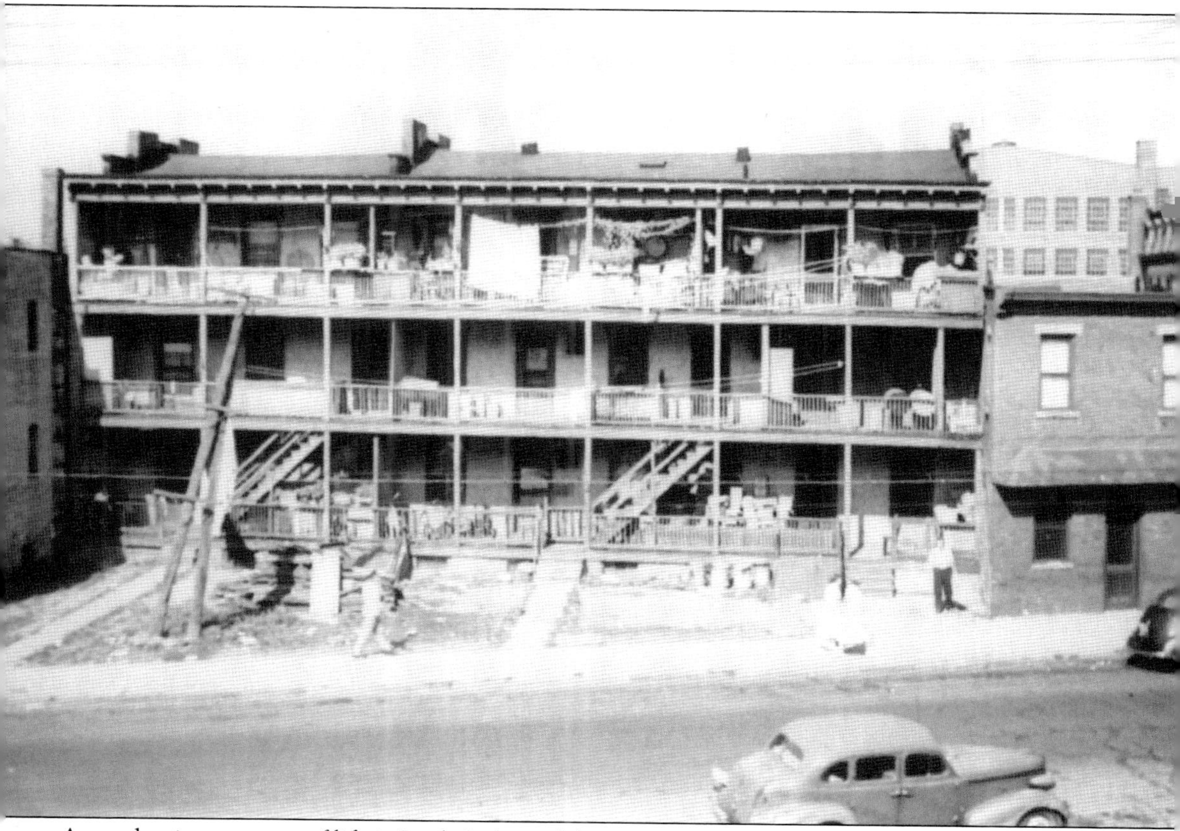

An endearing memory of life in Little Italy is of the tenement building Italian immigrants called "the boathouse" because it reminded them of the transatlantic liners that had brought them to America. Rev. Peter Havermans was responsible for its construction in 1853, first built for St. Mary's Female Orphan Asylum. The complex was sold eventually to private owners, first to Irish, then Italian families who converted the building into apartments. Philomena Bizzarro and Mildred and Anthony Ionata were the last longtime residents of the building to move before it was demolished in the mid-1960s. The earliest Italian residents were Nicolo and Gennaro Riggione, in 1914. The street numbers, originally 17, 19, and 21 Hill Street, were later changed to 57, 59, and 61. (Courtesy of Leonard DeMeo.)

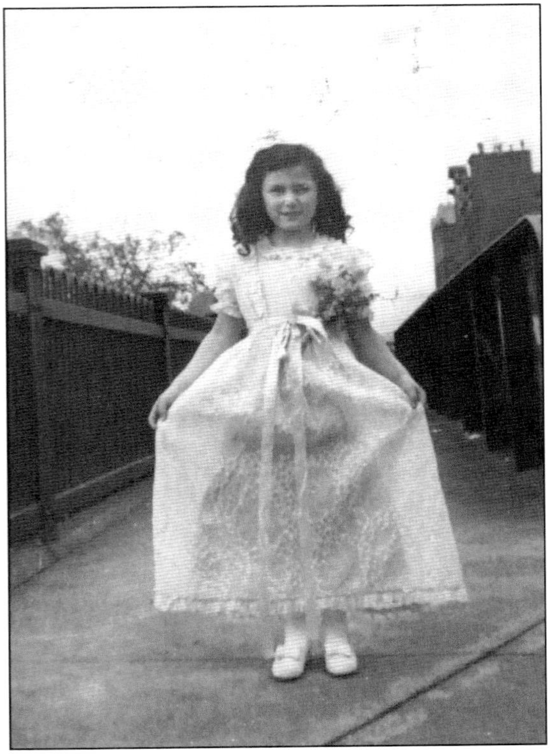

Catherine Pitaniello is modeling a new dress worn in a May Day procession at St. Mary's Church. The site of the photograph is the Fifth Avenue railroad bridge just south of Liberty Street, which was dismantled several years after passenger rail service was discontinued in Troy in 1958. The building in the background is Stanton's Brewery, demolished after a disastrous fire ravaged the building in 1963. (Courtesy of Mary Teta Pitaniello.)

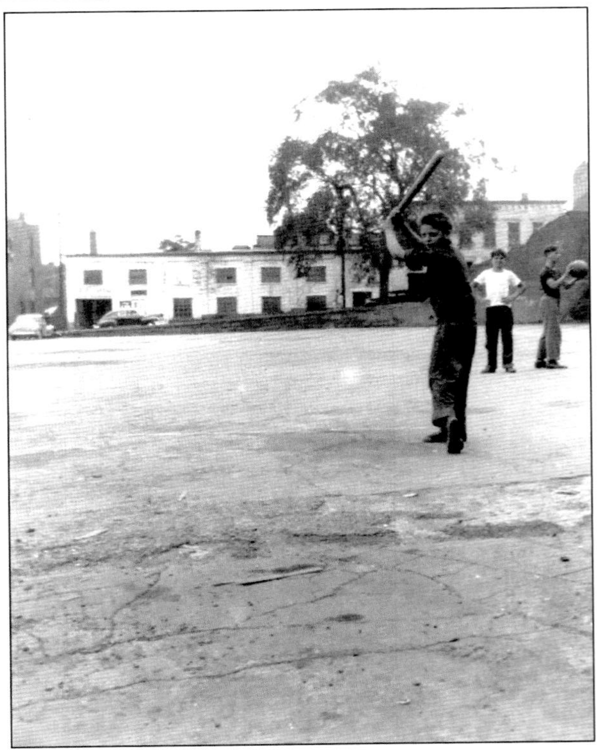

In the old market area, the neighborhood's four-season playground, are, from left to right, at bat Charles (Chuckie) Casale, Phillip (Philo) Germano, and an unidentified boy with a basketball. The market was a staging area for Troy parades and a small play area for a time containing swings, sliding boards, and other playground equipment. A huge election-eve bonfire (properly supervised by adults) was a fall tradition. (Courtesy of Jean Turriglio Cavallo.)

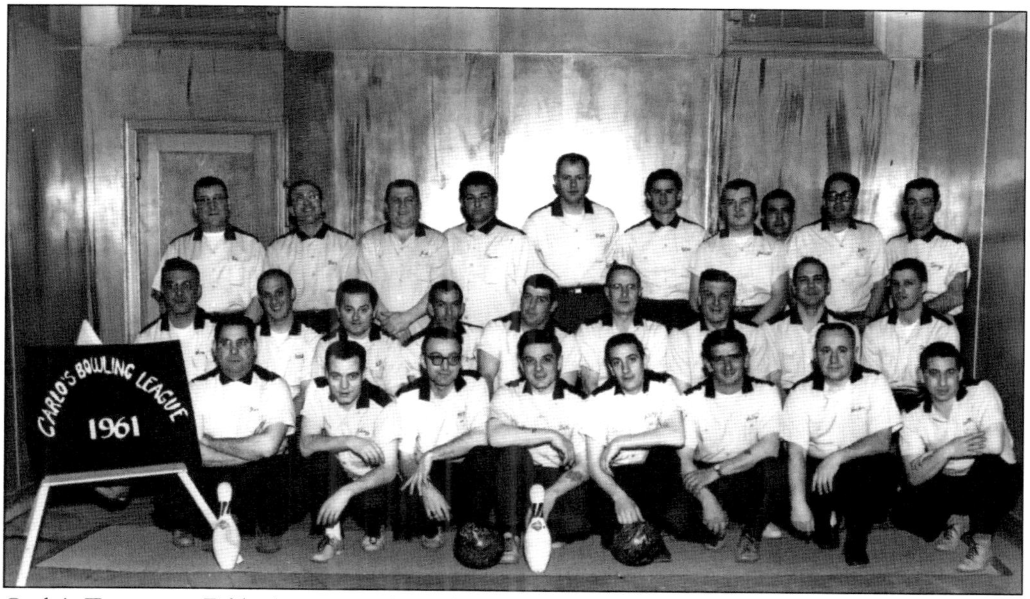

Carlo's Tavern, at Fifth Avenue and Washington Street, sponsored a bowling team. From left to right are (first row) Henry Merola, Dominic Montello, Frank Francese, Pat Pascarella, Joseph Montello, Dominick Mantello, Anthony Santora, and James Cardenuto; (second row) Sam and Nicholas Laiacona, Bill O'Connell, Frank Montello, Maurice Germinerio, Dominick Marro, Francis Berlino, Samuel Finelli, and Anthony Cioffi; (third row) Edward Brooks, Fred Testo, John Abrunza, Carmine Casale, unidentified, Anthony Teta, John Stapleton, Anthony Ragosta, Bob Teta, and unidentified. (Courtesy of John Merola.)

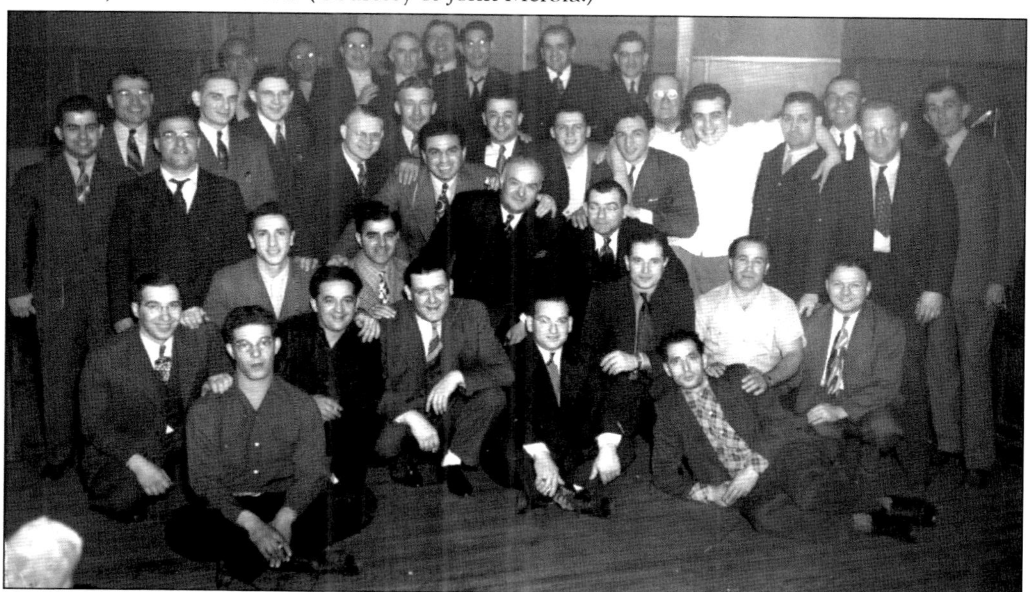

One of the oldest bowling leagues in the city, St. Mary's Bowling League was comprised of a group of neighbors that included a tavern owner, a baker, produce peddlers, a taxi driver, a politician, a shoe repairman, an insurance salesman, a barber, mill workers, truck drivers—tradesmen of all kinds. (Author's collection.)

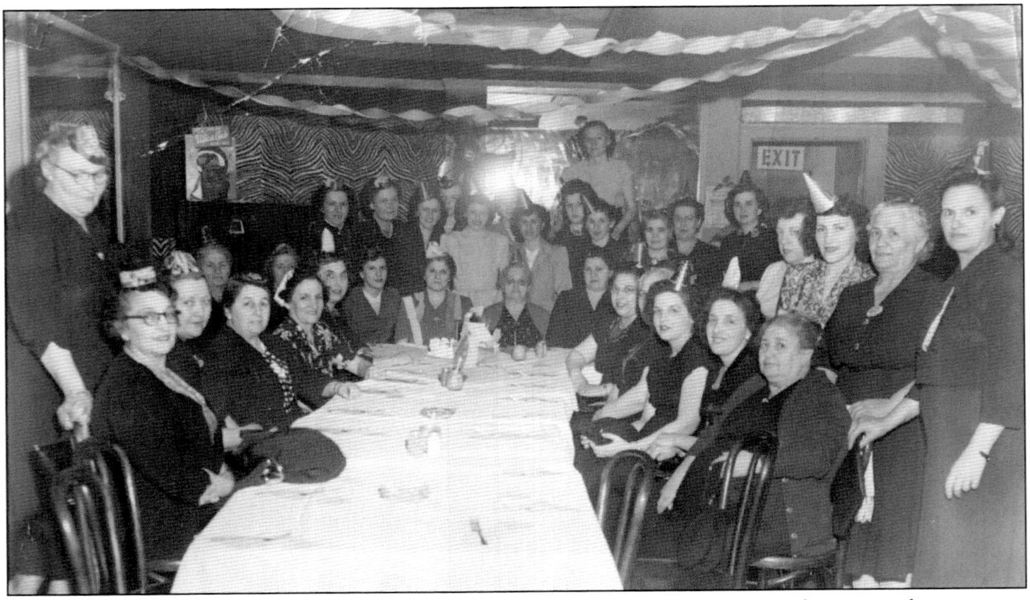

Relatives and friends gathered at Red Teta's Watervliet tavern to celebrate the impending voyage of Clara Terribile, who joined others from her parish, St. Anthony's, to attend the 1950 Holy Year Pilgrimage to Rome declared by Pope Pius XII. The first Christian Jubilee was held in 1300. The tradition of a pilgrimage to a sacred site is shared by several major religions. For Catholics, the site is Rome. (Author's collection.)

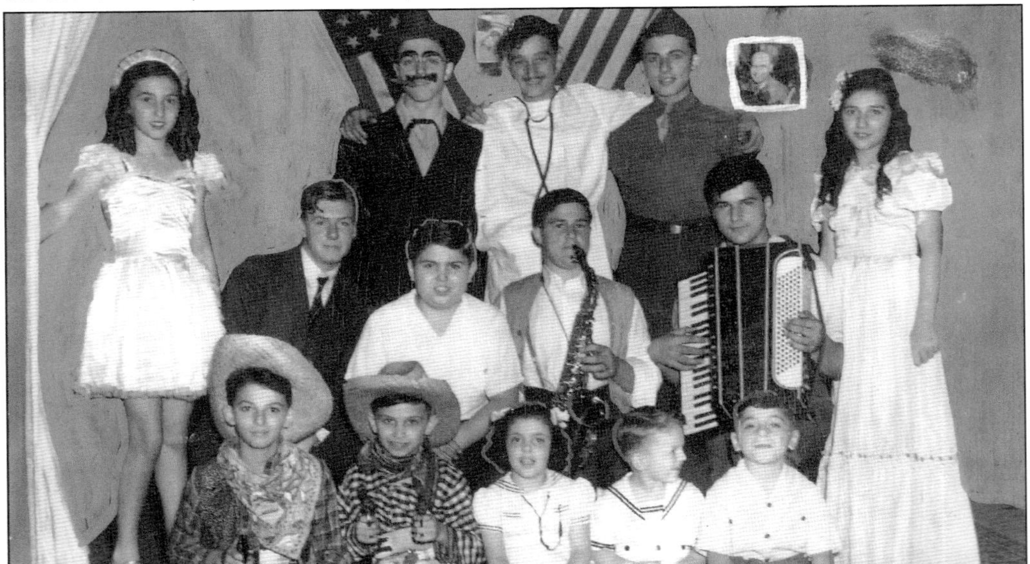

A USO show featuring neighborhood children was presented by Anthony G. Visk and William Pascarell on August 23, 1942. From left to right are (first row) Michael Milanese, Michael "Mickey" Visk, Mary Ann Tornincasa, Frank Visk Jr., and Louis Marchese Jr.; (second row) Irene DeThomas, Edward Brooks, Guy "Little Guy" Visk Jr., Carlo and Frank Sorrento, and Angie DeThomas; (third row) Anthony G. Visk, Jerry Clemente, and John Milanese. Before the war would end, both presenters would see action in Europe. (Courtesy of Mickey Visk.)

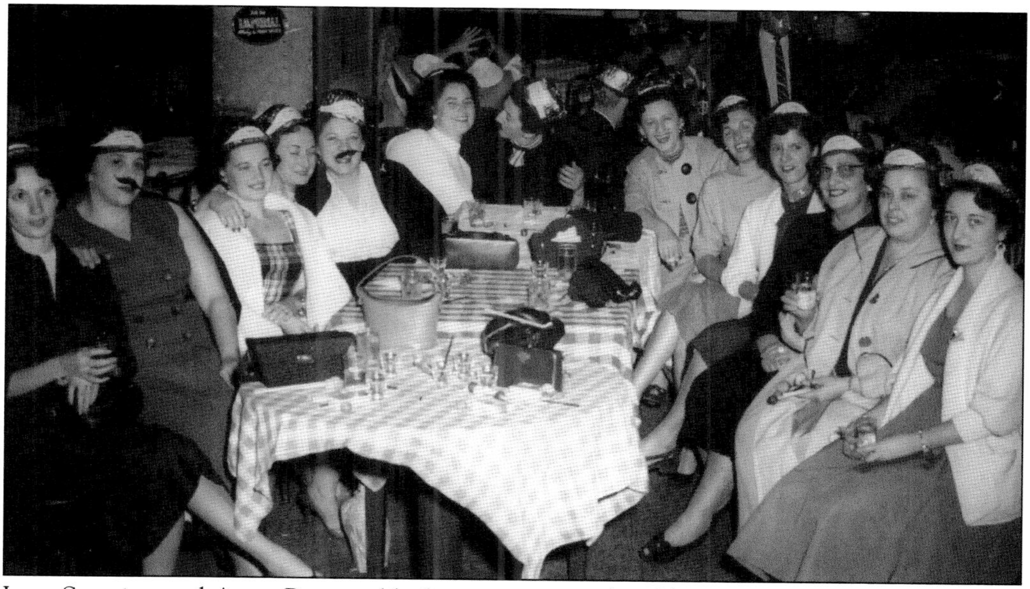

Lucy Saracino and Anna Reo would often organize weekend bus trips in September to attend New York City's Feast of San Gennaro in Manhattan's Little Italy. Usually, one evening's entertainment was at Sammy's Bowery Follies, the setting for this 1954 photograph. Seen here, clockwise from bottom left, are Betty DeBonis, Minnie DeLorenzo, Anna Cuozzo, Helen Testo, Lucille Salerno, two unidentified, Lucy Saracino, Rose Consuello, Toni Terribile, Anna Reo, Mary Martone, and Jean Cavallo. (Courtesy of Anna Cuozzo.)

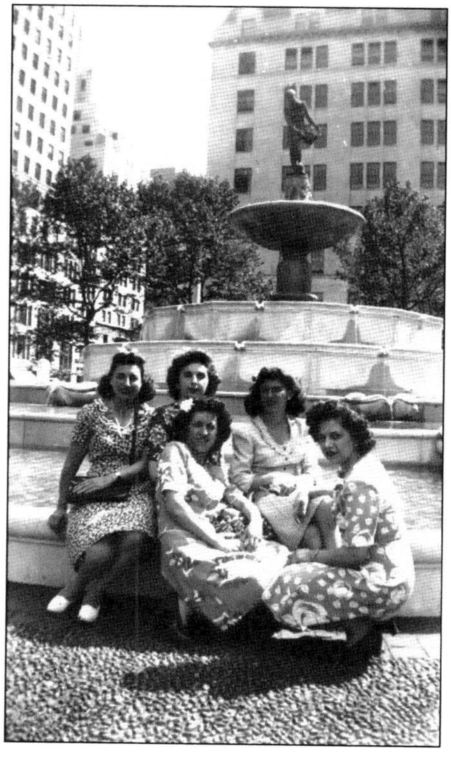

The height of rail passenger transportation at the Troy Union Station on Sixth Avenue was during the 1940s. Local residents made frequent one-day trips to New York City, often using the Sunday excursion fares. From left to right (first row), neighbors Dorothy Terribile and Louise Stellato; (second row) Catherine Sanzo, Anna Bruno, and Antoinette Dinova spend a pleasant break at the fountain on Fifth Avenue and Central Park South during an afternoon of sightseeing. (Author's collection.)

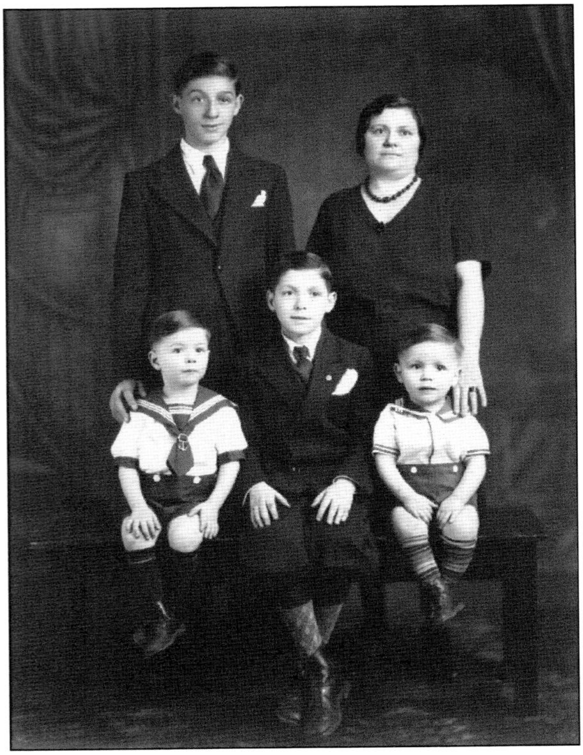

Assunta Comegna Cavallo, born in Candela, Foggia, was the widow (at 33) of Nicola Cavallo, also from Candela. In this 1938 photograph, she stands proudly with her four sons, from left to right (first row) Joseph, Anthony, and Vincent; (second row) Nicholas. Like many women of the neighborhood, Assunta worked in Troy's garment industry, as a presser at Browning and King. Her husband was also a presser, employed at Wul-Tex Clothes. (Courtesy of the Cavallo family.)

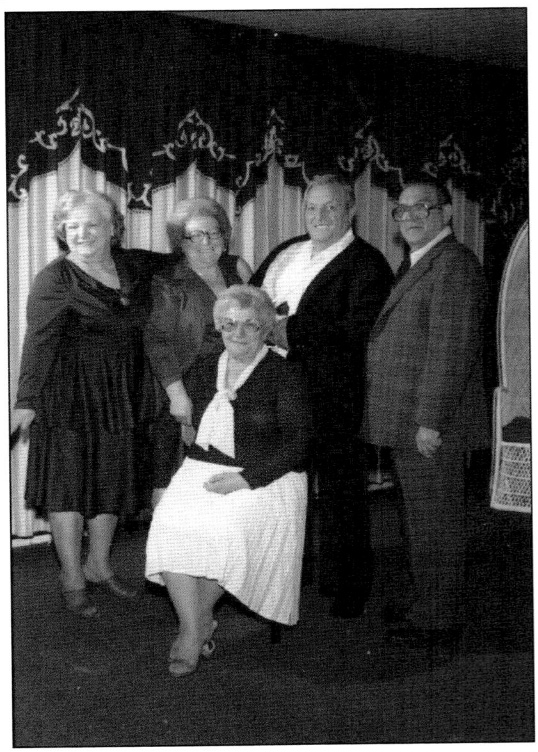

Members of the Riggione family were prominent business entrepreneurs from the earliest days of the Italian settlement in the neighborhood. Photographed are the children of Gennaro and Giovanina Riggione. Mildred Ionata is seated. From left to right are (standing) Mary Casale, Anna Gross, and brothers Nicholas and Louis Riggione. Among their longtime businesses were Jerry's Tavern, the Bowl-O-Torium Bowling Lanes, and the Malta Diner. (Courtesy of Anna Riggione Gross.)

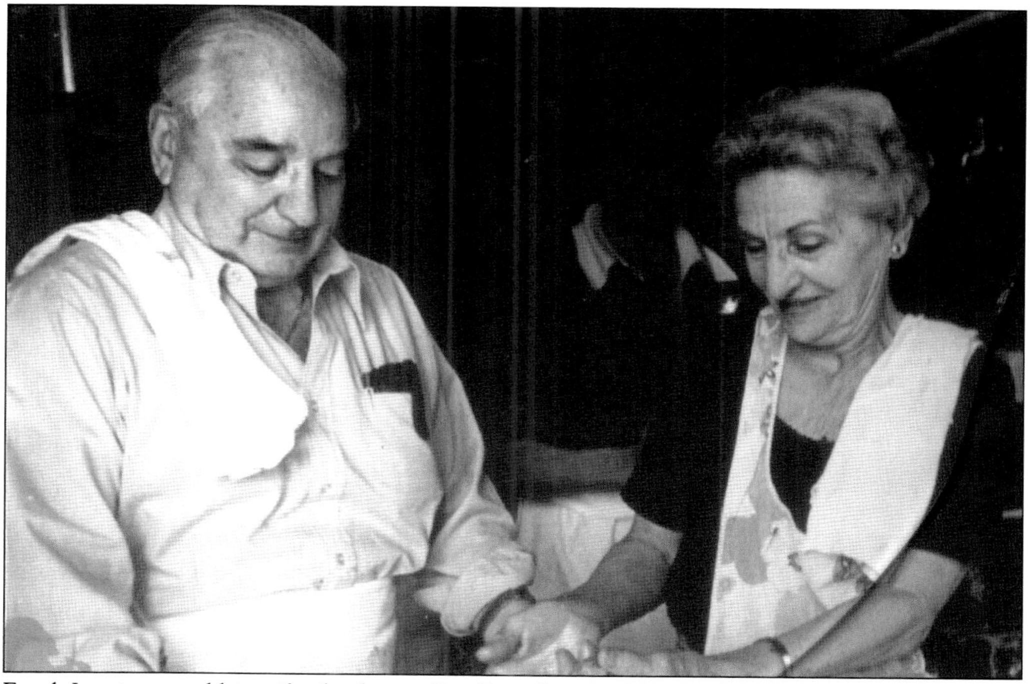

Frank Lamiano and his wife, the former Eva Spinelli, were New York City natives who moved to Troy when his employer, Tiny Town Togs, relocated here in 1935. Lamiano served many years as production manager for the children's dress manufacturer. Both were active in St. Mary's parish and the ICC and are often remembered for having organized countless spaghetti suppers, including the annual Election Eve Spaghetti Supper at St. Mary's. (Courtesy of the Lamiano family.)

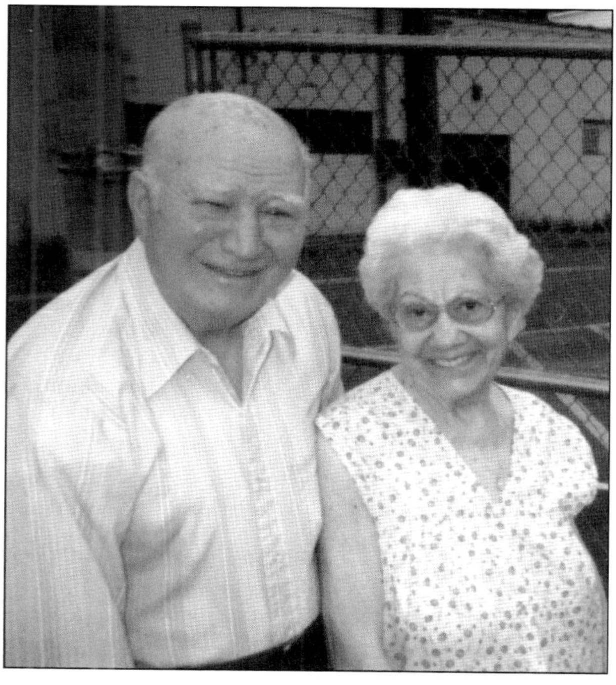

Josie and Tony DeFazio and their family were honored in September 2005 by the Rensselaer County Historical Society for service to the Troy community, including St. Anthony of Padua Church and parish, the American Committee on Italian Migration, the Friends of Little Italy, and several organizations that helped assimilate Italians and preserve Italian and Italian American culture. (Courtesy of the DeFazio family.)

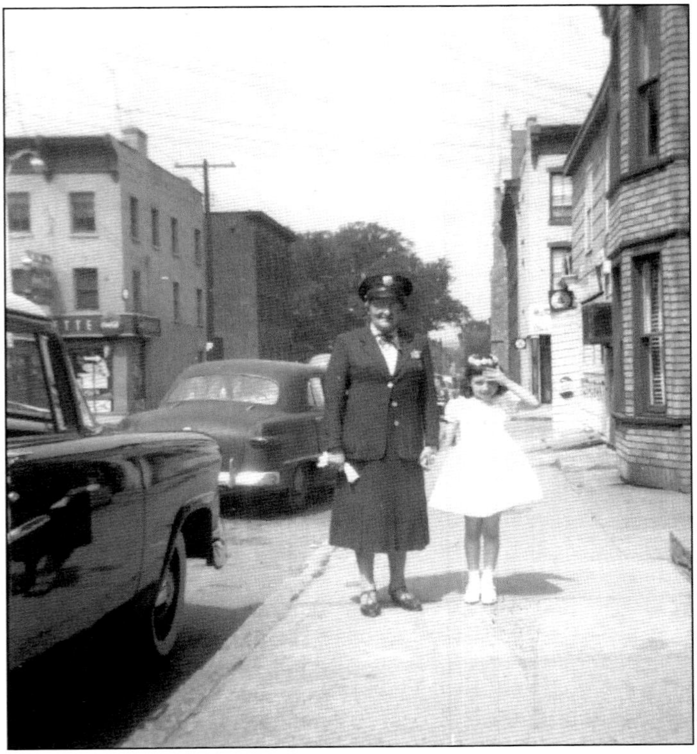

Crossing guard Philomena Donato, stationed for several years at the corner of Fourth and Washington Streets, stands next to Bonnie Lomaestro in this 1957 photograph. Students crossed the busy intersection to attend St. Mary's School on Third Street and LaSalle Institute on Fourth Street. The corner, a crossroads of the Little Italy neighborhood, was also the location of Stewart's Ice Cream Shop, Tony Testo's Luncheonette, and Americo Simpson's Fish and Chips. (Courtesy of Louise Donato Finelli.)

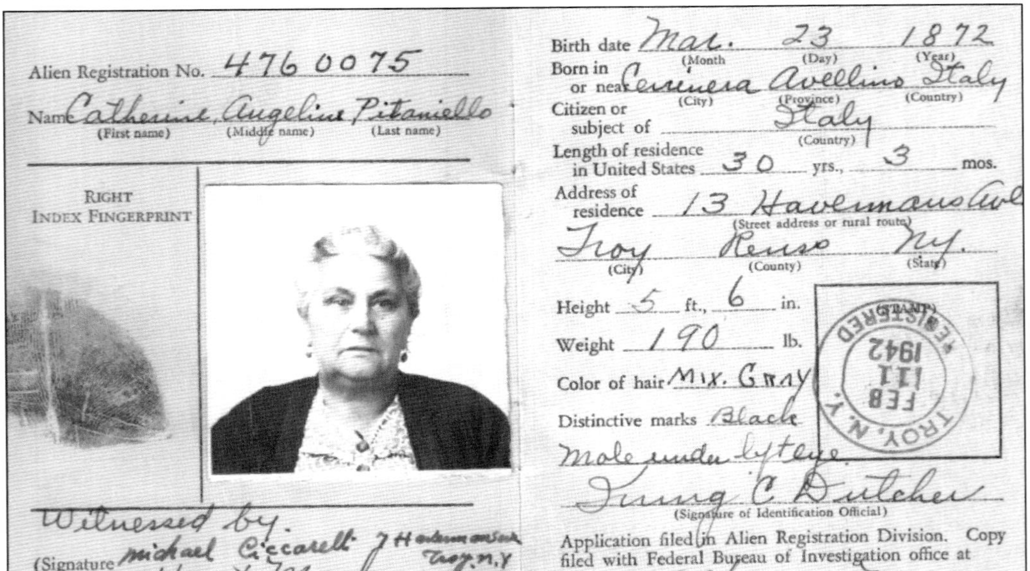

Alien Registration No. 4760075

Name Catherine Angeline Pitaniello
(First name) (Middle name) (Last name)

Right Index Fingerprint

Witnessed by.
(Signature of holder) Her X Mark

Birth date Mar. 23 1872
(Month) (Day) (Year)

Born in or near Cervinara Avellino Italy
(City) (Province) (Country)

Citizen or subject of Italy
(Country)

Length of residence in United States 30 yrs., 3 mos.

Address of residence 13 Havermans Ave
(Street address or rural route)

Troy Renss NY.
(City) (County) (State)

Height 5 ft., 6 in.

Weight 190 lb.

Color of hair Mix. Gray

Distinctive marks Black mole under left eye

(Signature of Identification Official)

Application filed in Alien Registration Division. Copy filed with Federal Bureau of Investigation office at Albany NY

This Alien Registration Certificate for Catherine Pitaniello was issued by the United States Department of Justice. Many Italians were required to register as aliens and to carry a registration card during World War II, to be produced if required by any police officer or other duly accredited official. A copy of the certificate was filed with the local office of the Federal Bureau of Investigation. (Courtesy of Mary Teta Pitaniello.)

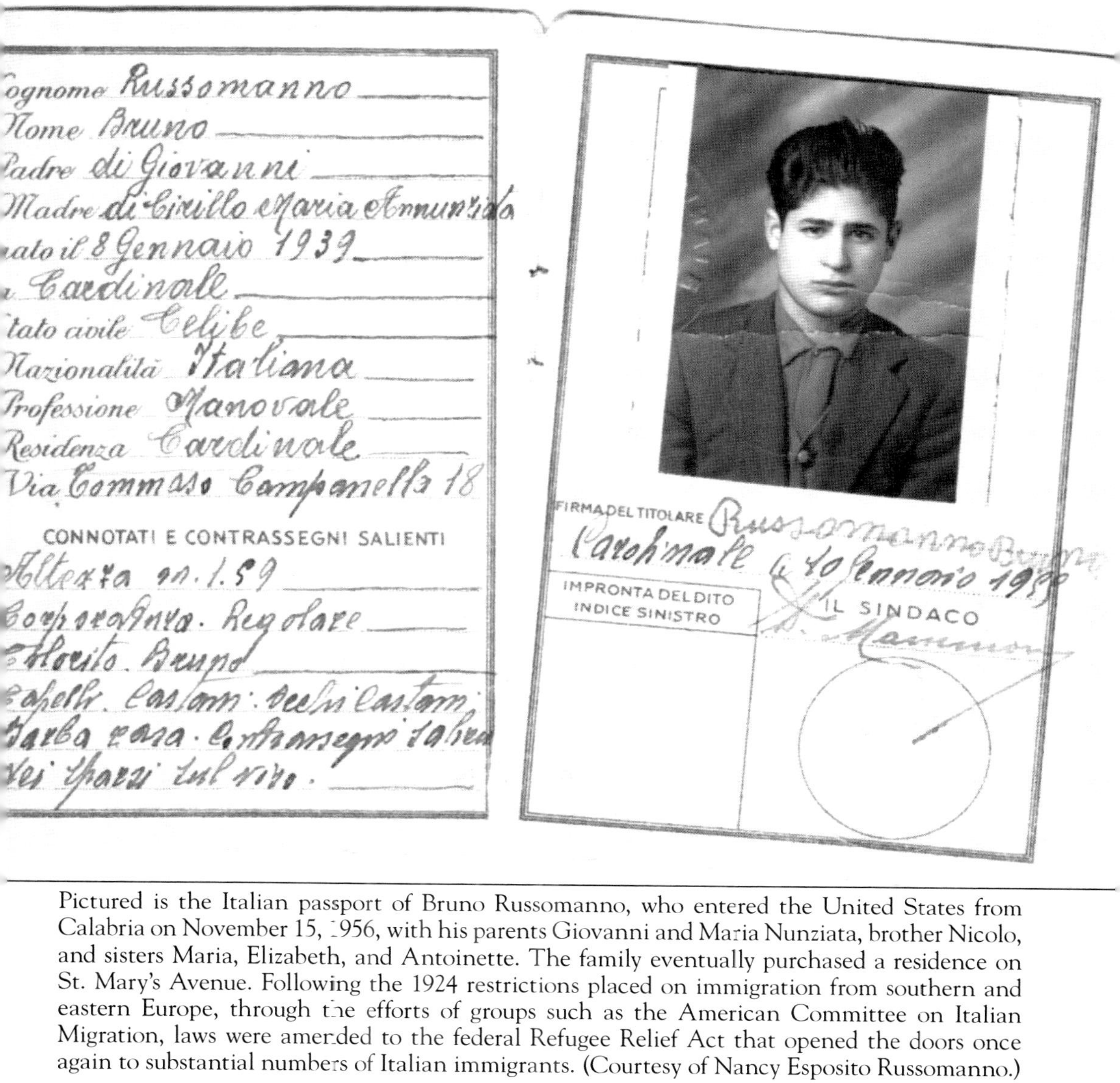

Pictured is the Italian passport of Bruno Russomanno, who entered the United States from Calabria on November 15, 1956, with his parents Giovanni and Maria Nunziata, brother Nicolo, and sisters Maria, Elizabeth, and Antoinette. The family eventually purchased a residence on St. Mary's Avenue. Following the 1924 restrictions placed on immigration from southern and eastern Europe, through the efforts of groups such as the American Committee on Italian Migration, laws were amended to the federal Refugee Relief Act that opened the doors once again to substantial numbers of Italian immigrants. (Courtesy of Nancy Esposito Russomanno.)

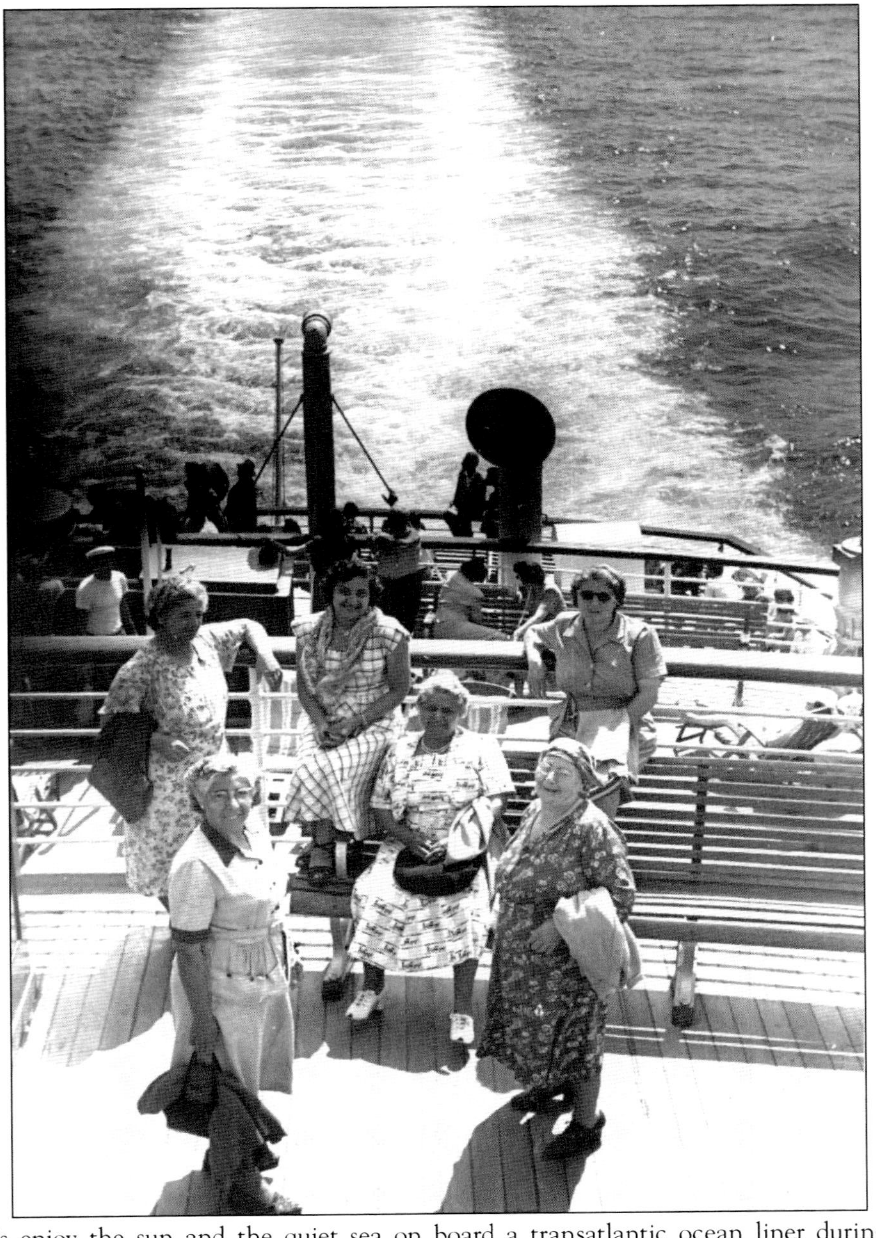

Friends enjoy the sun and the quiet sea on board a transatlantic ocean liner during their visit with family in Italy and touring the Italian peninsula. From left to right are (first row) Anita Tucci, Bernice Bove, and Filomena Calacone; (second row) Maria Clemente, Minnie Bove, and Clara Terribile. The return trip to their place of birth was quite different from the arduous voyage in steerage they and their families had made to America in the early years of the 20th century. While visits to Italy were infrequent for many family members and telephone or telegraph contact during the early years was rare, written correspondence was always available, often with the assistance of someone in the neighborhood who could read and write in both Italian and English. For many years, the availability of an Italian Consulate in Albany was also helpful. (Author's collection.)

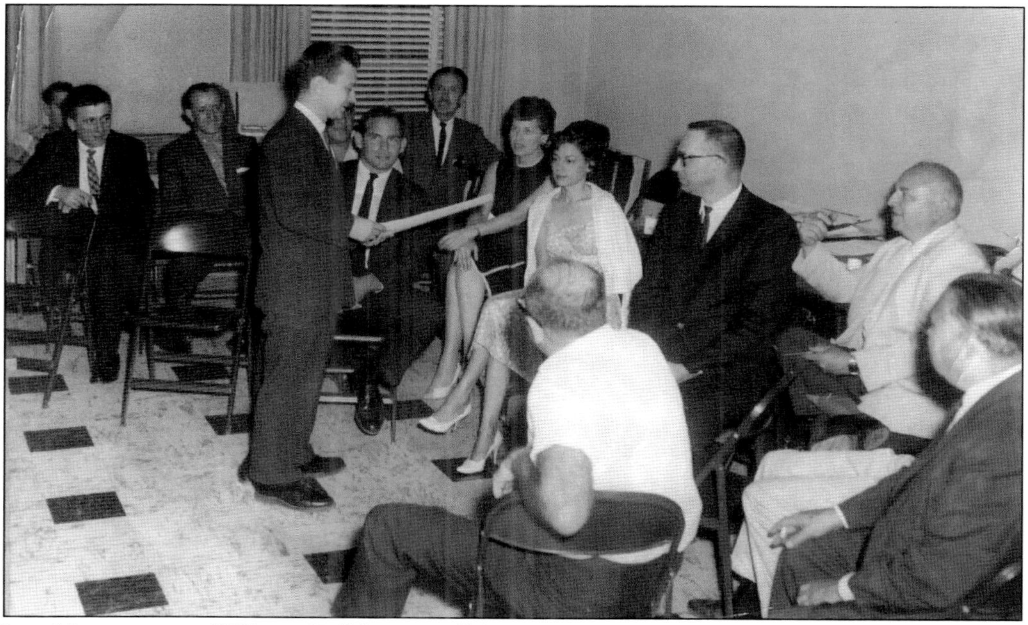

Local businessman William (Billy) Pascarell (a printer by trade) is pictured at the organizational meeting of a third-party movement he founded in 1962, Troy's Citizens' Party. Pascarell eventually served three terms on the Troy City Council, running as an independent with the backing of the Republican Party, representing downtown's Fourth Council District. His Fourth Street print shop was a popular hangout for politicos. (Courtesy of Frank Visco.)

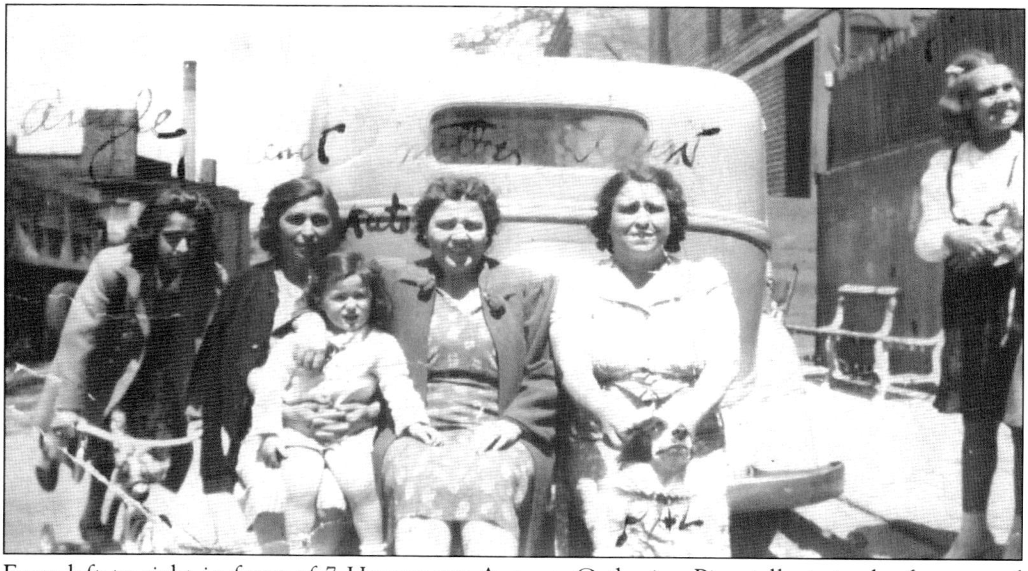

From left to right in front of 7 Havermans Avenue, Catherine Pitaniello is in the foreground with her cousin Angela Clemente and three aunts, the Pitaniello sisters—Carmella "Minuche" Clementi, Louise Sorrento, and Angela Ciccarelli—along with Pal, the family pet, and an unidentified neighborhood child. All of the women lost their homes on Havermans Avenue when the government bought their property through its right of eminent domain. (Courtesy of Mary Teta Pitaniello.)

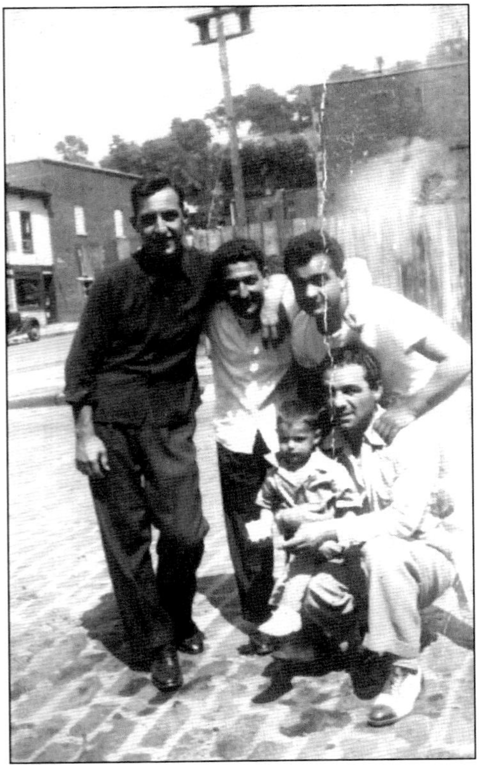

At the corner of Fourth and Washington Streets, in front of Mary's Luncheonette, are, from left to right, neighborhood buddies James "Tucker" Tedesco, Vito Furciniti, Anthony (Tony) Bove, and Salvatore "Mack" Casale holding young cousin Nicholas "Junior" Casale. Notice the block street pavement, which remained until the street was resurfaced a dozen or so years later in the 1950s. (Courtesy of Marie Casale Santora.)

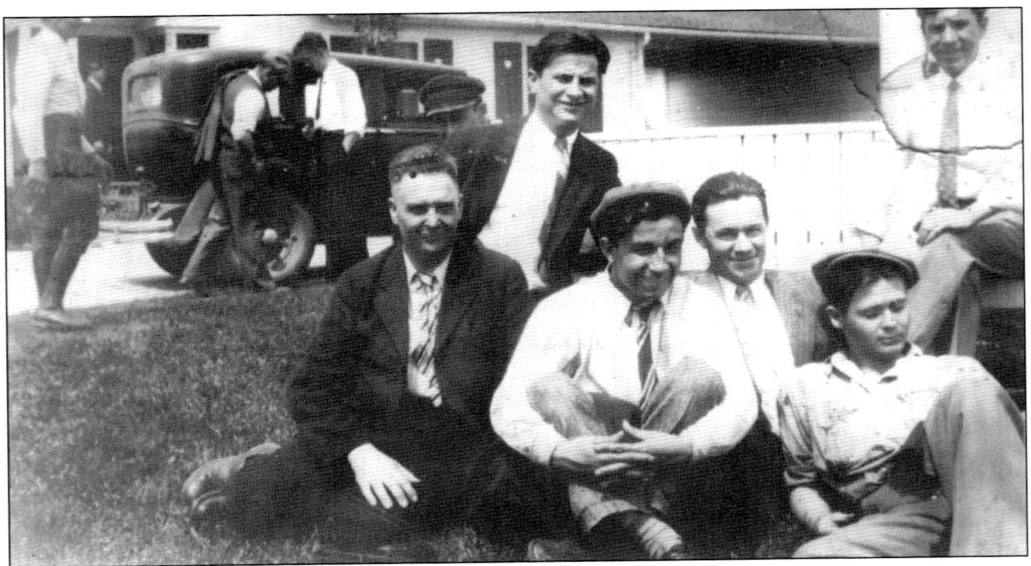

Salvatore Laiacona (center of group, with cap) is with classmates at Coyne American Institute, a Chicago trade school for electrical training, attending a nine-month motor-electrician course in 1934. The course was part of a work relief program during the Great Depression. Programs sponsored by Pres. Franklin Roosevelt's National Recovery Act helped millions of those unemployed find work in the trades and other occupations. (Courtesy of Frank Laiacona.)

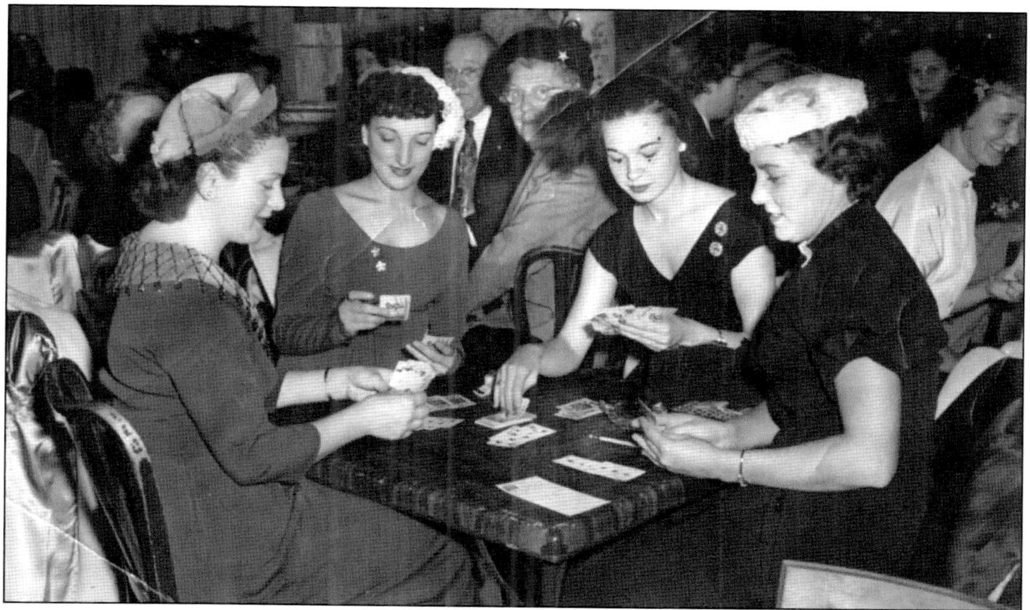

Organizations often held card parties, smokers, and variety shows to raise funds for projects and programs. Enjoying a friendly game of rummy at a Republican Party fund-raiser are, from left to right, Toni Valenti, Emma Esposito Valenti, unidentified, and Anna Mae DeLucia. A card party to benefit St. Mary's Church held in Washington Park was reported by the *Troy Record* on June 6, 1933. With 5,000 people in attendance, it may have set an area record. (Courtesy of the DeMaria family.)

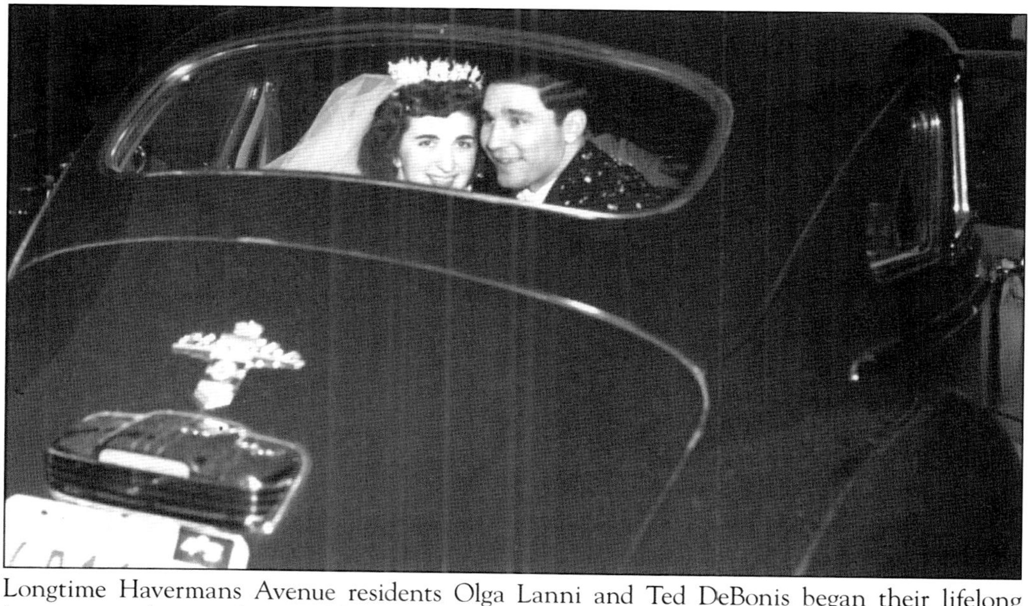

Longtime Havermans Avenue residents Olga Lanni and Ted DeBonis began their lifelong journey together on their wedding day in February 1949. Ted was a semipro ballplayer at the triple-A level with a Chattanooga, Tennessee, team in the American Associates League. He was also owner of Trojan Auto Supply. Olga was a seamstress at Cluett, Peabody and Company. (Courtesy of the DeBonis family.)

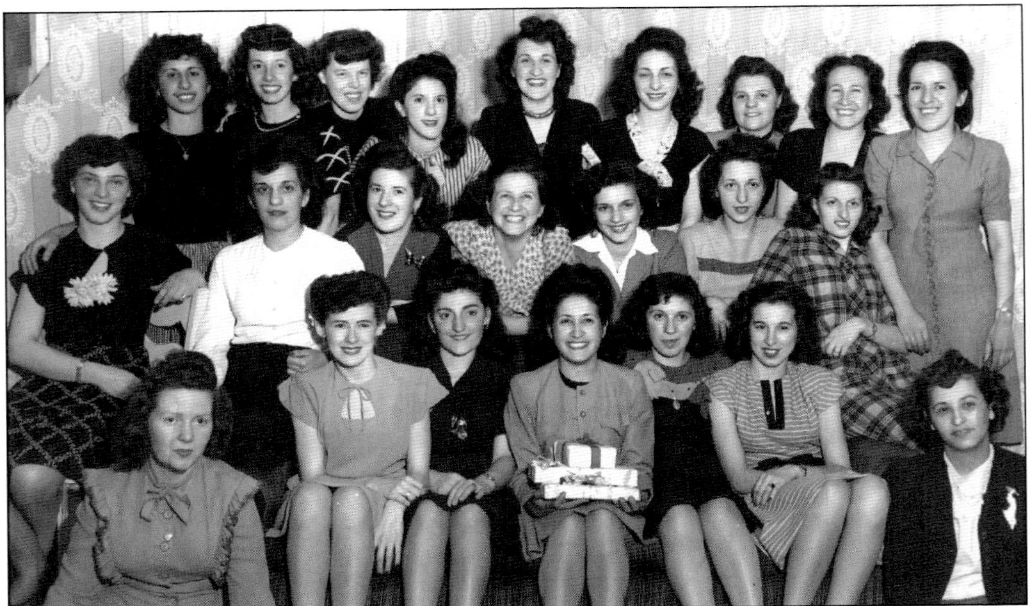

Friends of Julia Derrico gather at the home of Antoinette Dinova (maid of honor) to celebrate the soon-to-be bride at a bridal shower in this 1946 photograph. Most of the young women pictured lived within a block or two of the Dinova home and that of longtime friend Julia, a resident of Havermans Avenue. (Courtesy of the Roy family.)

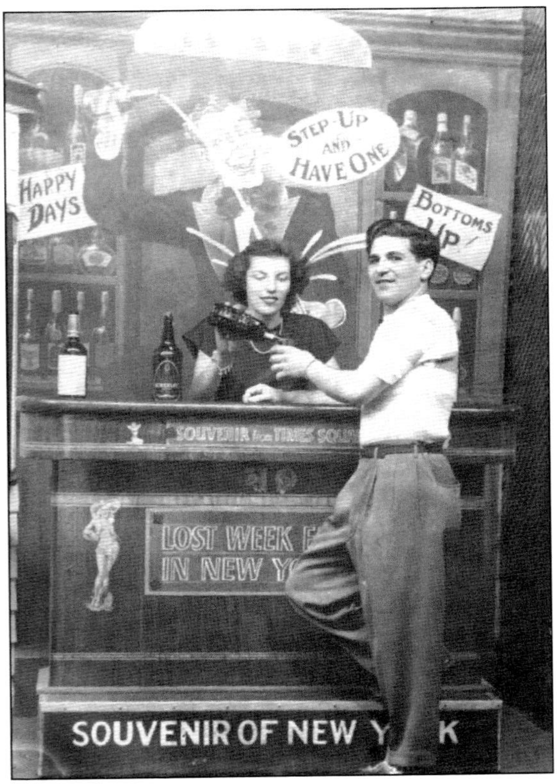

Adele and Nicholas Furciniti celebrated their honeymoon in the Big Apple in June 1947. Following World War II, many newly married couples were fortunate to spend a few days in New York City or along the Jersey shore. In the 1940s, air travel was not an option, and people either drove or traveled by train. (Courtesy of Colleen Furciniti Rogers.)

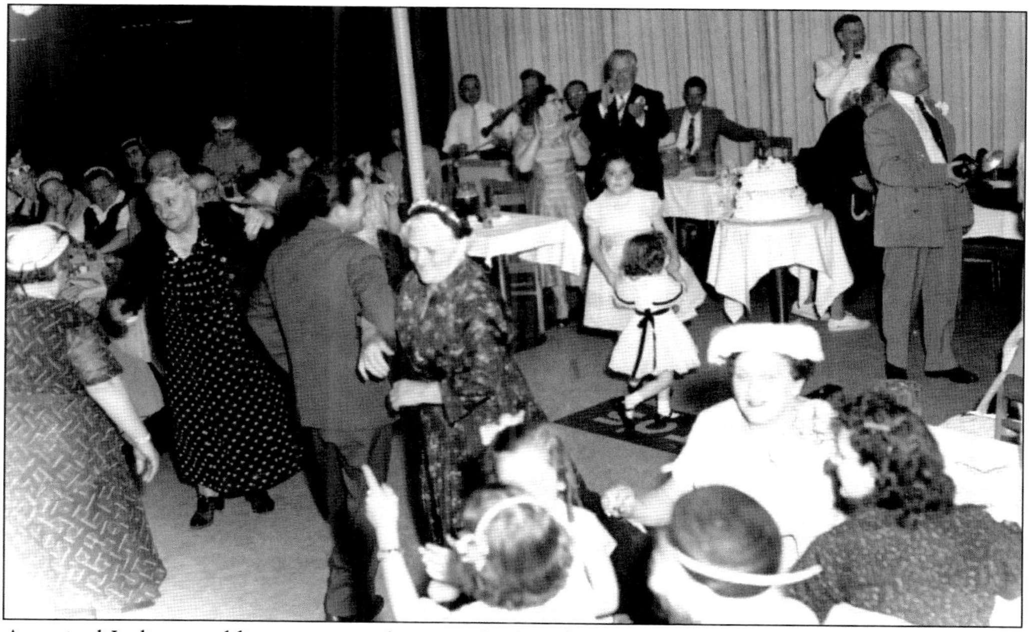

A typical Italian wedding scene is photographed as dancers from young to old join in when the music plays. In the background, Jennie Bizzarro and William Wade clap as, from left to right, young Rachel and Phyllis Bizzarro join Stella Lombardo, Joseph Miele, and Manil Longo on the dance floor. Ralph Bizzarro has his camera ready to capture the fun at the festivities. (Courtesy of Philomena Bizzarro DiSalvatore.)

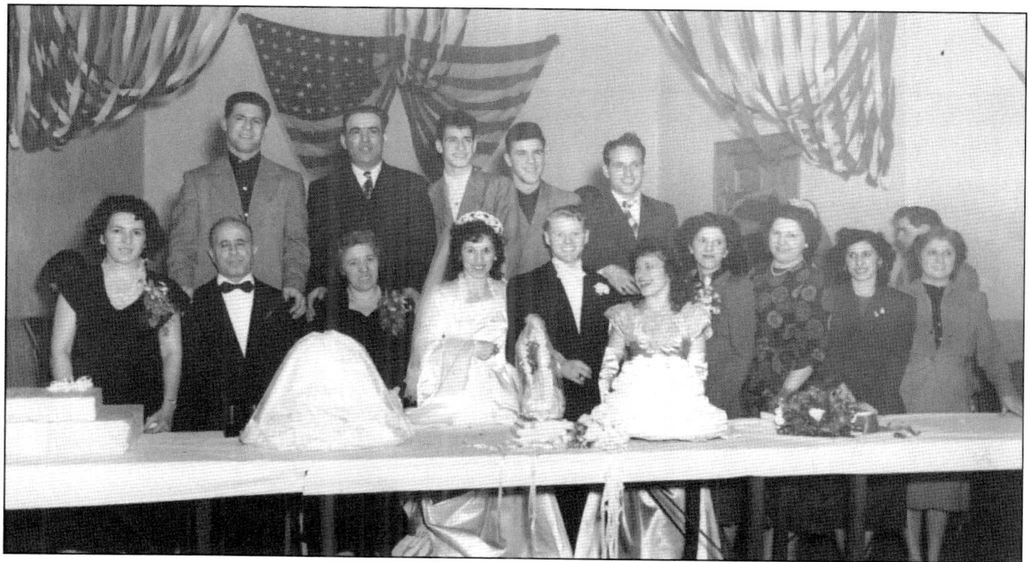

The Dinova family gathers at the head table for the reception at Troy's Polish American Club following Antoinette's marriage to Raymond Roy. Postwar receptions were simple affairs held in local restaurants, taverns, or veterans' posts. Food and decorations, along with beverages, a wine toast, an assortment of Italian cookies, and a wedding cake, were provided by family. The grand march started with the bridal party and ended with everyone at the reception on the dance floor. (Author's collection.)

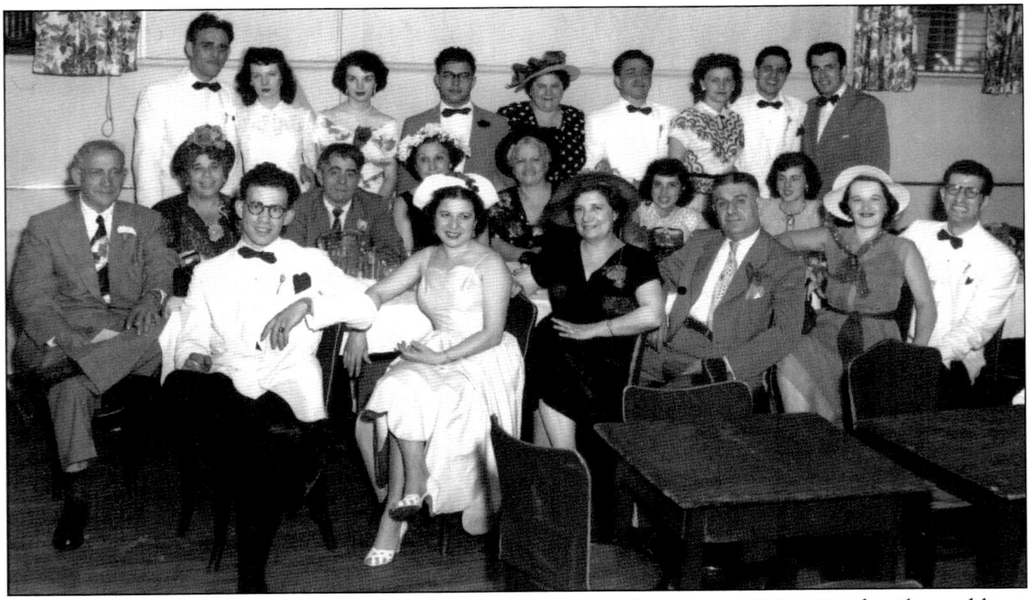

Frank A. Mancini Sr. (second row, left) joins family and friends at a Mancini family wedding. Mancini established a funeral home on Fourth Street in 1911 and frequently traveled to New York City to assist members of Troy's early Italian community in obtaining steamship tickets and passports, exchanging currency, and acting as interpreter for new arrivals. His sons, Vincent, John, and Frank Jr., and daughter, Angela, continued for more than 70 years in several family businesses. (Courtesy of the Mancini family.)

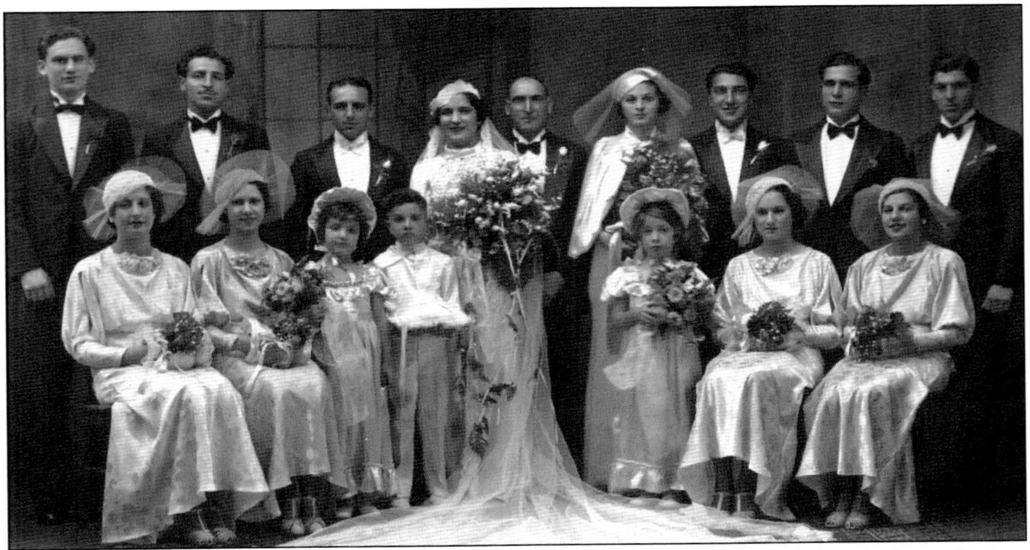

Principals and attendants gather for the official photograph of the wedding of Nicholas and Mary Consuello. From left to right are (first row) Theresa Riggio, Antoinette Terribile, and children Mary Pascale, George Genevive, and Angie Pascale with Mary Teta and Betty Esposito; (second row) William Teta, James Consuello, groom and bride Nicholas and Mary, father of the bride Anthony Consula, Rose Consuello, Nicholas Consula, Jerry Pitaniello, and Francis Consuello. (Author's collection.)

SAINT ANTHONY'S CHURCH

28 STATE STREET, TROY, N. Y.

Saint Anthony's Proteges

Pray

for Our Boys
in the Service

Attend

St. Anthony's
Devotions

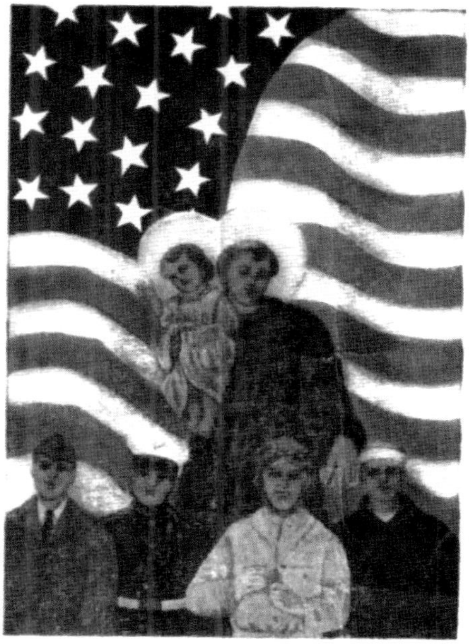

Devotions

in honor of St. Anthony
Every Tuesday
at
7:30 Mass
3:30 and 7:30 P. M.

Dear Saint Anthony, Protect OUR Boy

JOHN GORI

Troy, N. Y., MARCH 24 1943

Father Roger A. Imperiale, O. F. M., Pastor

St. Anthony of Padua Church honored members of the armed services during World War II with a beautiful tribute to its heroes, whom it called St. Anthony's Proteges. A prayer service was held at the church each week, and a service flag with a star was displayed prominently in the window of the family residence as a tribute to the armed services member. Among the World War II deceased were Lt. Anthony Iozzo, Pvt. Charles Decetise, Seaman Second Class Luciano Manzerra, Sgt. Patrick Comi, S.Sgt. Dominick Pitaniello, S.Sgt. Carmen Ciccarelli, Pfc. Dominick DiGiorgio, S.Sgt. Robert DelMonaco, Pvt. Gerald Furciniti, Sgt. Carmen DeCrescenti, Pvt. Felix Clementi, Cpl. John Rea, Pfc. Michael Ricciuti, and Pvt. Anthony Melia. (Courtesy of the Rea family.)

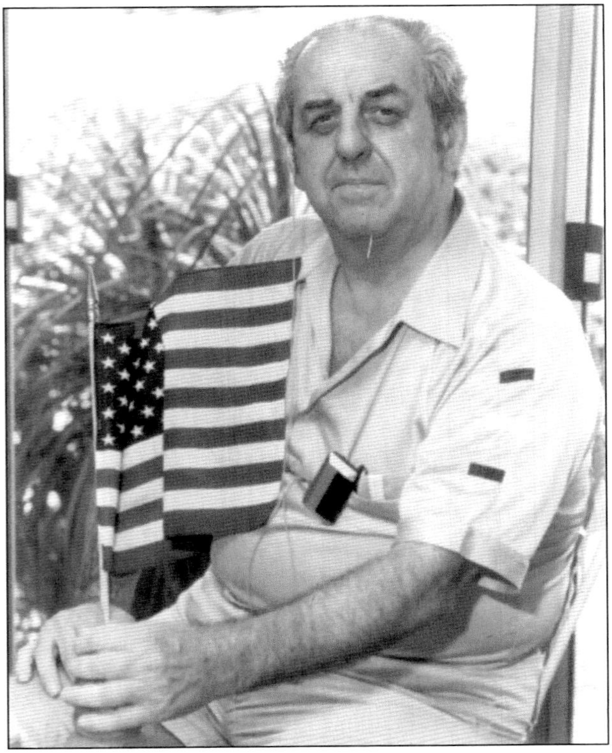

The late James Pasinella, a United States Marine veteran and retired postal carrier, was concerned about the disrespect shown for the flag during antiwar demonstrations in the 1960s. In 1967, Pasinella enlisted community support that eventually led to the formation of Troy's annual Flag Day parade, the largest in the country. The parade marches through the Little Italy community to downtown Troy, "the home of Uncle Sam." (Courtesy of Ed Verrillo.)

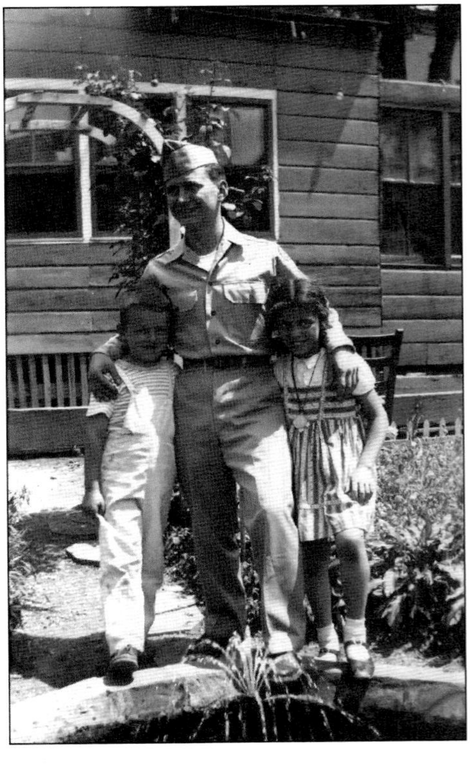

During World War II, many young Italian Americans found themselves back in the country their grandparents had left, fighting for freedom. Shown here during a military leave with cousins Frank Visk Jr. and Mary Ann Tornincasa is William (Billy) Pascarell, who drove a jeep to deliver mail to the front lines in Patton's army. His brother Anthony "Toto" was a tail gunner flying on bombing raids out of England. Cousin Anthony G. Visk helped liberate Italian towns from German occupation. (Courtesy of Frank LaPasta Visco.)

Little Italy residents Nicholas Grinaldo of Fifth Avenue (in the photograph) and Samuel Dinova of Havermans Avenue survived the July 7, 1944, Japanese suicide attack against the 105th Infantry at the World War II Battle of Saipan. A graphic documentary of the battle, which cited the two men, was part of the series *Day under Fire: WWII* produced for the National Geographic Channel. Sergeant Grinaldo was awarded a Purple Heart, a Bronze Star, and a New York State Conspicuous Service Award. (Courtesy of Nicholas Cristiano.)

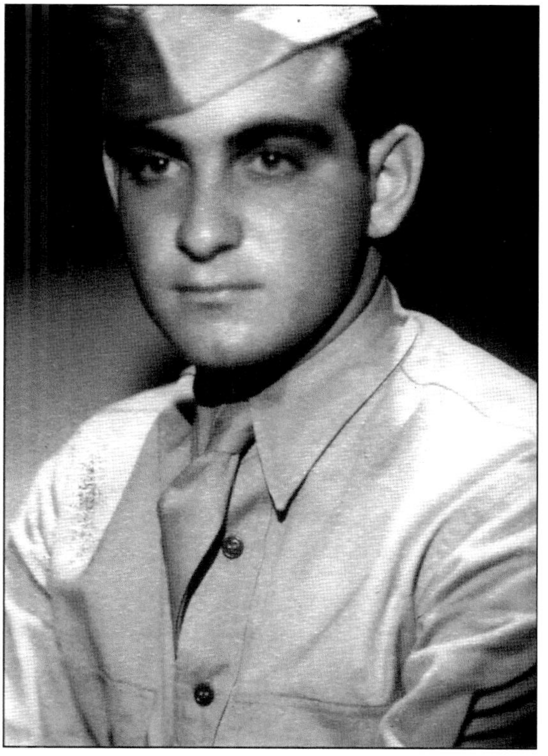

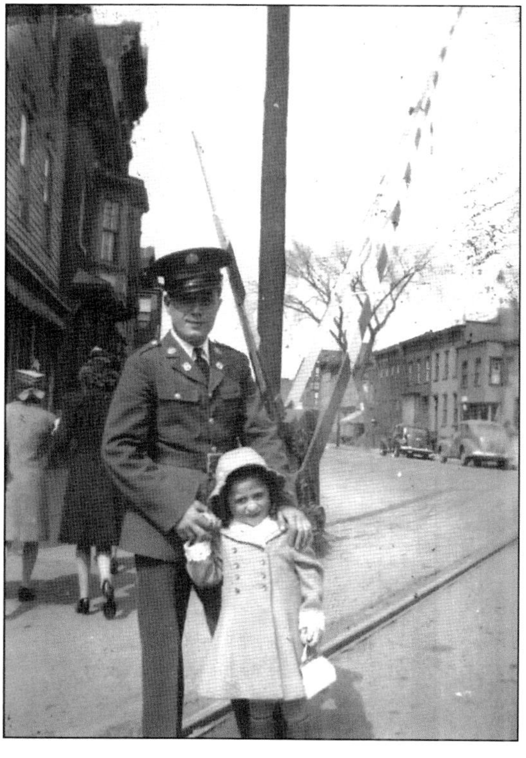

John DeFazio, on leave from the United States Army, stands next to Theresa Marchese near a railroad crossing on Fourth Street. Troop trains during World War II would occasionally be delayed en route, allowing local merchants and neighbors the opportunity to visit briefly with the troops and provide them with snacks and a cold beer; but it was the friendly conversations that were most remembered. (Courtesy of the DeFazio family.)

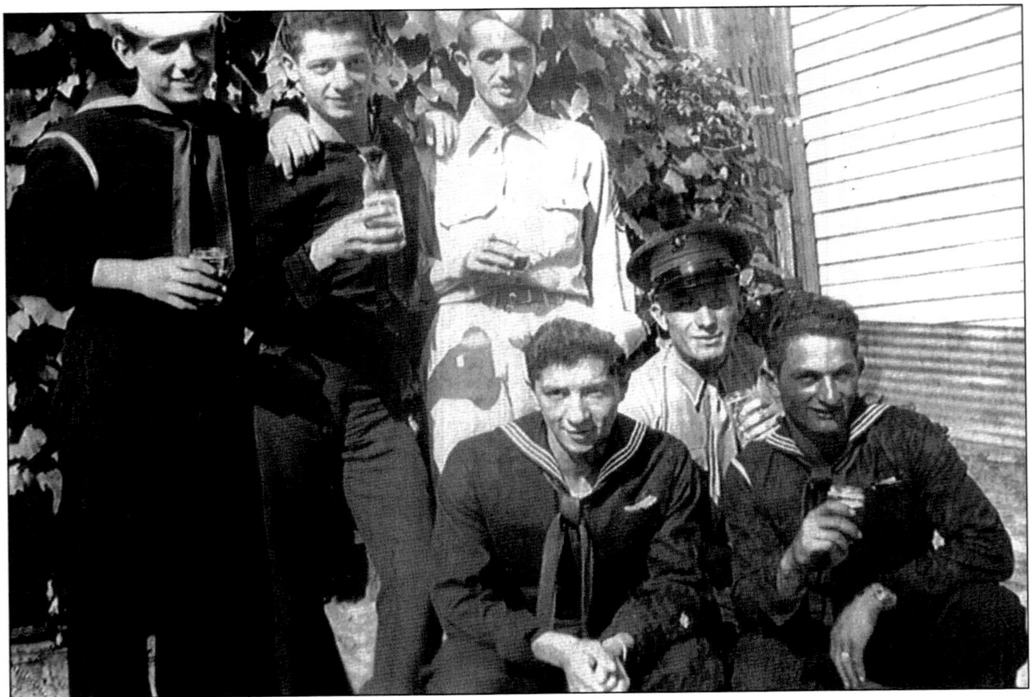

Neighborhood buddies gather for a well-deserved break while on military leave in the summer of 1944. This photograph was taken in the courtyard of the Stellato homestead at 256–258 Fourth Street. From left to right are (kneeling) Dominick Brignola, Francis Stellato, and Joseph Dinardo; (standing) Joseph Panza, James Bevevino, and William Stellato. Of the 12 million members of the United States armed forces involved in World War II, 1.2 million were Italian Americans. (Courtesy of the Bevevino family.)

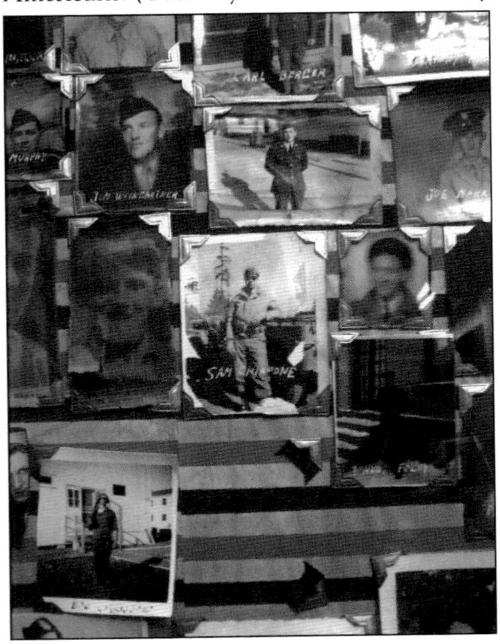

Tavern owner John J. Gerger maintained a display case containing photographs and letters sent by men of the neighborhood who were serving in World War II. Included was a photograph of Cpl. Sam Chiappone serving with the 83rd Infantry, involved in a battle at Hürtgen Forest on the German-Belgian border, where he would be seriously wounded on December 18, 1944. Gerger's family donated the collection to the Rensselaer County Historical Society. (Courtesy of the Rensselaer County Historical Society.)

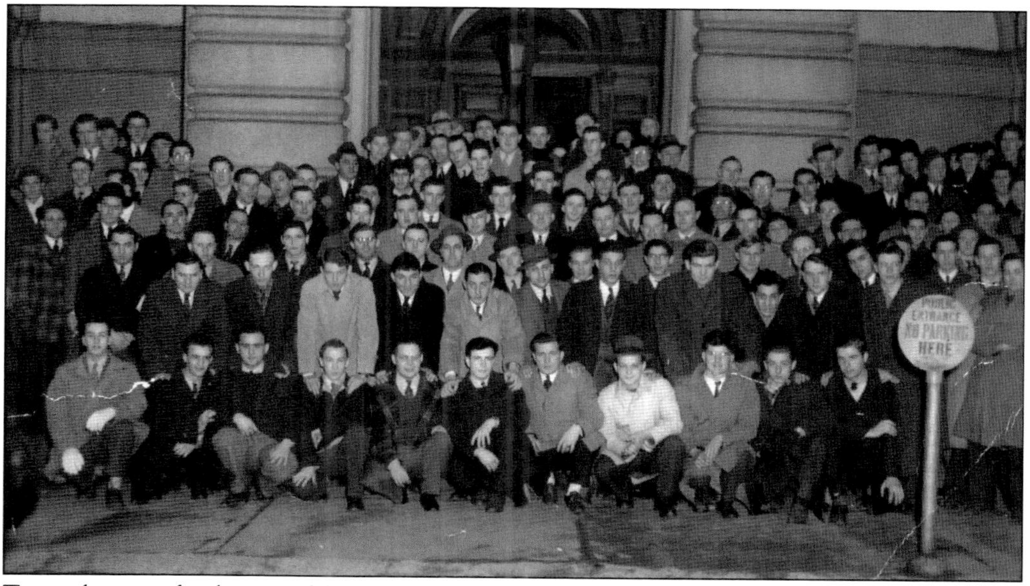

Troy volunteers for the armed forces gather at the Rensselaer County Court House before leaving for Fort Dix, New Jersey, in February 1943. Among those who can be identified are Michael Cuozzo, Michael Mariano, and Samuel Laiacona. Fort Dix, opened in 1917, was a training and staging ground for army units in both world wars, became a permanent United States Army post in 1939, a basic-training center in 1947, and is well known to thousands of Troy servicemen who trained there. (Courtesy of Michael Cuozzo.)

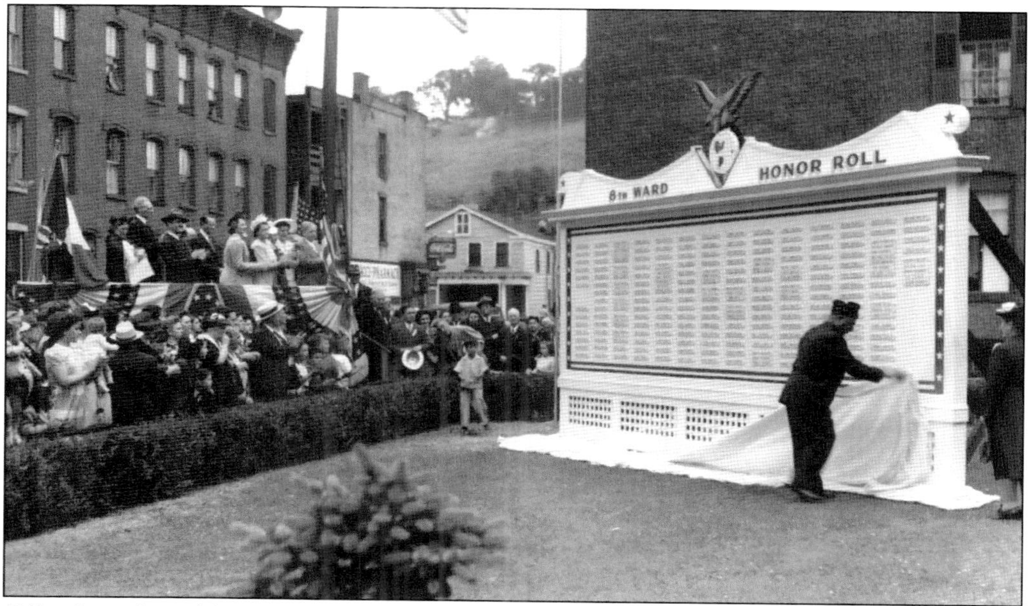

Officials and neighbors gather at the dedication ceremony for the Eighth Ward Honor Roll listing people from the ward serving in the armed forces during World War II. The memorial was in a small pocket park at the corner of Washington and Church Streets. Permanent stone memorials to veterans are located at the corner of Third and Division Streets, along fencing at Washington Park, and on Third Street below Adams Street. (Courtesy of Mickey Visk.)

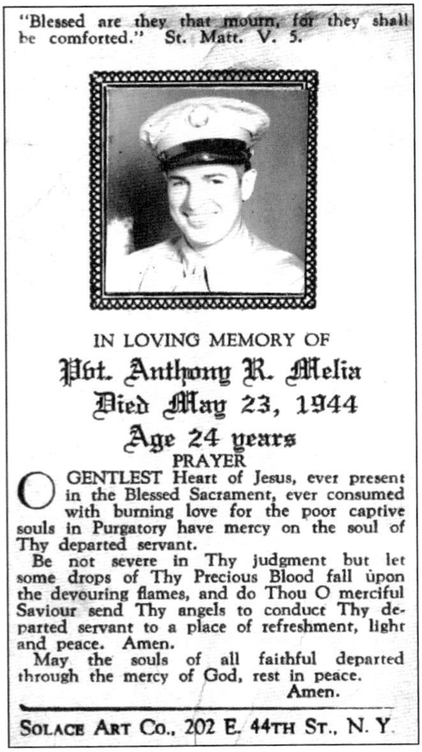
"Blessed are they that mourn, for they shall be comforted." St. Matt. V. 5.

IN LOVING MEMORY OF

Pvt. Anthony R. Melia

Died May 23, 1944

Age 24 years

PRAYER

O GENTLEST Heart of Jesus, ever present in the Blessed Sacrament, ever consumed with burning love for the poor captive souls in Purgatory have mercy on the soul of Thy departed servant.

Be not severe in Thy judgment but let some drops of Thy Precious Blood fall upon the devouring flames, and do Thou O merciful Saviour send Thy angels to conduct Thy departed servant to a place of refreshment, light and peace. Amen.

May the souls of all faithful departed through the mercy of God, rest in peace. Amen.

SOLACE ART CO., 202 E. 44TH ST., N. Y.

A remembrance card is shown for Pvt. Anthony R. Melia, killed in action in Italy on May 23, 1944. Less than five months later, his friend and neighbor Pvt. Gerald A. Furciniti, infantryman, was killed in the line of duty in Belgium on October 15, 1944. Both young men, residents of St. Mary's Avenue, had been employed at the Allegheny Ludlum Steel Company in Watervliet. (Courtesy of Leonard DeMeo.)

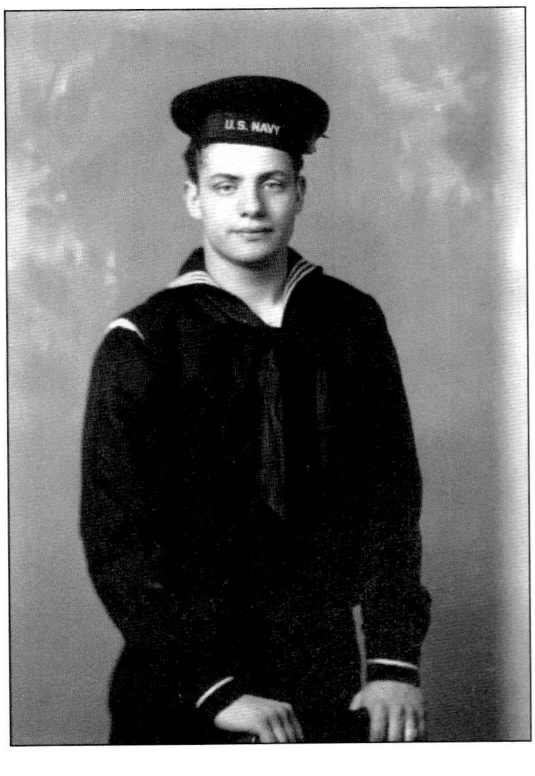

Seaman Second Class Luciano A. Manzerra, recipient of a Purple Heart, was killed in action on November 5, 1943, in the Mediterranean Sea aboard the USS *Bristol* when it was torpedoed and sunk. For months, he was reported missing in action. Nineteen-year-old Manzerra was the son of Louise and Joseph Manzerra of Fourth Street. (Courtesy of Sr. Mary Jane Manzerra.)

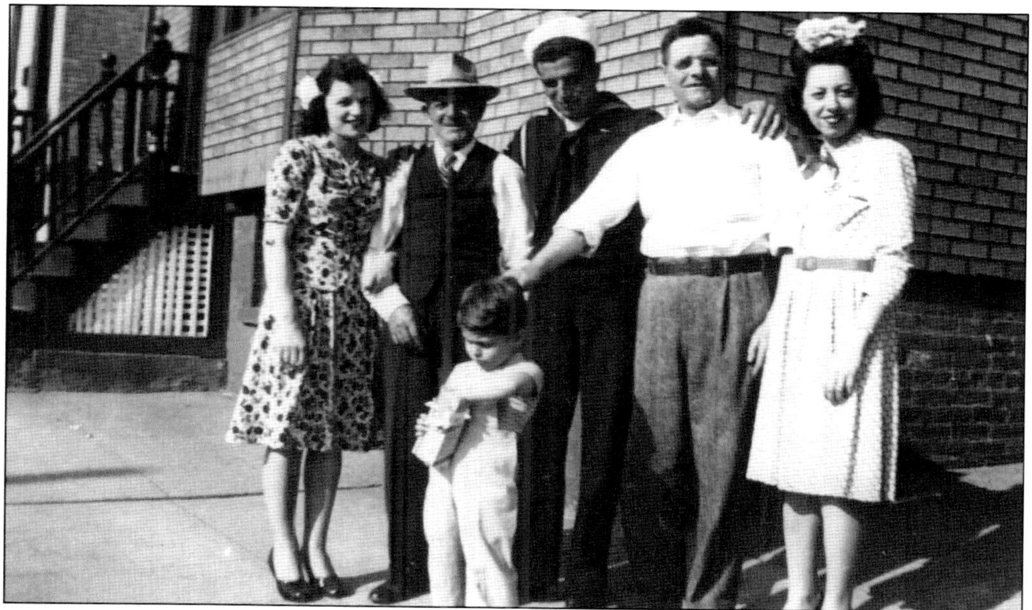

Standing behind young Nicholas Marro in this 1944 photograph taken in front of 1266 Fifth Avenue are, from left to right, Lena Marro, Sebastian Marro, Nick Marro, Saverio Gori, and Marie Marro. The site was adjacent to several important 19th-century institutions built by Rev. Peter Havermans, including Troy Hospital (later renamed St. Mary's Hospital) and St. Mary's Male Orphan Asylum. (Courtesy of Rose Gori Julian.)

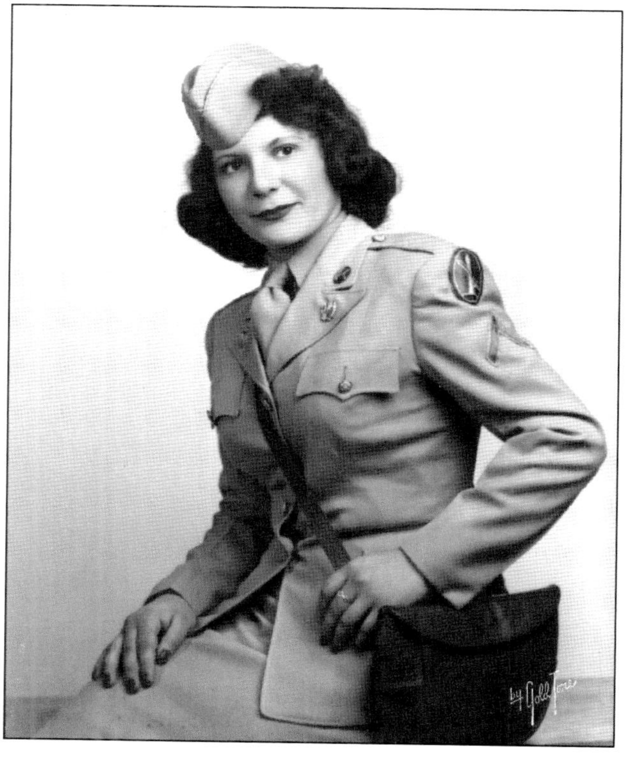

Josephine Rea Oswald entered the Women's Air Corps in 1944, shortly after hearing that her brother John had been killed in service to his country. Elizabeth Consuello, a member of the Women's Air Corps reserve unit, and Grace DeLucia Hoffman, a member of the Marine Corps, were among the women in the neighborhood who served proudly in the military. (Courtesy of Josephine Rea Oswald.)

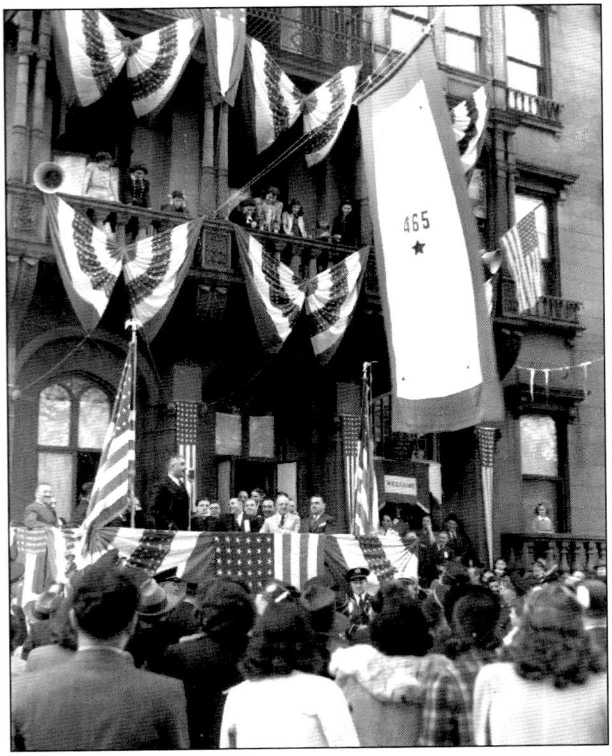

The ICC, 191 Second Street at Washington Park, was the setting for the World War II service flag dedication ceremony on October 11, 1942. Addressing the crowd is Dr. Nicholas Brignola, master of ceremonies. The Honorable Charles Poletti, New York State's lieutenant governor, was the keynote speaker. The number 465 on the flag indicates the number of armed-service members from the neighborhood at the time. (Courtesy of Mickey Visk.)

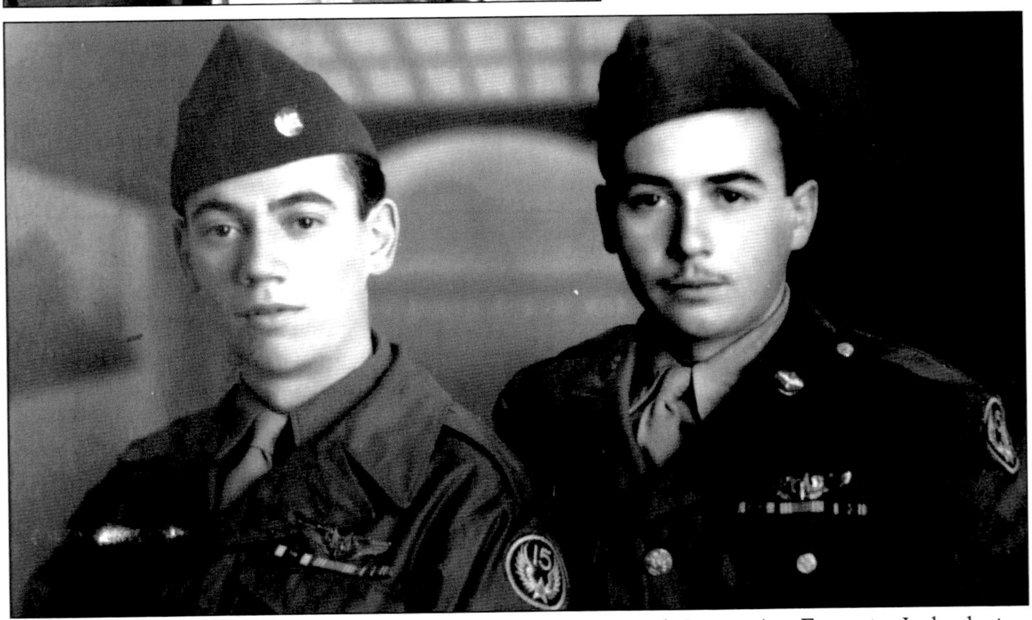

Brothers Anthony and Rocco DeMeo served in the United States Air Force in Italy during World War II. Rocco was a radio operator stationed in Spinazola. Tony was a flight engineer stationed in Castelucci. Both were near Foggia, not far from the birthplace of their parents, who had come to America from the village of Candela, Apulia, in southern Italy. (Courtesy of the DeMeo family.)

Eight

A Lot to Celebrate

The formation of the South Central Neighborhood Association in 1991 and its long success under the coordination of Lee Boyle, set the groundwork for the revitalization of Little Italy. From the adoption of the Canal Avenue tot lot to the organization of the Neighborhood Resource Center, partnerships developed, communication improved among neighbors, with city officials and other neighborhood groups, and participation in neighborhood activities enhanced the quality of life in South Central Troy.

The creation of the Friends of Little Italy was proposed by Rocco DeFazio in February 2003. One year later, Troy was the site of the first annual New York State Little Italy Heritage Tourism Conference. The Italian ambassador, the Honorable Sergio Vento, a guest of Sen. Hillary Rodham Clinton, addressed the group and reminded listeners of "the power of memory as a formula for a great project." This was a wake-up call to begin to research and document the history of the neighborhood. Troy Little Italy, Inc., was formed two years later to continue to develop and maintain a healthy and vibrant community. Its goals are to establish Little Italy as an ethnic tourism destination, to restore Troy's historic marketplace, and to make the neighborhood safe and clean. There is much to celebrate as Troy's Little Italy continues to enrich the life of the community.

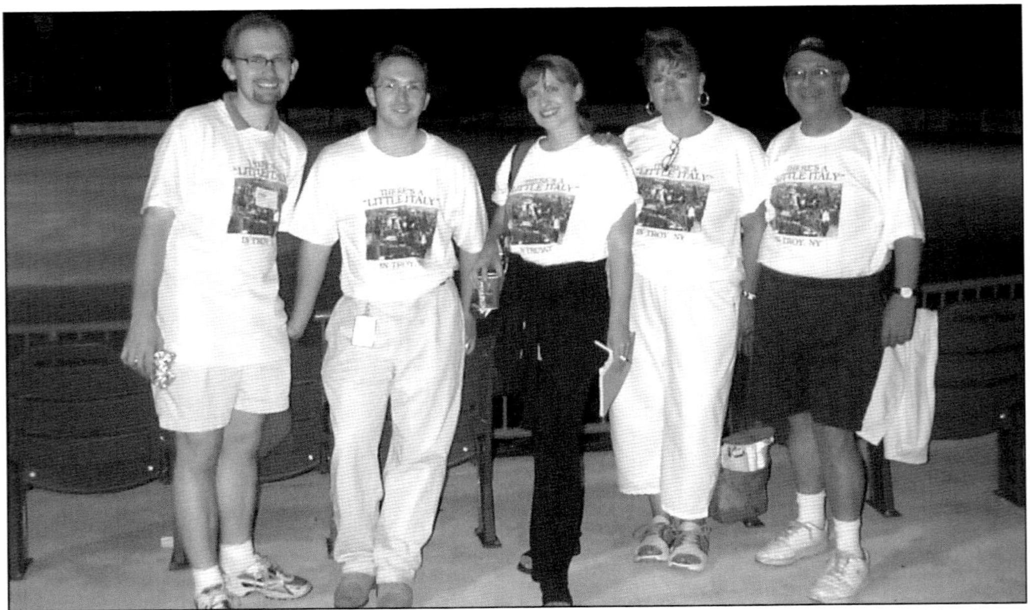

Volunteers from the South Central Neighborhood Association raised funds for the Neighborhood Resource Center by working at a concession stand for Italian Night at a Tri-City Valley Cats baseball game in August 2003. From left to right are Dan Lennon, Adrian and Lisa Graham, Lee Boyle, and Mike Esposito. During the three years the center remained open, the most successful fund-raiser was the annual Neighborhood Arts Stroll, cosponsored by the Washington Park Association. (Courtesy of Dan Lennon.)

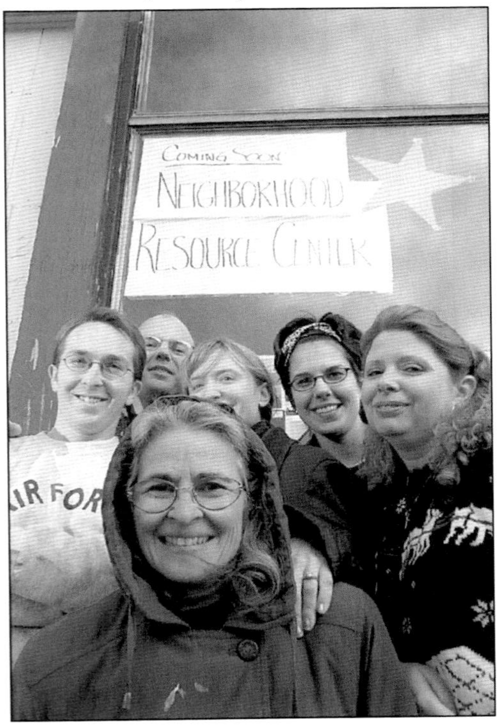

Volunteers gather to clean and paint the interior of the Neighborhood Resource Center in Little Italy. Claire Davis is in the foreground. Behind her are, from left to right, Adrian Graham, Jim Cardany, Lisa Graham, Amy Dow, and Julia Cardany. The center, a project by neighbors for neighbors, served as a place for meetings, community events, voter-registration drives, storytelling for children, a Saturday-morning "coffee chat," and a place to obtain information about the Troy community. (Photograph by Dan Lennon.)

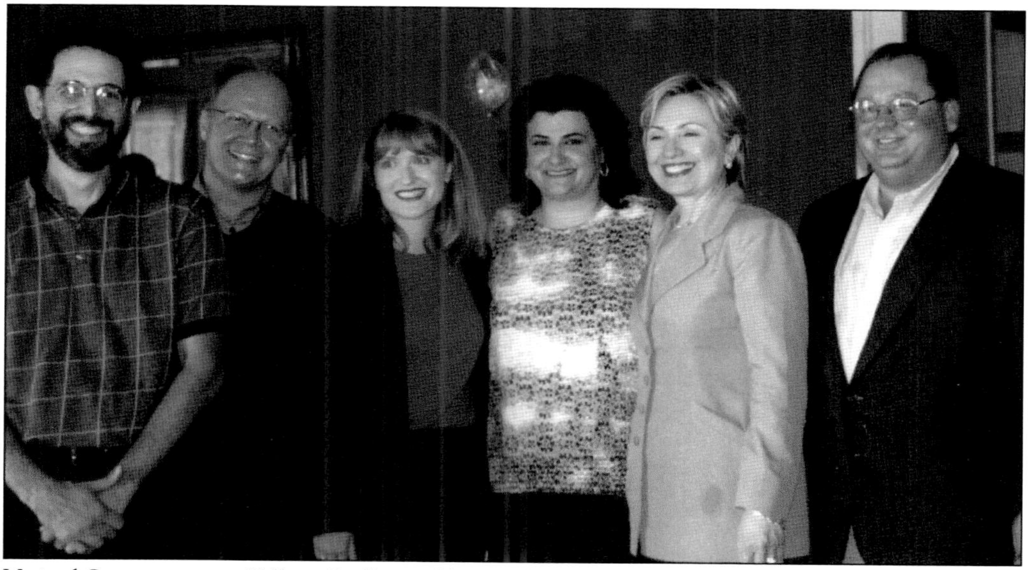

United States senator Hillary Rodham Clinton (second from right), on a visit to Troy in 2003, greets, from left to right, Joseph Fama, director of the Troy Architectural Program; community organizers Rocco DeFazio and Lisa Graham; Anna Lombardi Hunt, ICC office manager; and Mayor Mark Pattison. In July 2004, at the first annual New York State Little Italy Heritage Tourism Conference, Senator Clinton brought as her guest the Italian ambassador, the Honorable Sergio Vento. (Photograph by Janice DeFazio.)

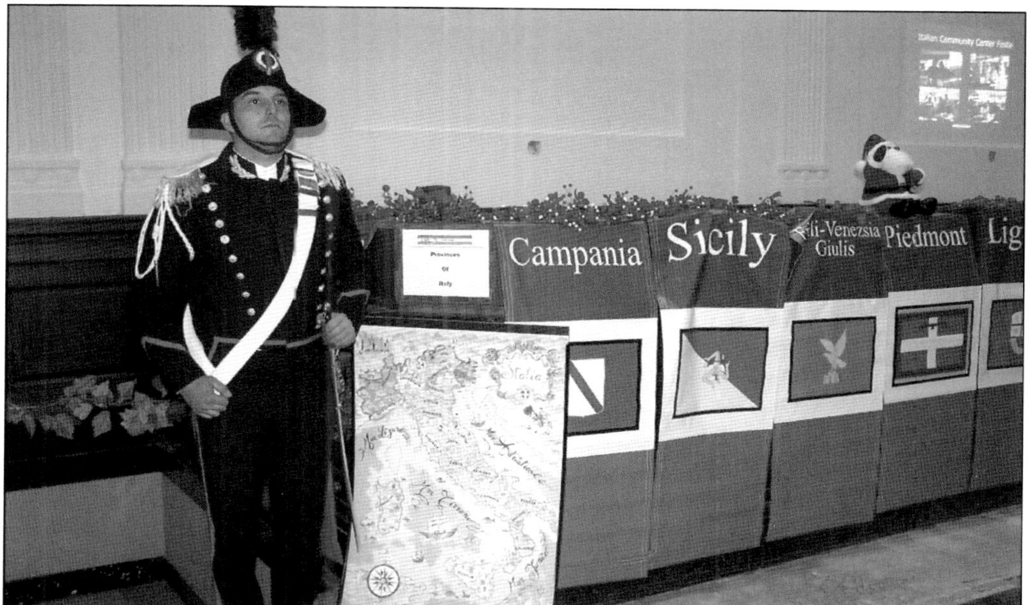

Colorful banners of the 20 regions of Italy were installed along the streets of Little Italy in 2008, interspersed among dozens of green-white-and-red banners with the inscription "Benvenuti! Little Italy" installed in 2004 to identify the neighborhood's boundaries. Fourth Street resident and ICC member Francesco Mamone stands guard dressed in the uniform of a carabiniere. (Photograph by Dan Lennon.)

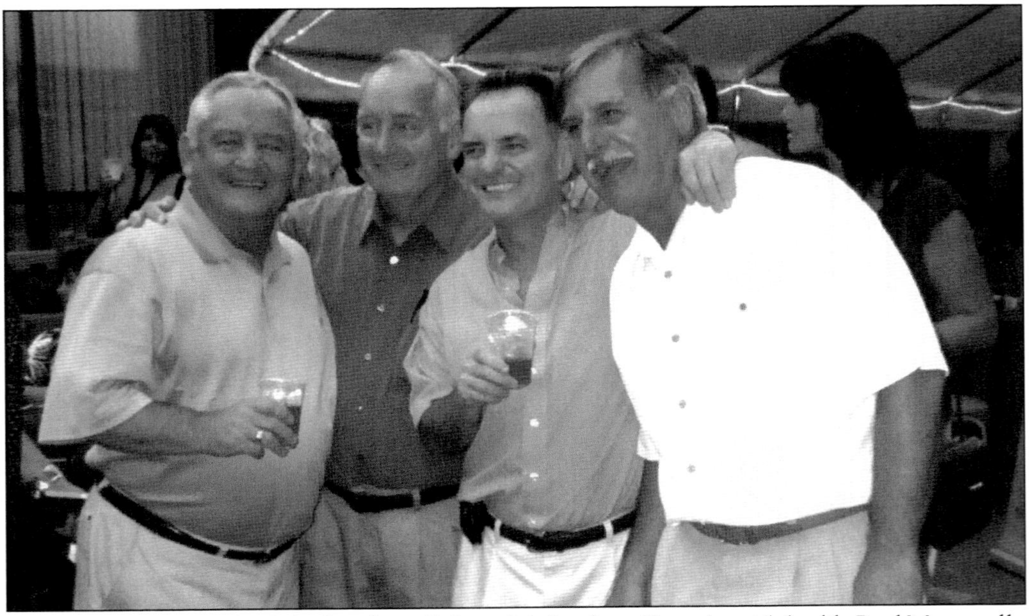

From left to right are the Riley brothers, Robert, Michael, and Joseph, with buddy Paul Montarello at a reunion of friends sharing the good times remembering the old public market. As people gather for future reunions, it will be to honor the memory of Joe Riley's dream of keeping people together and neighborhood history alive. Several hundred former and present residents attend the reunions first organized by Riley. (Courtesy of Geraldine DeBonis.)

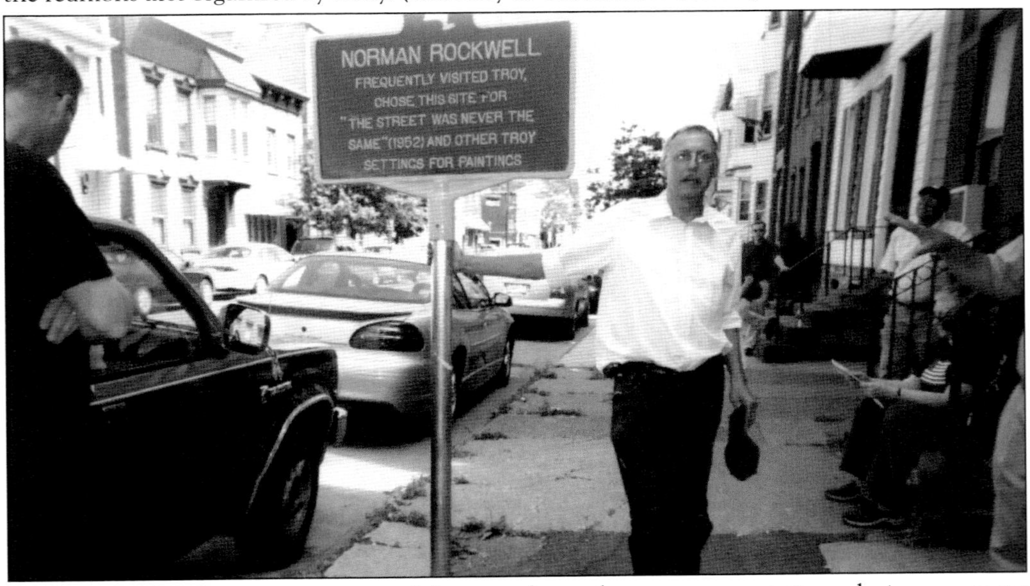

Troy artist John Conners was one of four speakers who gave presentations during an event in July 2007 sponsored by Troy Little Italy, Inc., and the Hudson Mohawk Gateway to celebrate neighborhood history. Historic markers were placed at sites to honor the remarkable 19th-century Dutch priest Rev. Peter Havermans, the beloved 20th-century American artist Norman Rockwell, and two local sites on the National Register of Historic Places—the Gasholder House and the Poestenkill. (Photograph by Jean Krueger.)